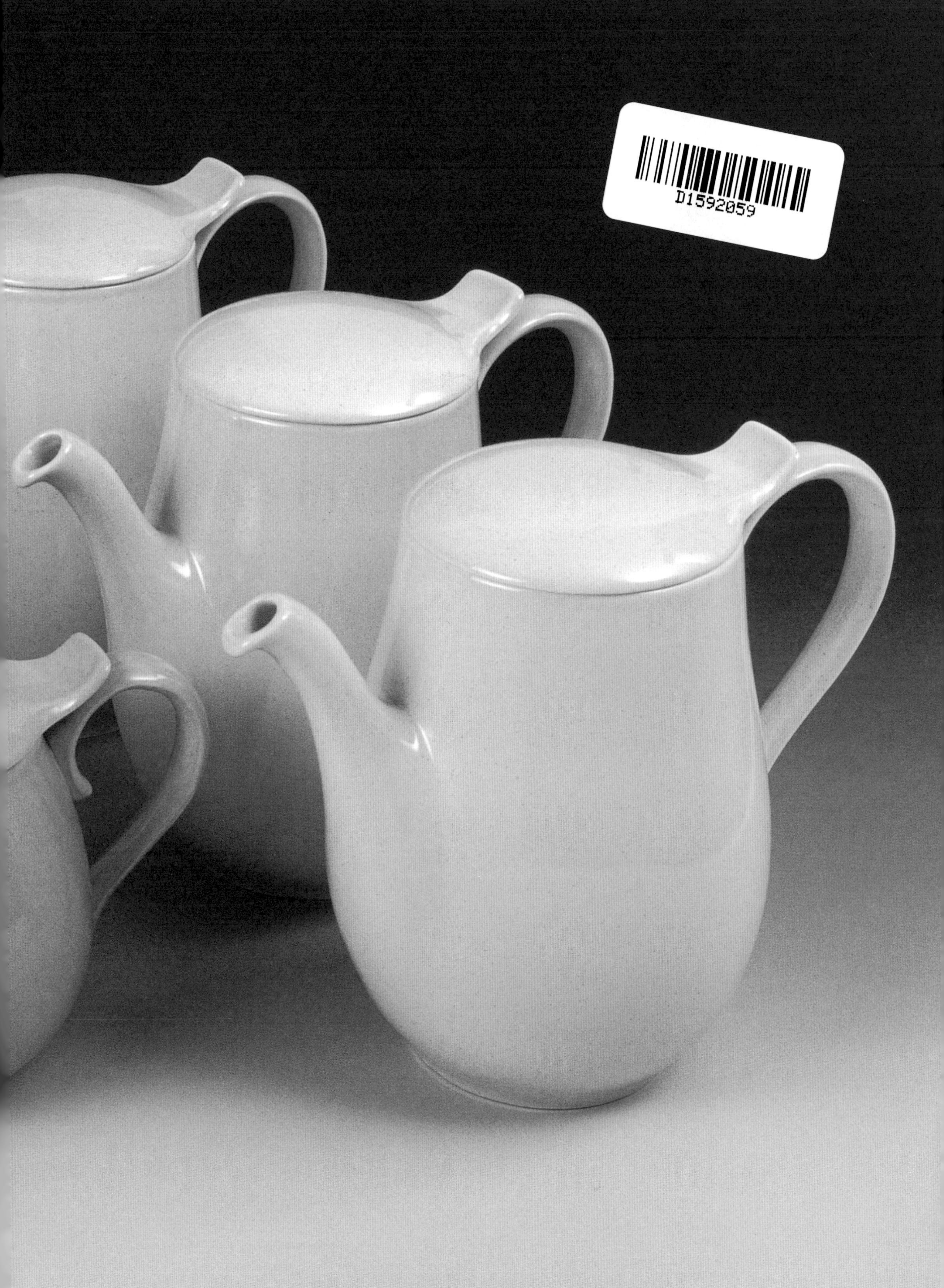

Mid-Century Modern Dinnerware:

A Pictorial Guide

Red Wing™ to Winfield™

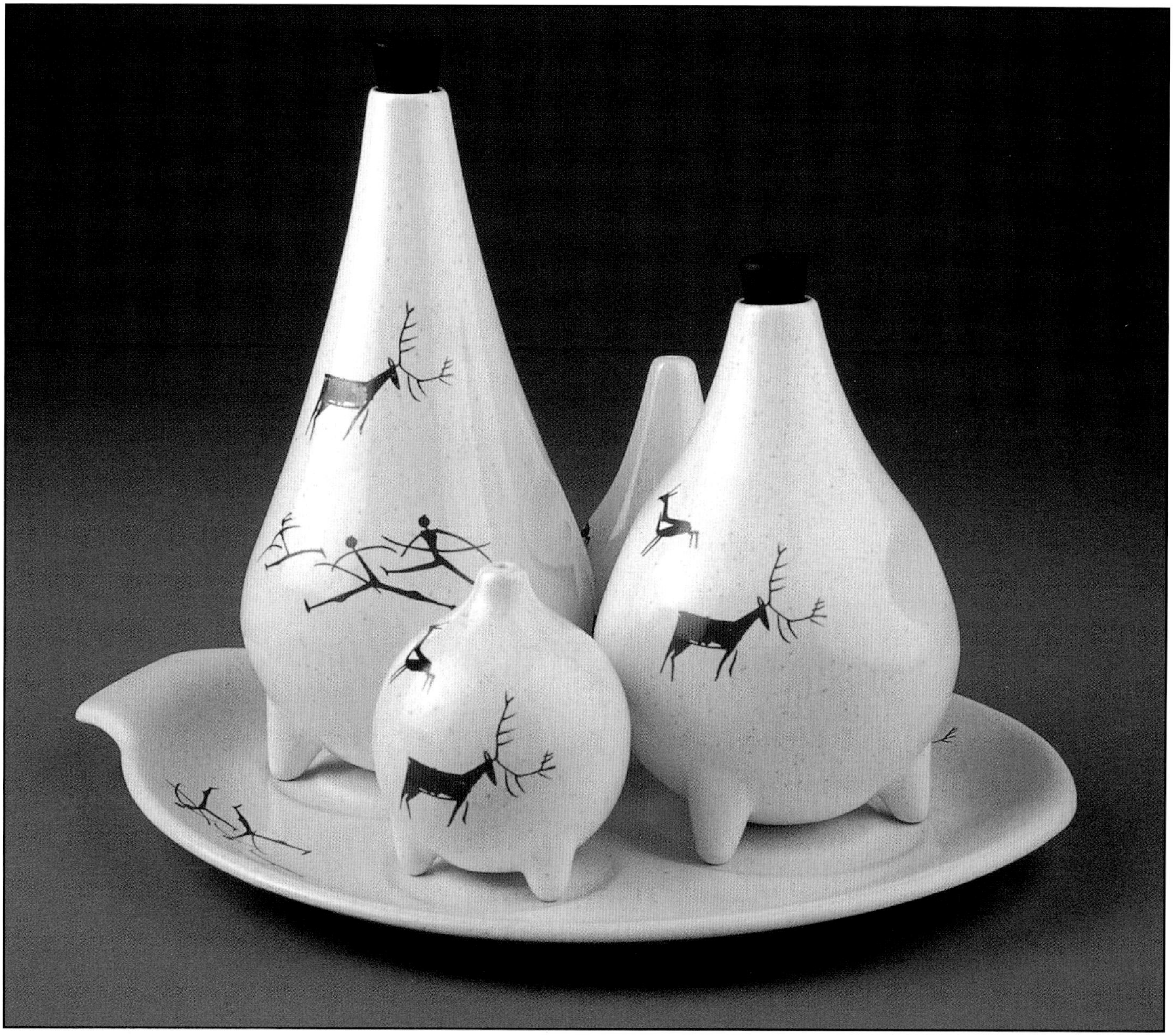

Michael Pratt

4880 Lower Valley Road, Atglen, PA 19310 USA

Dedication

This book salutes the men and women of America's pottery industry, past and present. Your competent innovation has blessed our lives with good design. Your vision and toil have given birth to compelling form and beauty. You have graced us with your inspired art and craft.

Neither the author nor the publisher may be held responsible for any losses incurred through the use of this price guide. This book is not intended to set values in the secondary market but only to provide a useful guide as to what one might reasonably expect to pay for *mid-century modern* dinnerware that is in *excellent* (A1) condition.

A number of the product lines mentioned in this book are copyrighted or trademarked by their manufacturers. Names such as Russel Wright and Eva Zeisel are the registered trademarks of individuals or companies. None of the trademark or copyright holders have authorized this book nor furnished or approved the information contained herein. This book is for the information and entertainment of collectors. This book in no way attempts to infringe on any copyright or trademark.

Library of Congress Cataloging-in-Publication Data

Pratt, Michael E.
Mid-century modern dinnerware : a pictorial guide Red Wing to Winfield / by Michael Pratt. -- (Updated ed.).
p. cm.
ISBN 0-7643-1914-0
1. Ceramic tableware--Collectors and collecting--United States--History--20th century--Pictorial works. I. Title.
NK4695.T33 P73 2003b
738'.0973'075--dc21
2003013655

Type set in Humanist 521 BT/Humanist 521 BT

ISBN: 0-7643-1914-0
Printed in China
1 2 3 4

Published by Schiffer Publishing Ltd.
4880 Lower Valley Road
Atglen, PA 19310
Phone: (610) 593-1777; Fax: (610) 593-2002; E-mail: Info@schifferbooks.com
Please visit our web site catalog at **www.schifferbooks.com**
We are always looking for people to write books on new and related subjects. If you have an idea for a book please contact us at the above address.

This book may be purchased from the publisher. Include $3.95 for shipping. Please try your bookstore first. You may write for a free catalog.

In Europe, Schiffer books are distributed by
Bushwood Books
6 Marksbury Ave.
Kew Gardens
Surrey TW9 4JF England
Phone: 44 (0)20-8392-8585 ; Fax: 44 (0)20-8392-9876; E-mail: Bushwd@aol.com
Free postage in the UK. Europe: air mail at cost

Contents

Acknowledgments

> I beg leave to express my sense of indebtedness to all who have contributed in any manner to the information contained herein...toward those who have refused or withheld information we shall not be uncharitable.
>
> – Edwin Atlee Barber, 1893

Mid-Century Modern Dinnerware: A Pictorial Guide, Red Wing™ to Winfield™, is both a photographic record of some mid-century modern dinnerware designs and a reference source for pertinent historical data. Sources for ceramic objects, research materials, and pricing intelligence used in this book would not have been possible without the support of many enthusiastic people. Those I want to thank include authors, collectors, designers, libraries, companies, museums, pottery owners and employees, and researchers.

First and foremost, I would like to thank Scott Vermillion, one of this country's premier enthusiasts of mid-century modern dinnerware and design. His ceramic assemblage is prominently featured in this book, along with the author's. Scott has the eye for spotting good twentieth century design and has been acquiring it since he was sixteen. He studied architecture as well as product and graphic design at the Institute of Design in Chicago. (Some will recall that the renowned Laszlo Moholy-Nagy had emigrated from Germany to America in the 1930s and opened a school known as the "New Bauhaus." The Institute of Design was its eventual successor.) Scott now heads the product and graphic design division of a major mid-western manufacturer. His interest in competent modern design is seen in his other outstanding collections, which include vintage cars, art deco and mid-century modern furniture, pottery, and other furnishings. He sells vintage modern design at the Broadway Antique Market in Chicago.

A very special thanks also go to Charles Alexander, Louise Dolak and family, Mary & Ray Farley, Gene Grobman & Pat Moore, Maxine Nelson, Richard G. Racheter, Rod Nelman & Anna Vikre, and McKinley Williams who graciously granted photographic access to their collections.

My deepest gratitude to Eva Zeisel and her family for affording me the opportunity to ask my questions and peer into her world. Her graciousness is much appreciated.

I am particularly grateful to Paul Cook, Alfred Dube, Curtis Fahnert, Gene Patterson, Don Schreckengost, and Ernest Sohn—all mid-century designers who generously assisted me with information about their work for companies featured in this book.

Many people assisted me in other ways. As mentioned previously, some provided pricing input while others provided access to information, permitted interviews, or just answered my questions. The following individuals and companies have helped both directly and indirectly over the years with this series of books. My heartfelt thanks go to:

California Designs

Jack Chipman (author: *Collector's Encyclopedia of California Pottery*)

Bill Stern (author: *California Pottery: From Missions to Modernism*)

Red Wing Potteries

Clifford Ekdahl

Scott Vermillion

Roseville Pottery (for Raymor)

Michael Kaplan

Paul Beedenbender

Royal China

Don Schreckengost

Curtis Fahnert

Gene Patterson

John Briggs

Charles Henderson

Nordic Capital

Salem China

Louise Dolak and family

Harvey Duke (author: *Official Price Guide to Pottery and Porcelain*)

Shenango China, Inc.

Beverly Zona and the Lawrence County Historical Society

Polly Stetler and the Susquehanna Pfaltzgraff Co.

Wayne Zitkus and the Syracuse China Corporation

Southern Potteries, Inc.

Mary & Ray Farley

Stangl Pottery

Robert Runge Jr. (author: *Collector's Encyclopedia of Stangl Dinnerware*).

Bob and Nancy Perzel

Harvey Duke (author: *Stangl Pottery*).

Sterling China Company

Bruce E. Hill and the Sterling China Company (www.sterlingchina.com)

Paul Cook

McKinley Williams

Stetson China Company

Philip Stetson

Alfred Dube

Burt Chudacoff

Mrs. Charles Murphy

Al Lass

Steubenville Pottery Company

Mrs. Harry Wintringer, Jr.

George and Janet Wintringer

R. D. Schonfeld (co-author: *Russel Wright: Creating American Lifestyle*)

Syracuse China

Wayne Zitkus and the Syracuse China Corporation (www.syracusechina.com)

Cleota Reed

Tamac

Rod Nelman and Anna Vikre

Vernon Kilns

Maxine Nelson

Kevin Souza

Wellsville China Co.

Bruce E. Hill and the Sterling China Company (www.sterlingchina.com)

Winfield China

Bill Stern

Jack Chipman

Mid-century Modern Designs

Joel Albert

Bruce Arnold

Robert Culicover (www.hiandlomodern.com)

Herb Fogel (www.fiftysdish.com)

Jim Medeiros & Ken Paruti (www.fiestajim.com)

The Retrospection list members (groups.yahoo.com/group/retrospection)

Ben Seibel Designs

Paul Beedenbender (www.abenseibeldesign.com)

Michael Kaplan

Richard G. Racheter

Eva Zeisel Designs

Pat Moore (Eva Zeisel designs and Eva Zeisel Collectors Club: www.zeiselmostly.com and www.evazeisel.org)

Eva Zeisel

Jean Richards

Scott Vermillion

Russel Wright Designs

Annie Wright

Dennis & Eve Mykytyn

Charles Alexander

Joe Keller (co-author: *Russel Wright® Dinnerware, Pottery & More: An identification and Price Guide*)

David Ross (co-author: *Russel Wright® Dinnerware, Pottery & More: An identification and Price Guide*)

The Russel Wright list members (listserv.aol.com/archives/russel-wright.html)

I am indebted to institutions as well. The New York Public Library houses a mother load of research materials. Literally many hundreds of hours were spent at NYPL's research and branch libraries including the Science, Industry, and Business Library; the Humanities and Social Sciences Library; and the Mid-Manhattan Library. Thanks also go to the Newark Public Library, the Newark Museum Library, and the Morris County (NJ) Library.

Additionally, I would like to thank the Museum of Modern Art library, the Smithsonian Institution, the Thomas J. Watson Library at the Metropolitan Museum of Art, the Cooper-Hewitt National Design Museum library, the Ohio Historical Society, Lori Carson and the Ohio Historical Society's Museum of Ceramics, the Ohio State University Libraries, and the Scholes Library and Archives at Alfred University.

Many thanks to Ken Thorlton for his cover concepts, proofreading, and encouragement. I am especially grateful to Charles Henderson, Maxine Nelson, and Philip Stetson for their kind help. My sincerest gratitude to Robert Armstrong, Michael Kaplan, Pat Moore, Cleota Reed, and Bill Stern for their friendship and assistance. It is always a pleasure to work with the Schiffer Publishing team. Special thanks to Peter Schiffer, Jeff Snyder, & Bruce Waters. It is always enjoyable to work with you.

Some of the historians, collectors, dealers, and friends who have assisted me over the years include Kevin Cole, Tim Colling, Robert Cullicover, Barrett Gould & Aline Griffith, Irene Guber, Gus Gustafson, Michael Haas, Brett Harrison, Ted Haun, Laura Kaspar, Marty Kennedy, Ron Linde, Jim Medeiros, Philip Northman, Ken Paruti, Richard G. Racheter, Tom Rago, Karen Silvermintz, Reba Schneider, and Fran Stone.

There is nothing more treasured to me than the acquaintances and friendships I have made over the years. I have had the great fortune of meeting so many individuals during this project. It is heartwarming to know that there are so many wonderful and generous people in this world. I salute you all and am truly indebted. To those individuals, institutions, and manufacturers not mentioned here, who either helped me with content not featured in this particular book or were inadvertently forgotten, you have my sincerest thanks.

Introduction

> Problem: How shall we impart to this sterile pile, this crude, harsh, brutal agglomeration, this stark, staring exclamation of eternal strife, the graciousness of those higher forms of sensibility and culture that rest on the lower and fiercer passions? How shall we proclaim from the dizzy height of this strange, weird, modern housetop the peaceful evangel of sentiment, of beauty, the cult of a higher life?
>
> – Louis Sullivan, 1896

What is Modern Design? Observations and Historical Perspective

In considering modern design it is helpful to ask: What is traditional design? By *traditional* we mean the inherited cultural elements from past generations that are familiar, provide continuity, and often give us a sense of security in the present. Traditional design, then, is evident in the architecture, fashion, and decorative furnishings that predominate in any period and is shaped by that which has gone before.

Modern is tradition's maverick sibling. It is a forward-looking inquiry that questions the established rules and sensibilities of any era and speculates about what the present is and where it is going. Modern asks: Why this belief, this rule, this construct? Modern design asks: Why this material, this structure, this style? By challenging the comfort of the past and an easy status quo, modern design risks being provocative, uneasy, and new!

The English word *modern* is more than four hundred years old and was derived from the Latin term, *modo*, meaning "right now." While the word *modern* invokes a sense of newness or the *au courant*, over the last century it has taken on a gamut of historical connotations that range from contemporary to futuristic, state-of-the-art to avant-garde, bizarre to hideous, impractical to functional, organic to technological. The seemingly oxymoronic expression, *classical modern*, has even been used to imply a restrained, almost *traditional* modern, not given to wild paroxysms of structure or fashion.

During the early nineteenth century, America focused more on mechanical invention than artistic innovation. The role of the craftsman languished as mass production burgeoned. American products, while utilitarian, lacked aesthetic appeal. Artists and designers industriously copied established styles and soon lost touch with their own creativity.

By the mid-1800s, England's Sir Henry Cole, co-organizer of the first world's fair—the *Great Exhibition of the Works of Industry of all Nations* (1851), sought to give practical application to art and design by encouraging manufacturers to introduce aesthetically competent products for the masses. William Morris, a founder of the arts and crafts movement, denounced mass production and responded to the problem by promoting hand craftsmanship.

However, the world could not turn its back on progress. Structures and products, no longer constrained by traditional tools and materials, were soon benefiting from innovative manufacturing technology, materials, and processes—all born of engineering and scientific advance. High-rise structures made of steel and concrete, along with the elevator, were bringing to America's outer and inner spaces a new verticality. Edifices and household furnishings, once constructed with ponderous effort, were reaching new heights—not solely on the backs of workers—but increasingly on the back of science.

Architecture was leading a design revolution rooted in ideas. In 1896, Louis Sullivan, famed American architect, eloquently articulated that *form follows function*, a landmark concept in modern design:

> Whether it be the sweeping eagle in his flight, or the open apple-blossom, the toiling work-horse, the blithe swan, the branching oak, the winding stream at its base, the drifting clouds, over all the coursing sun, *form ever follows function*, and this is the law. Where function does not change form does not change. The granite rocks, the ever-brooding hills, remain for ages; the lightning lives, comes into shape, and dies in a twinkling.

> It is the pervading law of all things organic and inorganic, of all things physical and metaphysical, of all things human and all things superhuman, of all true manifestations of the head, of the heart, of the soul, that the life is recognizable in its expression, that form ever follows function. *This is the law.*

One year after Sullivan's famous dictum, Josef Hoffmann helped found the *Viennese Secession*, a movement that identified the artist's creative source as residing in the dynamism of personality. A simple philosophy directed the *Secessionist's* design, which found stylistic reproduction and modification anathema. A relationship with the material object must be developed in which the object's purpose is comprehended. The product's use dictates its architecture. Materials utilized in manufacture must never simulate another material, but naturally integrate into the artistic expression. Principles for good modern design were finally becoming more evident.

The *début de siècle* world was reawakening to innovation in architecture and everyday life. Inspired by his mentor Louis Sullivan, Frank Lloyd Wright introduced America to a new style of integrated home construction and furnishings based on functionality and "organicity." His Prairie architecture was American in style, despite its Asian influence. It was characterized by a down-to-earth linearity that integrated landscape, structure, and occupant. Ornamentation was derived from essential form. Structures were simple, honest, and practical.

The writings of Frank Lloyd Wright helped inspire architect Walter Gropius, founder of Germany's premier school of art, design, and crafts known as the Bauhaus in 1919. Gropius established the school with the purpose of reuniting all the arts into a *Gesamtkunstwerk*, or synthesis of the arts. The synergism of the practical with fine arts would result in reclaiming the architectonic vigor that structures and products had lost during the beginning of the nineteenth century.

Nazi antagonism of the Bauhaus, during the early 1930s, led to the school's premature closure. Gropius, Mies van der Rohe, Moholy-Nagy, and others sought refuge in America and brought with them the dynamic ideas and principles that gave birth to good mid-century modern design.

What is Mid-Century Modern Design?

> "Modern Art" is so unusual and new that it is hard to find words to describe it...One of the first essentials is real simplicity, depending on form and color for beauty instead of elaborate detail, and we are fast beginning to realize freedom in form.
>
> – *Crockery and Glass Journal*, 1928

What is mid-century modern design? While *mid-century modern* speaks more to style than a particular period, objects created in this mode predominantly originated from 1935-1965. The genre has also been referred to as *Fifties* design since the style flourished during that decade.

Pure mid-century modern, like all the faces of modern design, is not traditional in its styling. For some, first encounters with this alien élan trigger a tradition-driven volley of disparaging comments that reveal non-acceptance of the unfamiliar. For others, there is an immediate appreciation of the compelling aesthetics fashioned from simplicity and honesty. Still others find good mid-century modern designs a koan: an *ah!* of surprise and wonderment, forcing the mind to go beyond preconception.

The best mid-century modern design incorporated the principles of good design and was concerned with attractiveness, functionality, construction, and cost. Edgar Kaufmann, Jr., the director of the Museum of Modern Art's Good Design exhibitions (1950-1955), articulated the precepts for competent modern design in 1950. The principles he enumerated were derived from historical precedent.

Summarizing his philosophy, Kaufmann believed that good modern design is: contemporary, practical, and technologically advanced. It is visually and functionally unified and avoids excessive embellishment. Its purpose is clearly stated and its function dictates its design. Furthermore, it demonstrates a proficiency in new materials and methods. Appropriate materials are used in a way that showcases their inherent beauty. Good design celebrates the method of manufacture and demonstrates machine mastery. Finally, the product is affordable for a large audience.

The experience of good mid-century modern design defines it best. Dinnerware created in this style may speak quietly or assertively, predictably or unexpectedly, informally or elegantly, but always simply and honestly. Superfluous ornamentation disrupts the poetry of contour and space. Mid-century forms can be free flowing, futuristic, and fun. The best glaze finishes add dimension. The best groupings possess thematic commonality, communicating through simplified relational surfaces and geometries; counterpointing structures and space; and even innuendo, be it cultural, technological, biomorphic, or anthropomorphic.

During the mid-century, some ceramic and industrial designers were eager to manufacture dinnerware that was substantially innovative and devoid of global precedent—dinnerware that was truly American in style. Many diverse lines emerged that showcased America's unique inventiveness. Tamac's ***Free-Form Dinnerware*** featured playful shapes drawn from simple protoplasmic contortion while Frankoma's ***Lazybones*** dinnerware masterfully abstracted skeletal anatomy. ***Bantu*** ware by Denwar, inspired by an egg, monumentalized an African tribe's sacred symbol of life. The aesthetic commentary transfigured purpose, as egg morphed into novel American forms. Eva Zeisel's ***Town & Country*** by Red Wing, featured ergonomically-derived shapes that were heartfelt, communicative, and amusing. This circus of characters revealed the *fun* in *function*.

Economic realities moved the post-World War II middle class household away from traditional formality. Large shelters, full table services, and servants begat a more casual lifestyle typified by bungalows, buffets, and barbecues. Outdoor themes enlarged a family's shrinking inner space: outer space, seashore, tropical, circus, and western themes prevailed.

During this time, foreign competition was capturing American dollars and market share by undercutting domestic products with decorative, low-priced ware. Imports were particularly appealing to younger households that were both cost and fashion conscious. Through technological advancement, America was challenging the competition with cost-effective and compelling contemporary design. The ceramic artist and designer was increasingly appreciated and even celebrated. American tableware garnered kudos throughout the world. The finest examples of mid-century modern production dinnerware became respectable pieces of modern art and design.

America's finest ceramic and industrial designers—Fong Chow, John Frank, David Gil, Edith Heath, Erwin Kalla, Belle Kogan, Charles Murphy, Glidden Parker, Charles Scarpino, Don and Viktor Schreckengost, Ben Seibel, Simon Slobodkin, Ernest Sohn, Sergio Strologo, Russel Wright, and Eva Zeisel (to name a few)—all sought inventive ways to enhance the drama of dining while addressing functionality. Their solutions were diverse. Some groupings were formal and restrained while others were casual and freeform. Some designs were not just ergonomic, but intended extensions of the human form. Others were space-saving and multi-purpose. Still others were intentionally comical or interactive. The best were honest expressions of innovative simplicity and function, and are as contemporary, today, as the day they were created.

By the mid-twentieth century, the country had already seen many outstanding examples of design and artistry in modern tableware. They included: Russel Wright's ***American Modern*** (Steubenville, 1939) and ***Vitrified China*** (Sterling, 1949) and Eva Zeisel's ***Stratoware*** (Universal, 1942), ***Riverside*** (Riverside, 1947), and ***Town & Country*** (Red Wing, 1947). The 1950s continued this trend with Ben Seibel's ***Raymor Modern Stoneware*** (Roseville, 1952) and ***Raymor Contempora*** (Steubenville, c.1953), Viktor Schreckengost's ***Free Form*** (Salem, 1955), and Charles Murphy's *Smart Set* (Red Wing, 1953).

While these lines and patterns are almost universally lauded, many thousands more were created during this period. Some of the exceptional lines featured in this volume include: Tamac's ***Free-Form Dinnerware*** (1946); Belle Kogan's *Desert* (Red Wing, 1952); Alf Robson's ***Vogue*** (Universal, 1952); George Nelson's ***Raymor Fine China*** (Walker China, 1953); Ben Seibel's ***Raymor Universal*** (Universal, 1957); Vernon Kilns patterns *Imperial* (1955), *Dis 'n Dot* (1957), and *Lollipop Tree* (1957); and Charles Murphy's *Kermis* (1955) and *Continental Buffet* (Red Wing, 1957).

One amazing outcome from the war against foreign imports was the determination of some American manufacturers to make attractive tableware available to everyone. Any family in American could enjoy good modern design on a budget. Stetson China's *Hiawatha* (1953) and *Country Casual* (1955), Salem China's *North Star* (c.1958), and Royal China's *Blue Heaven* (c.1961) were but a few of the many affordable lines gracing American tables. Should good design be measured by the volume of sales, these companies would certainly garner top awards.

Such affordable dinnerware must be evaluated both on its merit *and* its target audience. Some of the same designers who created award-winning lines for the classes, also designed for the masses. The fact is that most dinnerware produced during this era was designed by talented creative artisans, whether prominent or obscure. These lines are worthy of your collecting consideration. Many can be found even today in abundance and are relatively inexpensive.

Collect What You Like!

> Harmony for you is in your own eye, ear, and mind; and no other mind can make that harmonious to you...Perhaps you may be laughed at, but the chances are that you will set a good example to your friends by following your own free fancies...
>
> The study of ceramic art and the collection of specimens, whether for cabinet purposes or for home decoration, should lead to freedom and independence of taste. The collector who follows the opinions of others, and guides himself by what others consider good in color or art, will get small good to himself...
>
> – William Prime, 1877

More than a decade ago, I took a leisurely stroll through an antique mall in Centerville, Indiana. In those days I collected old works on the history of Wall Street. As I was scanning the room, a brightly colored plate seemed to call to me from a distant aisle. I walked over to the plate and examined it. Its reddish swirls and near black trim danced through my imagination. This was not like anything I had ever encountered. Our conversation was captivating, as if we were old friends. Bold, freeform, and honest, it bore no resemblance to the dainty Victorian floral.

My search began for more ware in this style. It was not long before the first plate I discovered, a Stetson platter, had turned into a diverse collection. Each new piece was prized and had its own story.

When on the road, I would ask antique dealers, "Do you have any mid-century modern dinnerware?" They would pause for a moment, stupefied, and then remark disparagingly, "Oh, you want that Russel Wright art deco stuff." After encountering this same scenario innumerable times, I abandoned the question. Today most antique dealers know what mid-century modern dinnerware is and the prices some items command.

More than a decade ago, I collected neither art deco nor Russel Wright tableware. Being of independent ilk, I wanted to follow a less traveled path. I limited my collection to abstract, geometric, and highly stylized American mid-century modern patterns and shapes. These were wildly attractive to me and seemed to resonate with my own personal values. When I soon realized that others enjoyed similar design sensibilities, the discovery was validating. Later, I also became a Russel Wright enthusiast.

My first dinnerware project showcased some of my rescued treasures on the web, with what may have been the first *cybercollection*, complete with animated pictures of rotating ware. The popularity of the site led me to my latest labor of love, a series of books on mid-century modern dinnerware.

About the Book

Mid-Century Modern Dinnerware: A Pictorial Guide, Red Wing™ to Winfield™ is the second volume of a two book set. It is arranged alphabetically for the rapid location of tableware from almost thirty different potteries. These volumes catalog a range of well-known and obscure lines and patterns. Not all are purely modern. Many are hybrids, demonstrating both traditional and modern elements in both decoration and form, fashioned to appeal to mixed sensibilities.

Through the use of this set, collectors will undoubtedly encounter designers, lines, and patterns that are new to them. This book does not, by any means, attempt to be comprehensive—that would fill a set of encyclopedias—but this book does present the collector with an overview of the scope of what was available. There are nearly five hundred photographs, some documenting items rarely seen. Many facts have been referenced from their primary sources and others have been obtained from sources listed in the bibliography.

Although many new findings have been unearthed, captions present information compactly so as not to be overwhelming. The lead caption for each pattern contains the most complete information about each pattern. Conventions are used to present information quickly and a *Convention Key* is included so the book can be fully utilized as soon as the reader is familiar with it.

The dates that one encounters in the captions generally refer to the earliest year that a line, pattern, or glaze decoration was introduced to the trade. Introduction to the consumer could lag trade introduction by one month to six months or more. If the date of introduction to the consumer is well known or easily established and it differs from the year of trade introduction, then this date may be used. Dates do not always reflect when a shape was first introduced or when a line was actually designed.

As has been previously stated, much new information has been revealed for the first time. In these pages, you will find answers to the following questions and many more. What are the names for ***American Modern's*** decorated patterns? What are the modern lines by Vincent Broomhall, Simon Slobodkin, and John J. Gilkes? What were ***Stratoware's*** color names? Who designed Universal's ***Ballerina***? What was the trade name for Blue Ridge's [***Spiderweb***]?

In Conclusion

Many people derive a great deal of satisfaction from collecting mid-century modern tableware, whether it be an item created by Eva Zeisel or a designer long forgotten. Acquiring this ware is a great way to study and appreciate America's design heritage, as well as meet many wonderful people. I am hopeful, that through these pages, you, too, will discover the enjoyment of mid-century modern dinnerware.

Pricing Mid-Century Modern Dinnerware

One of the biggest problems novice collectors face, is determining how much money they should pay for an item. Whether beginner or advanced, most collectors eventually refer to price guides. I remember, as if it were yesterday, the frustration I felt using these books. More than infrequently, I observed that book prices were lower than the retail prices charged by specialist dealers, pottery shows, and antique malls. Was I paying too much if I bought this item above the book price? Experience soon taught me that mid-century modern collectors share similar sensibilities and frequently want the same items. Aggressive competition meant that I would typically have to pay a premium for the most sought-after items.

I often wondered why book values varied so much from my own observations. Over the years, I gradually learned that there are a number of reasons for such large price differences. Condition, supply and demand, dealer subjectivity, dealer type (specialist versus generalist), geographical location (the coasts versus the mid-west, major cities versus small towns), economic climate, auction fever, market or store type (garage sale, flea market, thrift store, antique shop, antique mall)—all contribute to widened price ranges for an item. If an author's pricing is obtained primarily from flea markets, thrift stores, and garage sales, values will tend to be lower. If pricing is derived from specialist dealers, upscale modernism and pottery shows, and finer antique malls, values will likely be higher. Furthermore, prices obtained on the East and West coasts, as well as the larger metropolitan areas, are typically higher than those found in the heartland.

Mid-century modern dinnerware prices are not static. Values can fluctuate from minute to minute. Never is this so apparent as when observing prices realized from online auctions. It is not uncommon for two identical items in the same condition—selling only minutes, hours, or days apart—to fetch significantly different prices.

This presents a challenge for the author of a price guide. When reviewing auction results, aberrant price blips on the upside or downside are not as important in determining value as the price at which the majority of collectors buy. Such values tend to be median values, and are more characteristic of the actual market. Of course, this can be difficult to determine with a thinly traded item. Moreover, it has also become more apparent that online prices do not always reflect offline retail. Generally speaking, the prices realized by *brick and mortar* dealers are often higher than prices obtained in certain online venues. What this means for the collector is that he or she will likely find some bargains online. At other times, it is clear, that online prices push the high-end of the envelope because of aggressive competition: you have found that piece you always wanted, but paid the price.

In this guide, values have been determined both objectively (pricing intelligence has been gathered from a variety of sources—antique malls, shops, auctions, replacement services, online stores, specialist dealers, and collectors) and subjectively (from years of observation and comparison).

Despite an author's intentions to provide meaningful numbers, the moment a price guide is published, it can already be out of date because of the lag time involved in book production and publication. Another factor is that the publication of new material can directly affect the market that it hopes to accurately reflect. More specifically, a book can pique collector interest, which in turn can dramatically increase demand and prices; a book's prices can be outdated by its own success. Yet another problem is that thinly traded items, which have no established market, can experience more volatile swings before settling into a trading range.

Since prices are always in flux, the true value of a guide such as this is not in the price ranges it presents, but in the intuitive understanding it can impart regarding the relative valuation of one object when compared with another. Actual prices may vary outside published ranges, even substantially.

The three key ingredients to learning modern dinnerware pricing are observation, observation, observation. Collectors may start with a guide or encyclopedia, but must realize that this information needs to be supplemented with current market intelligence. Experienced collectors have developed a feel for pricing based on observing prices online, in the antique mall and shop, and at pottery shows. In time, the neophyte collector will also gain an objective and intuitive sense for the current valuation of mid-century modern dinnerware.

This chapter is adapted from the author's book entitled: *Mid-Century Modern Dinnerware: An Encyclopedia of American Design & Production (Ak-Sar-Ben, Denwar Ceramics, Iroquois China Company, Laurel Potteries of California, Royal China Company, Stetson China Company)*. Atglen, PA: Schiffer Publishing Ltd.

Conventions Key

continued from previous page

Convention		Explanation	Example/Comments
Definitions			
Hybrid		The combination of modern and traditional elements in a single pattern, line, grouping, or shape.	Detailed floral decorations tend to reduce simple modern shapes into hybrid lines.
Line		Typically, a grouping of similar dinnerware patterns often on identical shapes. Line names are capitalized and in bold italics.	***Town & Country*** by Red Wing.
Mid-century modern		A contemporary style (1935-1965) that resolved the "extravagances" of Art Moderne with simplicity and functionality.	Mid-century modern design may be: abstract, biomorphic, casual, comical, dramatic, ergonomic, futuristic, geometric, innovative, and/or multi-purpose.
Pattern		The manufacturer's name given to dinnerware with a particular decal (decalcomania), stamp, hand painted, or glaze decoration. Pattern names are capitalized and in italics.	*Seeds, Grass,* and *Botannica* are Russel Wright patterns in the ***Esquire*** line by the Edwin M. Knowles China Company.
Shape		The name given to a grouping of related forms. Sometimes the same shape comprised a line. Other times, different shapes comprised a single line. Shape names are bolded and capitalized to distinguish them from line names which are capitalized and in bold italics.	W. S. George created so many patterns on the **Ranchero** shape, that it will be difficult to develop a complete accounting of all the patterns.
Pricing			
	$ - $	Number ranges are especially useful for comparative purposes. Prices may vary or trend outside the ranges given. Prices change with condition, demand, supply, economic climate, dealer, geography, marketplace, presentation, and time. Recently, market conditions have widened the price ranges for many items. Prices realized from online auctions do not necessarily reflect the retail values obtained at pottery shows, antique shops, and antique malls (virtual or brick & mortar).	*Starburst* coffee mug, $38-55.
	ND	When the price is unknown either because the item trades infrequently or because it is hard-to-find, *ND* (not determined) may be used instead of a price range.	Russel Wright ***Nasturtium***, ND.
	+	The plus sign indicates the price range of an item could exceed the high end of the range.	*California Mobile* salad bowl, 450-500+.
Punctuation & Word Treatment			
Italics		Italics are used to denote a book title and patterns. They are sometimes used for special emphasis or in place of quotation marks.	*Fantasy* was produced by Hall China.
Bold italics		Bold italics will denote a line name or grouping.	The ***American Heritage*** grouping by Stetson China.
Bold		A capitalized bold term without italics refers to a shape name. This convention is used for rapid identification of shape names.	The **Museum** shape by Castleton was formerly called the **Zeisel** shape.
Parentheses	( )	Parentheses signify additional information or explanation of preceding information. If they are found after item, they are usually of manufacturer origin. Brackets will be used instead of parentheses for additional author information that might be confused with a manufacturer's terms.	Harvey Duke authored the eighth edition of the *Official Guide to Pottery and Porcelain*. (This book lists more than 21,000 prices!)
Square Brackets	[ ]	Square brackets identify unofficial collector names or invented names that are not the manufacturer's chosen terms. Manufacturer's pattern/glaze names will precede a bracketed name when known. Bracketed items also denote non-manufacturer descriptions and measured dimensions that differ from factory dimensions.	*Turquoise* [*Aqua*] creamer.

Conventions Key

continued

Convention		Explanation	Example/Comments
Abbreviations			
	(s)	Shape designer	Simon Slobodkin (s).
	(p)	Pattern or glaze designer	Curtis Fahnert (p).
		Designer created both shape & glaze or pattern.	Eva Zeisel.
Captions			
	caption	Roseville Pottery Company (Zanesville, Ohio) for Raymor (Richards Morgenthau & Co. New York, New York).* ***Raymor Modern Stoneware***. Ben Seibel. *Terra Cotta*. 152. Dinner plate, 12", $20-30.	Please note: the most complete information is found only in the lead caption for each pattern.
		Captions will present information in the following order: manufacturer; ***line or grouping name***; **shape name**; shape designer (s); *pattern or glaze name*; pattern, decal, or glaze designer (p); date the pattern/shape was introduced to the trade or consumer; shape number on item underside; item; dimensions (if available); and price range. Some captions include comments.	Each lead caption will present as much pertinent information as is currently known by the author.
	*	An asterisk following the company name indicates that non-bracketed items use manufacturer nomenclature.	
Dates			
	date	The caption date is the earliest year found for an item with a particular shape, pattern or glaze, and clay. Dates are obtained from trade journals, archival materials, manufacturers' catalogs and brochures, and authoritative reference works. Trade journal dates often lead introduction to the consumer market by 1-6 months or more. The caption date does not reflect the year the designer began or finished creating the line. Dates are best approximations and may change as new findings are discovered. Items clearly introduced to the trade in December for the following January's introduction to consumers, are sometimes given as an introduction date for that following year, especially when that date is well known.	Despite the fact that Frankoma's *Brown Satin* was first used on ***Lazybones*** during 1961, the presence of post-1980 Sapulpa clay dates the creamer to after 1980.
	c.	The circa abbreviation, *c.*, identifies that a year is not known with certainty, but is believed to be close to the time mentioned.	Pfaltzgraff's ***Country Time***™ line was previously thought to have been introduced c.1952. *China Glass & Tablewares* reported its introduction by Raymor (Richards Morgenthau Company) in its April 1956 edition.
	<year	The year that is the mentioned year or earlier.	Denwar's *Benin Blue* glaze on ***Bantu*** was introduced <1951.
	year>	The year that is the mentioned year or later.	Iroquois ***Casual*** *Cantaloupe* was introduced in 1959>.
	<year>	A year that is the mentioned year, earlier, or later. This is used to indicate less certainty than a date listed with the circa (c.) abbreviation.	The Iroquois ***Casual*** AD (after dinner) coffee cup was introduced in <1949>.
Definitions			
Coupe		Flat and rimless, with an outer perimeter that curves up.	Coupe-shaped plates often seem more informal.
Finial		The projection on top of a lid used for lifting.	
Flatware		Low profile items such as plates, platters, and saucers.	These items were often jiggered.
Holloware (hollowware)		Dinnerware items such as the coffeepot, teapot, gravy boat, shakers, cream and sugar, cups, and bowls.	These items were often cast.

The Potteries

Red Wing Potteries, Inc.™

Red Wing Potteries, Inc. (Red Wing, Minnesota).* ***Town & Country***. Eva Zeisel. *Forest Green, White, Peach, Dusk Blue, Sand, Rust, Metallic Brown.* 1947. Cups & saucers, $18-45, each. *White* commands the highest values for the standard glazes in ***Town & Country***. *Metallic Brown* is also favored by collectors, while other glaze decorations are more commonly found and less expensive. (The author strongly urges the reader to review the ***Conventions Key*** prior to reading the captions.)

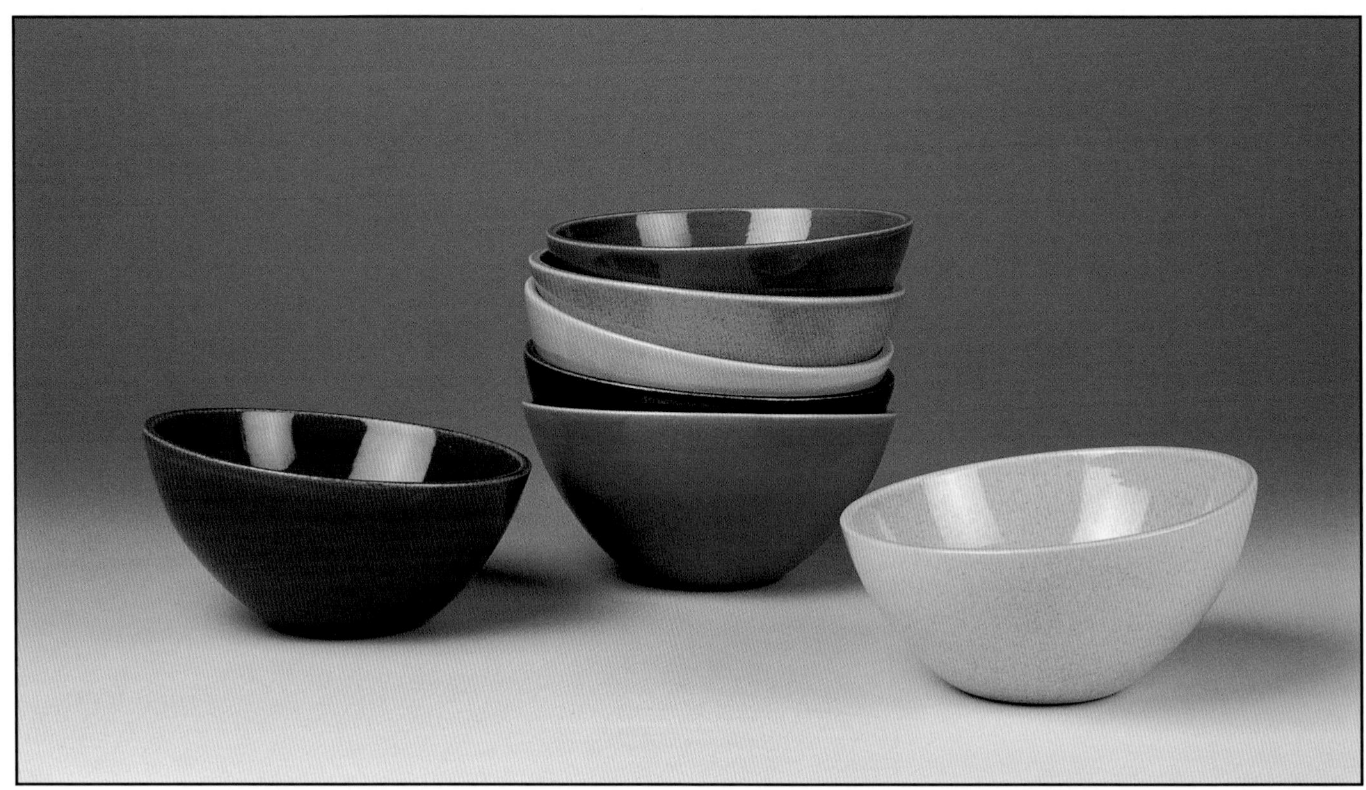

Red Wing.* ***Town & Country***. *Rust, Forest Green, Peach, Grey, Metallic Brown, Dusk Blue, Sand.* Cereal bowls, 8 1/2" x 3 3/4", $60-80, each. ***Town & Country's*** shapes are unexpected and humorous. Careful examination of each piece reveals sophisticated ergonomics and captivating theater that naturally heightens the dining experience.

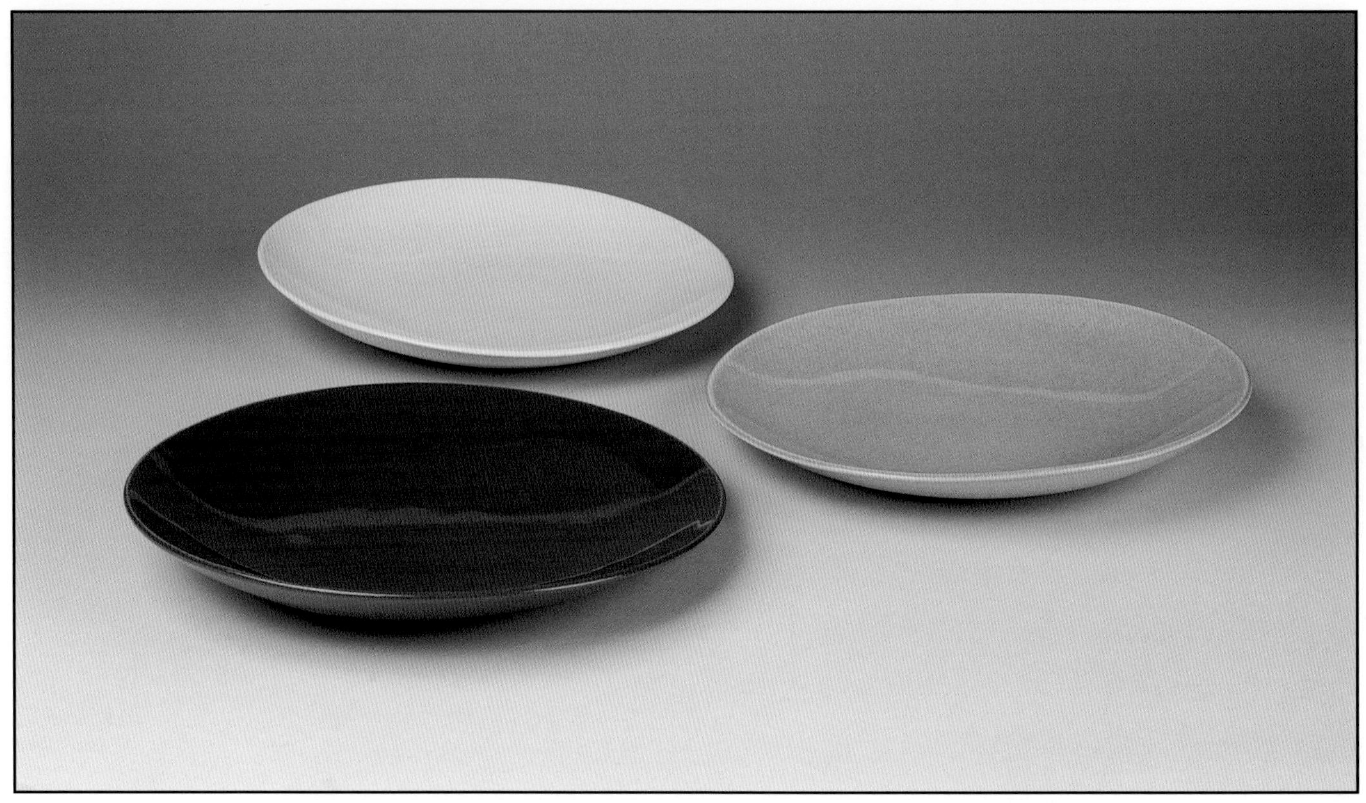

Red Wing.* ***Town & Country***. *Rust, White, Sand.* Plates [dinner], 10 1/2", *Rust/Sand*, $30-50; *White*, $50-75. Asymmetrically raised rims promote easier handling, while adding a touch of levity. Will food slide off the plate?

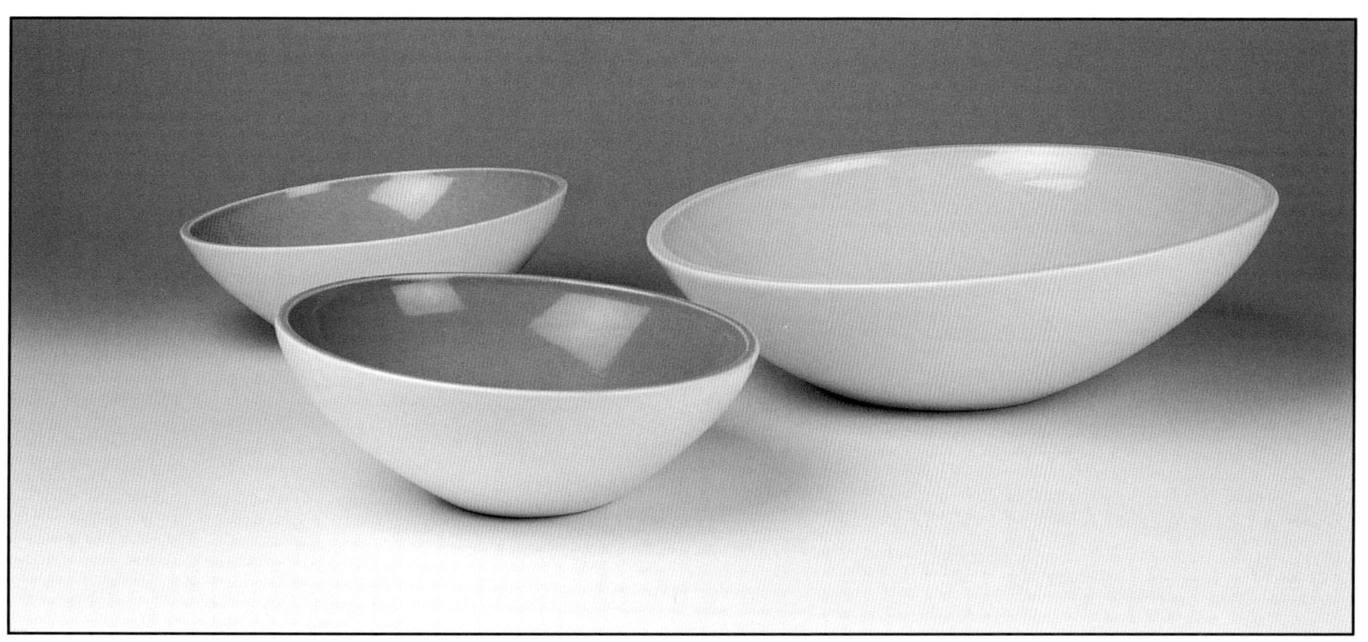

Red Wing.* ***Town & Country***. *Dusk Blue.* Salad bowl, 8" x 3 3/4", $50-75. *Peach.* Salad bowl, $50-75. *Gray.* Salad bowl, 13" x 4", $80-125.

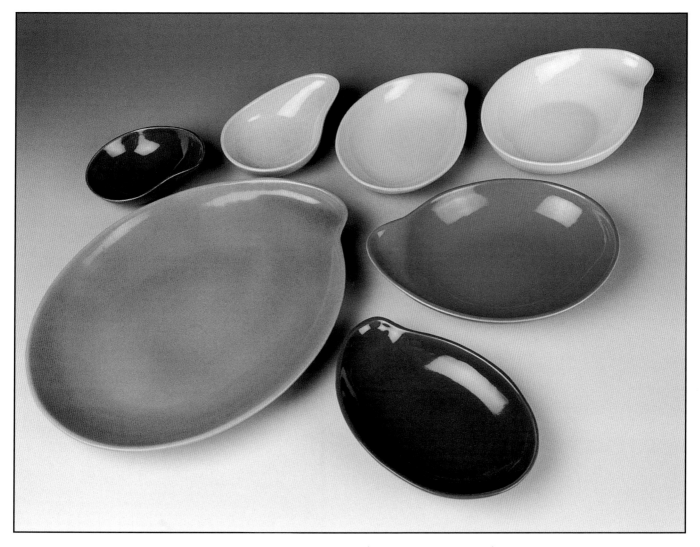

Red Wing.* ***Town & Country***. *Peach.* Platter, 15" x 11 1/2", $70-100. *Rust.* Sauce dish, $15-25. *Sand.* Relish dish, 7", $30-40. *Chartreuse.* Relish dish, 9", $35-45. *White.* Baker, 11"; $65-90. *Dusk Blue.* Baker, 11", $25-40. *Forest Green.* Relish dish, 9", $35-45. Dishes and platters have organically-shaped, built-in handles.

Red Wing.* ***Town & Country***. Lazy Susan with 7 relish dishes, 7" x 5", and condiment server or mustard, ND. Eva Zeisel's designs have won her innumerable accolades and honors throughout the world. In addition to two honorary doctorates (Royal College of Art, London and Parsons School of Design, New York), she has also been awarded America's most prestigious ceramic honor, the Binns Medal.

Red Wing.* ***Town & Country***. Another view.

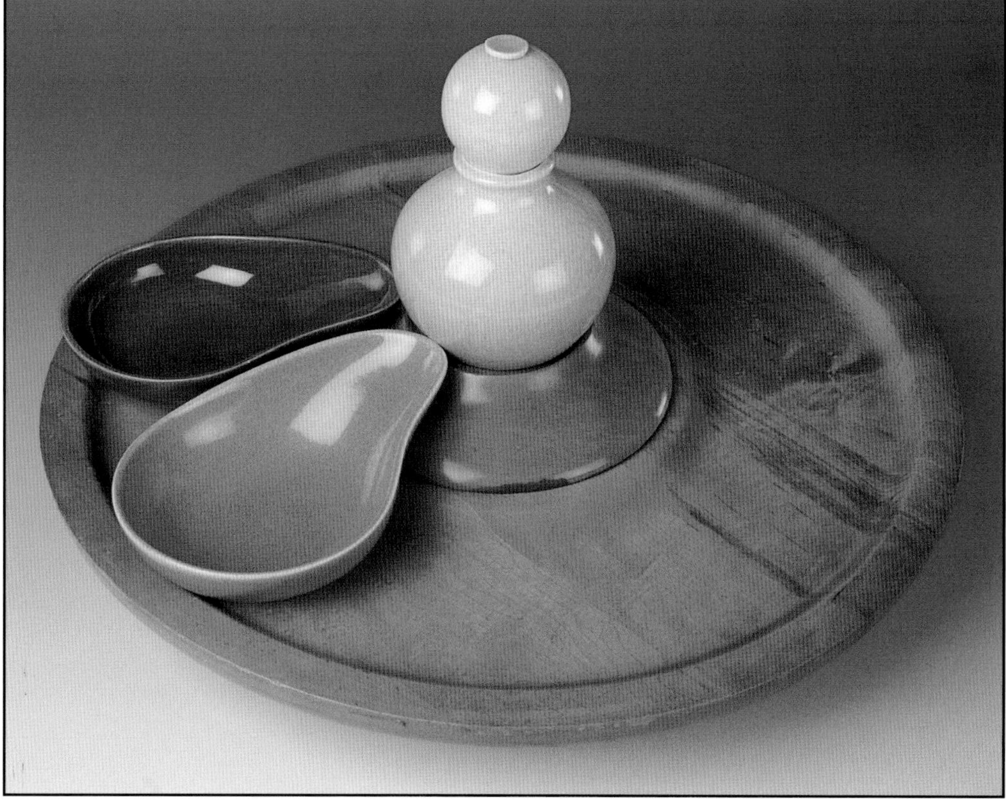

Red Wing.* ***Town & Country***. Two pieces of wood comprise the Lazy Susan's wooden stand.

Red Wing.* ***Town & Country***. *Dusk Blue*. Condiment server or mustard, $150-170+.

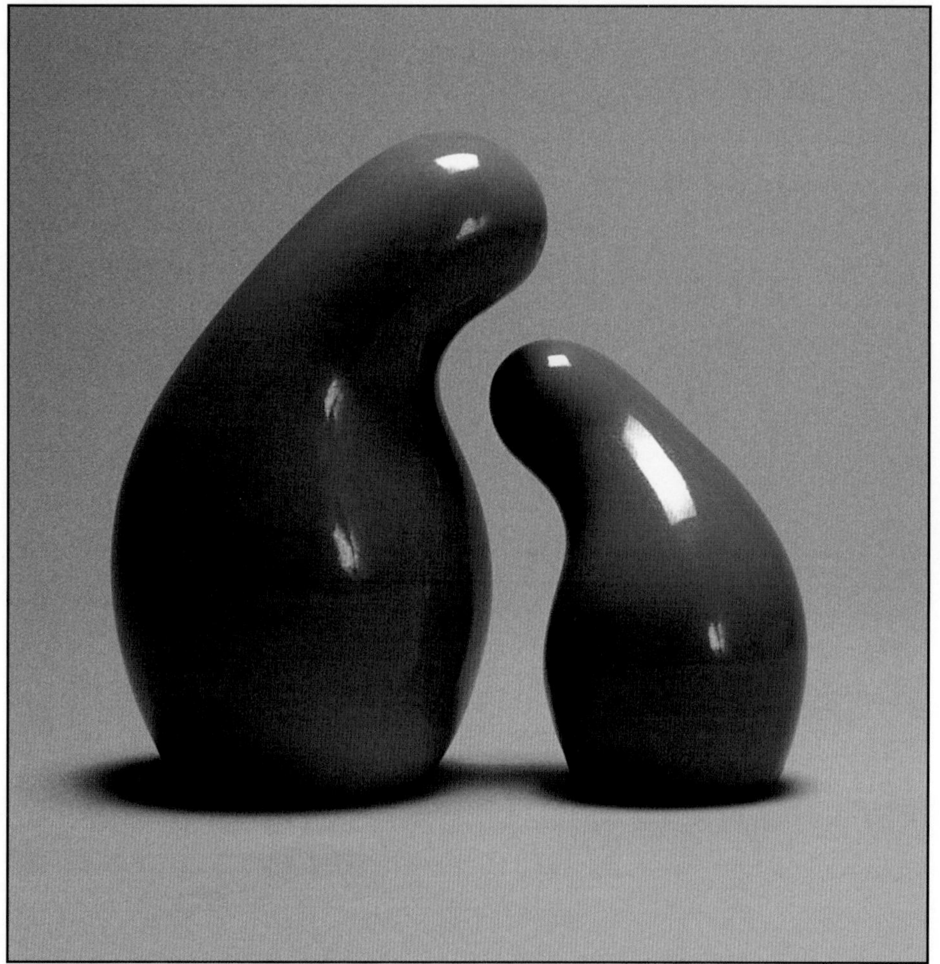

Red Wing.* ***Town & Country***. *Dusk Blue*. Salt & pepper shakers [schmoos], $75-100, pair.

During the late forties and early fifties, these ***Town & Country*** shakers were referred to as *schmoos* because of their similarity to the popular, seal-like Schmoos in Al Capp's Li'l Abner® comic strip. In a letter to the editor of *Interiors* magazine (January 1950), Eva Zeisel, responding to one such magazine reference, noted that her shapes had been introduced (1947) before the birth of the "Schmoo®" (1948). To this day, these cuddly shakers are highly regarded and collectors still affectionately refer to them as "schmoos."

Red Wing.* ***Town & Country***. *Chartreuse* (***Quartette***). Creamer, $150-200. *Peach.* Pitcher, 2 pint, $95-110. *Gray.* Pitcher, 3 pint, $140-150. The creamer and pitcher shapes are intriguingly biomorphic. The ***Quartette*** colors in ***Town & Country*** are not ***Town & Country's*** standard glazes, but are highly prized and hard-to-find. The ***Quartette*** colors included: *Ming Green*, (***Quartette***) *Chartreuse*, *Copperglow*, and *Mulberry*. ***Quartette*** *Chartreuse* has more yellow and vibrancy than the standard *Chartreuse*.

Red Wing.* ***Town & Country***. *Dusk Blue, Metallic Brown, Peach, Rust, Sand, Gray, White, Ming Green.* School of salt & pepper shakers, $75-120, pair; *White* & ***Quartette*** colors, ND.
These shapes evoke a feeling of love and bonding between mother and child, especially when paired.

Red Wing.* ***Town & Country***. *Forest Green.* Mug, $75-85. *Rust.* Coaster, $15-25.

Red Wing.* ***Town & Country***. *Metallic Bronze, Rust, Sand, Dusk Blue, Forest Green.* Mugs, $75-85 each; *Metallic Bronze*, $100-125.

Red Wing.* ***Town & Country***. Coasters [spoon rests], $25-35 each.

Red Wing.* ***Town & Country***. *Dusk Blue*. Vinegar with stopper, $100-150. *Forest Green.* Oil with stopper, $100-150.

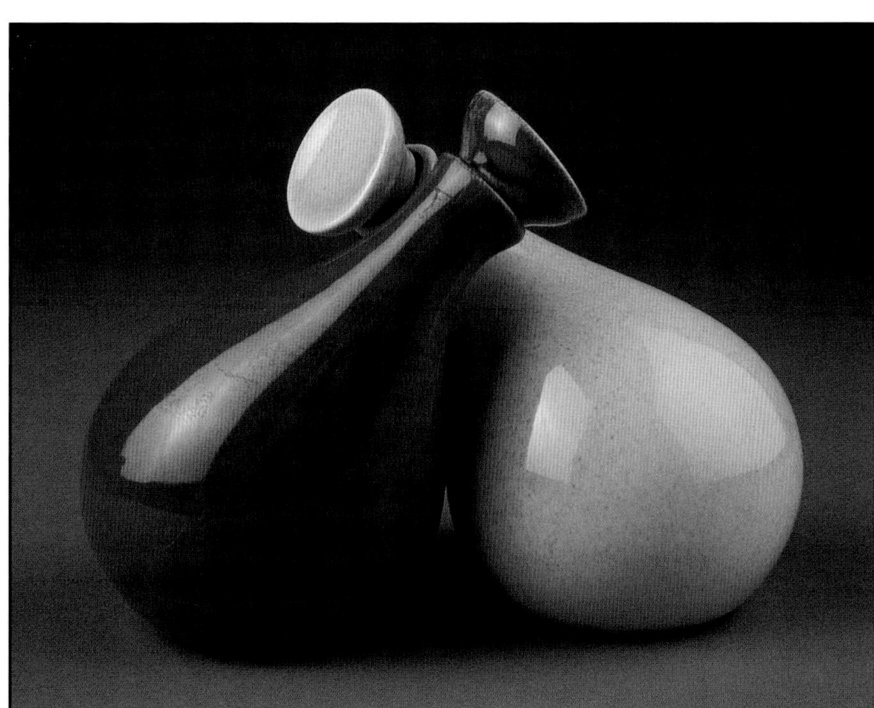

Red Wing.* ***Town & Country***. *Rust*. Vinegar with stopper, $100-150. *Sand.* Oil with stopper, $100-150.

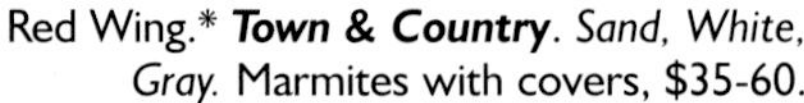

Red Wing.* ***Town & Country***. *Sand, White, Gray.* Marmites with covers, $35-60.

Red Wing.* ***Town & Country***. *Sand.* Marmite with cover, $35-60. *Gray.* Casserole with cover, $100-150.

Red Wing.* ***Town & Country***. *Sand, Rust.* Mixing bowls, 9", $125-180. The mixing bowl was engineered to comfortably fit the hand, permitting a firm grip.

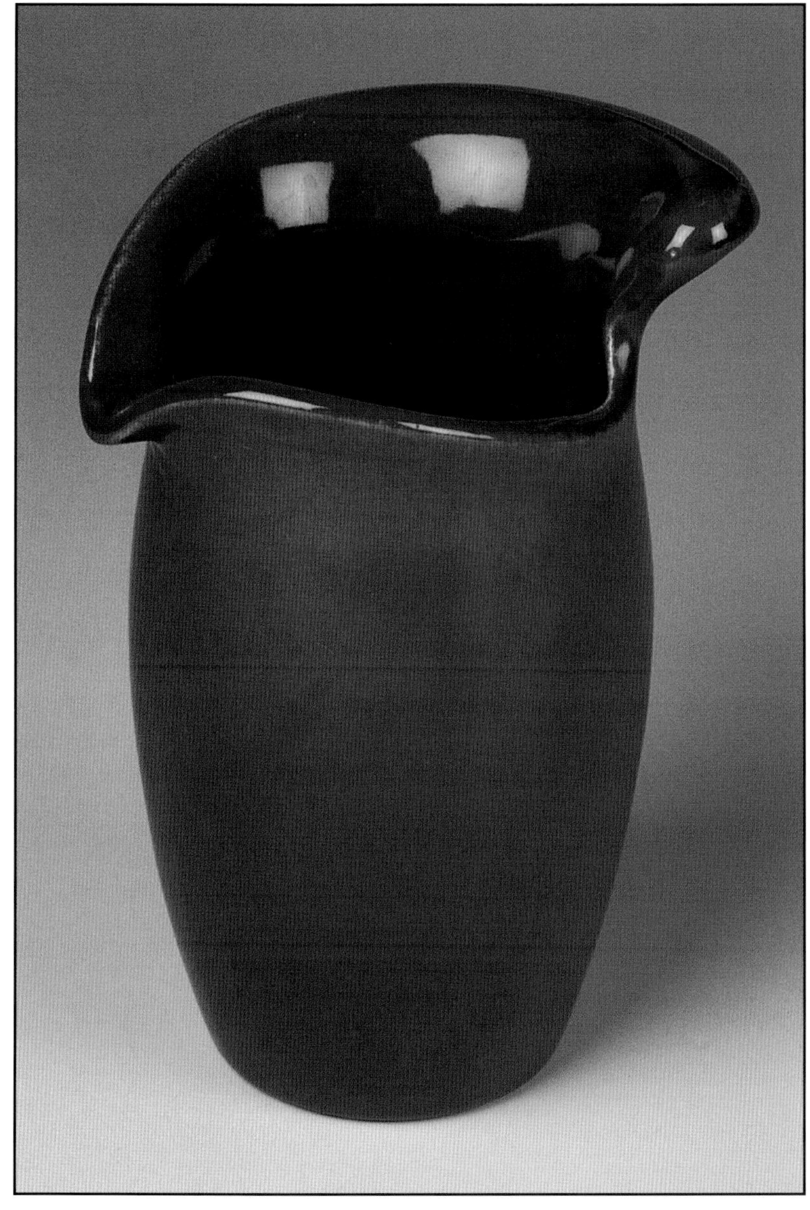

Red Wing.* ***Town & Country***. *Rust.* Syrup jug, $90-125. The shape of the syrup jug fits the hand comfortably. The syrup jug and mixing bowl, when used together, were intended to form a "waffle set."

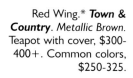

Red Wing.* ***Town & Country***. *Metallic Brown.* Teapot with cover, $300-400+. Common colors, $250-325.

Red Wing.* ***Town & Country***. *Metallic Brown.* Soup tureen. Common colors, $700-800+; *Metallic Bronze* (shown here), $800-1200+. The soup tureen and ladle were marked "discontinued" in the January 1950 ***Town and Country*** brochure.

Red Wing.* ***Town & Country***. *White.* Left salad spoon, 14 1/4". The left and right salad spoons were also marked "discontinued" in the 1950 brochure. ND. *Sand.* Soup tureen ladle, 14 1/4", ND.

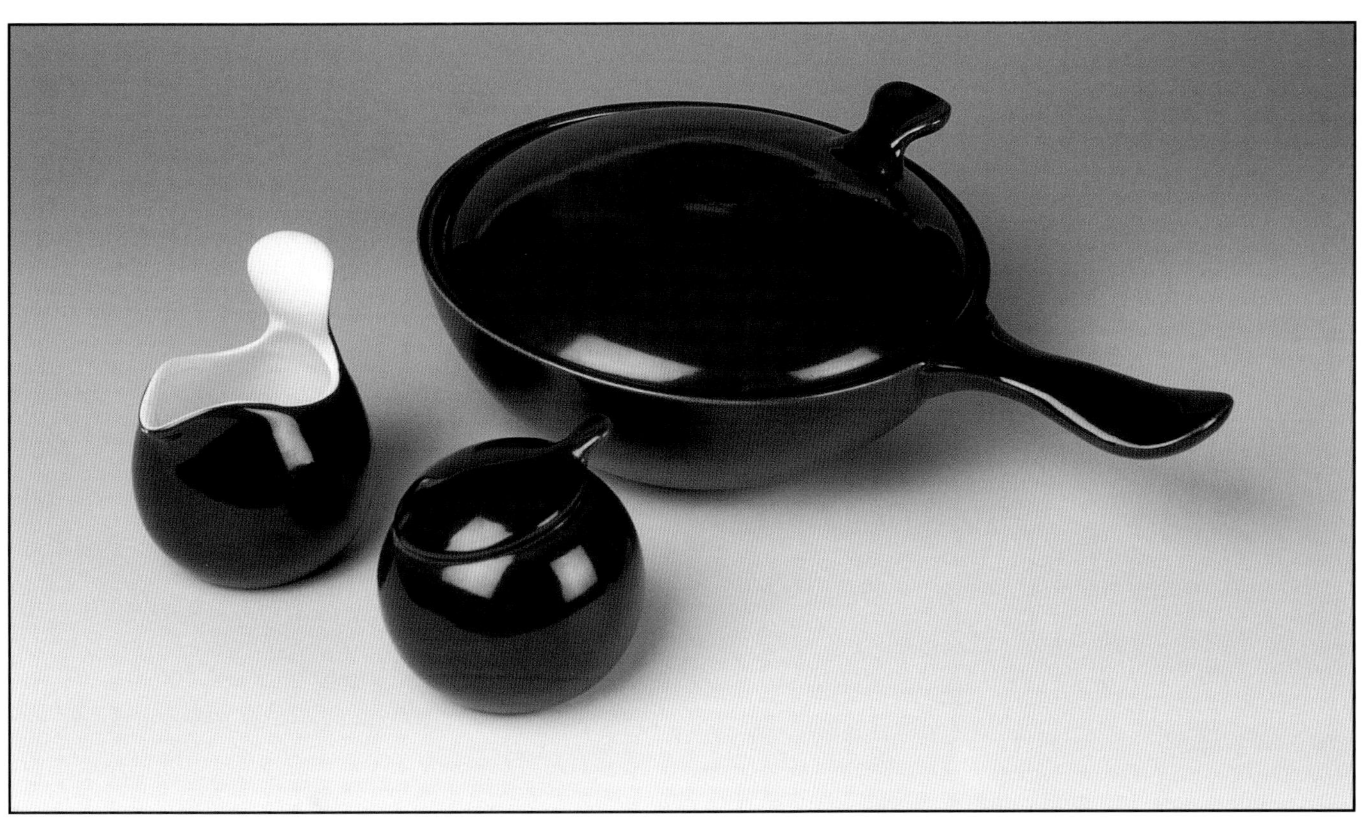

Red Wing.* ***Town & Country***. *Mulberry* (**Quartette**). Creamer, $175-250 (estimate). Sugar with cover, $250-300 (estimate). Casserole with cover, ND.

Red Wing.* ***Town & Country***. *Ming Green*, (**Quartette**) *Chartreuse*, *Copperglow*, *Mulberry*. **Quartette** colors on ***Town & Country***.

Red Wing.* ***Town & Country***. *Chartreuse* (***Quartette***). Relish dish, 6 7/8", $35-55 (estimate).
Provincial Luncheon Ware. *Chartreuse* (***Quartette***). <1951. *Festive Supper Service*, 12 1/8", $40-55.

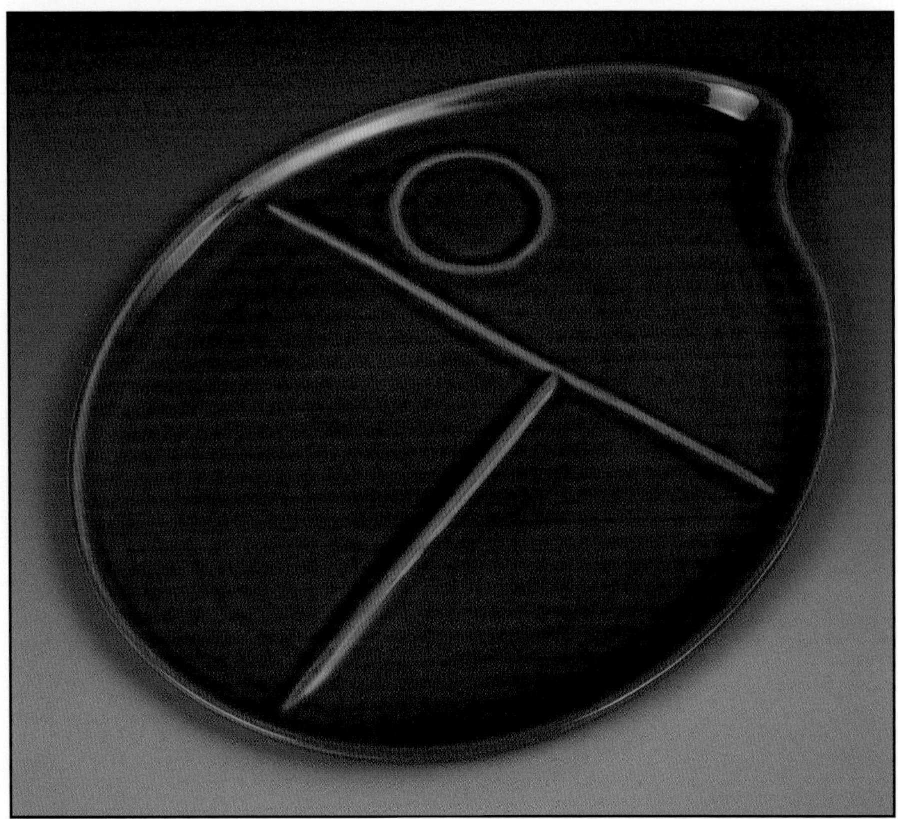

Red Wing.* ***Provincial Luncheon Ware***. *Copper Glow.* <1951. *Patio Supper Service*, 13" [without ceramic cup], $25-35.

Red Wing.* ***Quartette***. **Concord**. *Mulberry, Chartreuse, Ming Green, Copper Glow*. 1950. Plates, 10 3/8", $8-12 each.

Red Wing.* ***Quartette***. *Copper Glow.* Gravy boat, $25-30; creamer, $12-15; sugar with cover, $15-22; salt, $4-7.

Red Wing.* ***Quartette***. *Copper Glow.* [Bowl], 8 1/2" x 2 1/4", $6-12; plate, 10 1/2", $6-10; teacup & saucer, $8-12.

Red Wing.* ***Quartette***. *Mulberry.* Casserole with cover, 2 1/2 qt., $45-50.

Red Wing.* **Concord**. *Fantasy.* Belle Kogan (p). c.1951. Divided vegetable dish, $15-22; cup & saucer, $10-15. This author has not determined who designed the **Concord** shape.

Red Wing.* **Fancy Free**. Belle Kogan. *Desert.* 1952. Dinner plate, 10 1/2", $60-100; bread & butter plate, 6 1/2", $30-35; teacup & saucer, $60-75. Belle Kogan was one of America's leading industrial designers from the 1930s to 1960s. She was highly regarded for her innovative, contemporary design in the gift and housewares industry. Her client list included more than fifty companies, including Boonton Molding Co., Cameron Pottery, Commercial Decal Co., Ebeling & Reuss, The Gailstyn Company, Haviland China Co., Nelson McCoy Pottery, Roseville Pottery, and Vontury, Inc.

Red Wing.* *Desert.* Celery dish, 9", $75-100; pickle dish, 11 1/4", $65-90; relish dish, 12" [doubly divided], $80-125; platter, 13 3/4" x 11", $100-125.

Red Wing.* *Desert.* Creamer, $50-75; teapot and cover, $150-250; sugar with cover, $65-85.

Red Wing.* *Desert.* Beverage server with cover, $150-250; water pitcher, $150-200.

Red Wing.* *Desert.* Casserole with cover, 2 1/2 qt., $200-250; sauce or fruit dish, 5 3/4" x 1 1/2", $20-30.

Red Wing.* *Desert.* Salt & pepper, $70-80, pair; butter dish with cover, $125+.

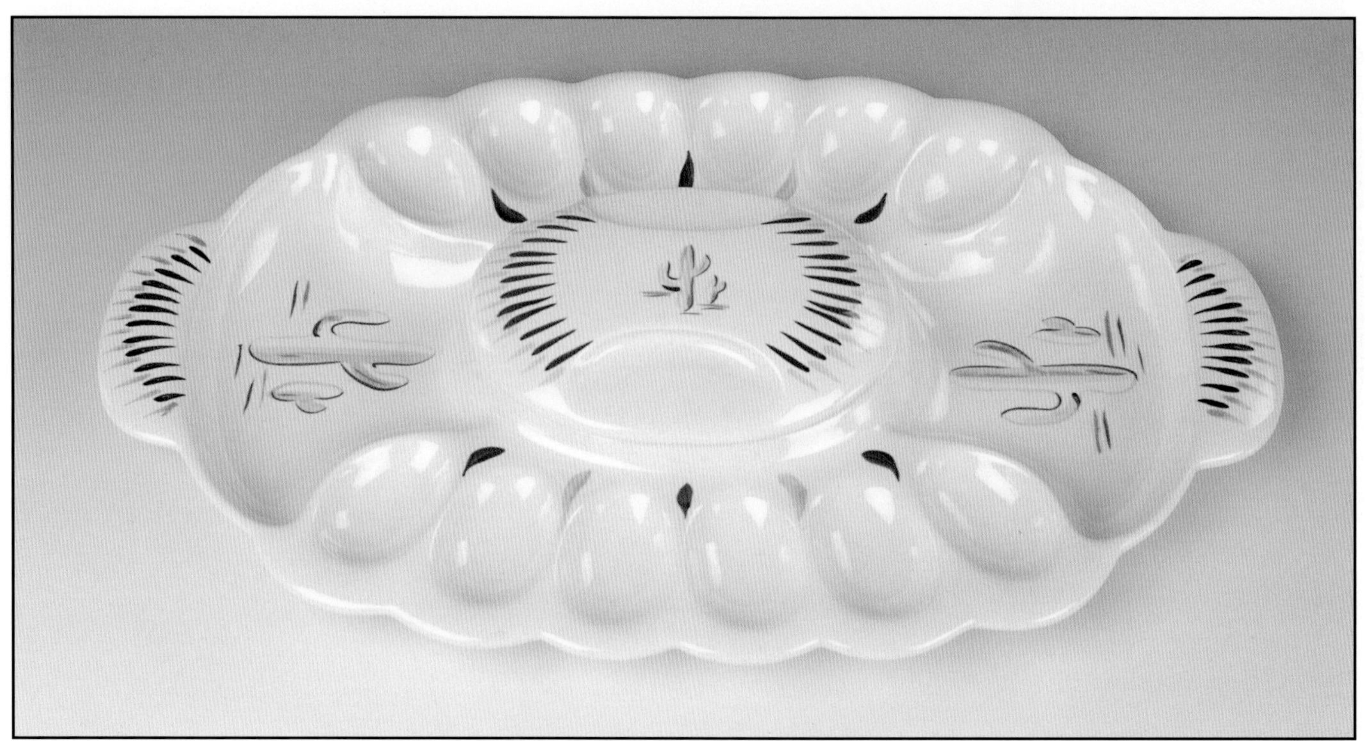

Red Wing.* *Desert.* Egg plate, $275-$350.

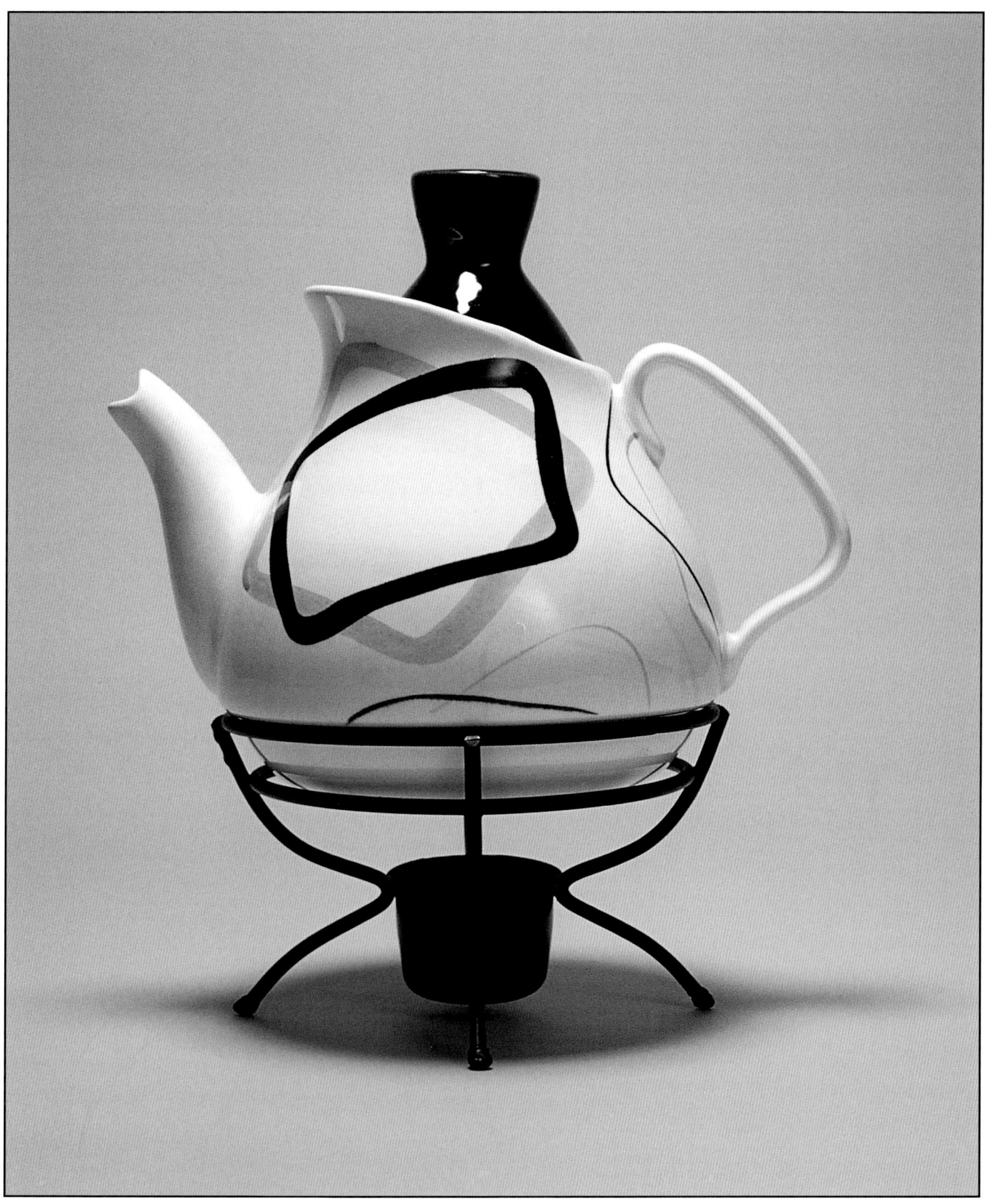

Red Wing.* **Casual**. Charles Murphy. *Smart Set.* 1953. Teapot with cover & iron warmer, $95-150. Many of Charles Murphy's ceramic shape and pattern designs are outstanding examples of mid-century modern style and highly regarded. His early accomplishments included a large mural honoring the pottery industry at the 1939 New York World's Fair. His work for Red Wing as artist and designer spanned more than twenty years. After Red Wing closed, Murphy became a respected wildlife artist.

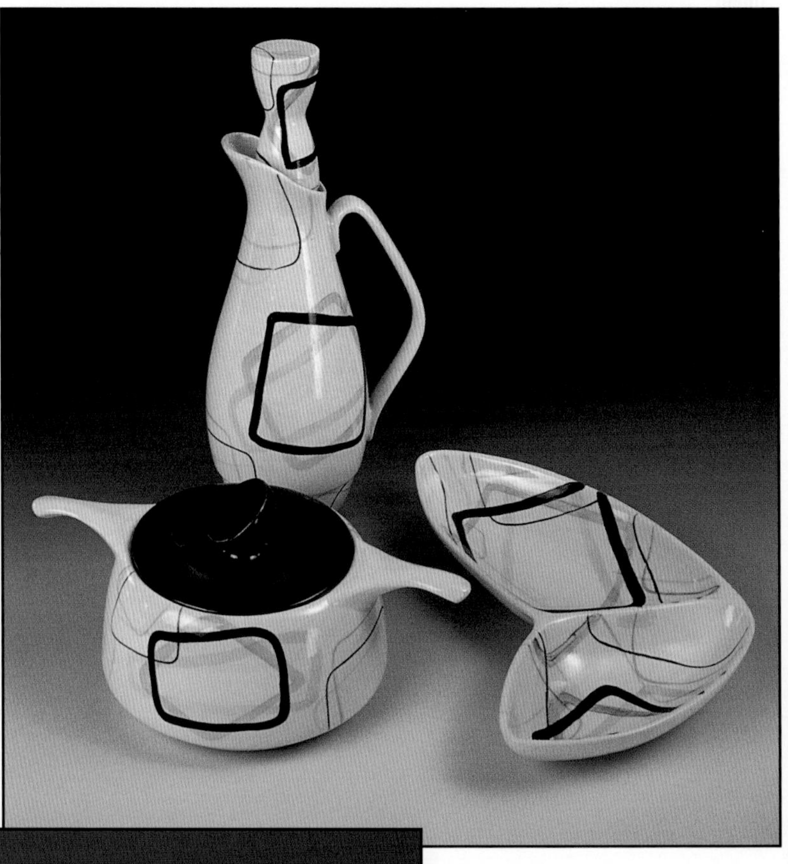

Red Wing.* *Smart Set.* Beverage server with stopper, $90-150; 2 qt. casserole with cover, $55-80; divided vegetable, $45-65. Both the beverage and casserole were available with stands (not shown.)

Red Wing.* *Smart Set.* Divided vegetable, $45-65; cup & saucer, $15-25.

Red Wing.* *Smart Set.* 2 Qt. casserole with cover, $55-80.

Red Wing.* *Smart Set.* Cup & saucer, $15-25; handled marmite with cover, $40-55.

Red Wing.* *Smart Set.* 3-compartment relish tray, $50-60.

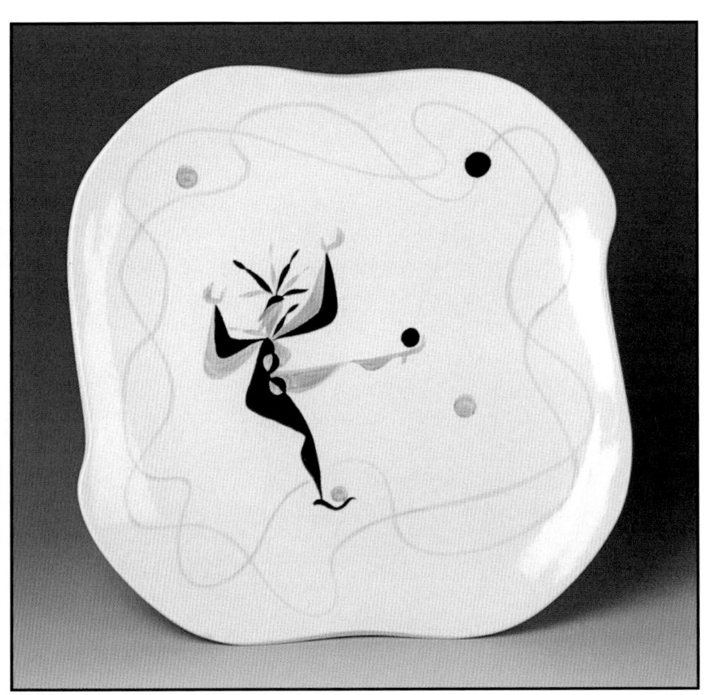

Red Wing.* Charles Murphy. *Kermis.* 1955. Sandwich tray, 14 1/2", $150-175. Charles Murphy designed the large majority of Red Wing's modern shapes and patterns.

Red Wing.* *Kermis.* 8 1/2" plates, $100-125, each.

Red Wing.* *Kermis.* Salad bowl 13" [13 1/4" x 4 3/4"], $200-250+; salad bowl, 10" [x 3 1/2"], $150-175.

Red Wing.*
Kermis. Beverage server and cover, $350-450+.

Red Wing.* *Kermis*. Sugar and cover, $100-125; creamer, $75-85.

Red Wing.* *Kermis*. Cup & saucer, $60-85.

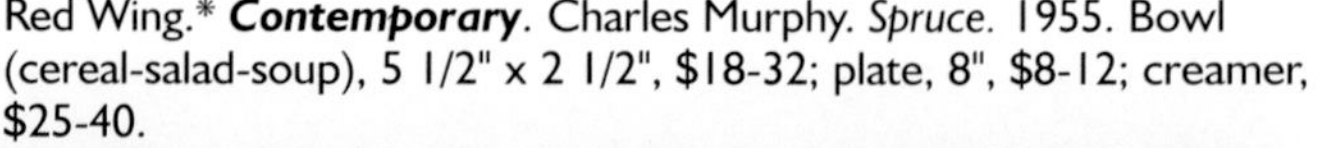

Red Wing.* ***Contemporary***. Charles Murphy. *Spruce*. 1955. Bowl (cereal-salad-soup), 5 1/2" x 2 1/2", $18-32; plate, 8", $8-12; creamer, $25-40.

Red Wing.* **Futura**. Charles Murphy. *Crazy Rhythm*. 1956. Dinner plate, 10 1/2" [10 3/4" x 10"], $10-16; coffee cup & saucer, $10-16.

Red Wing.* *Crazy Rhythm*. Sugar and cover, $30-40; creamer, $20-27.

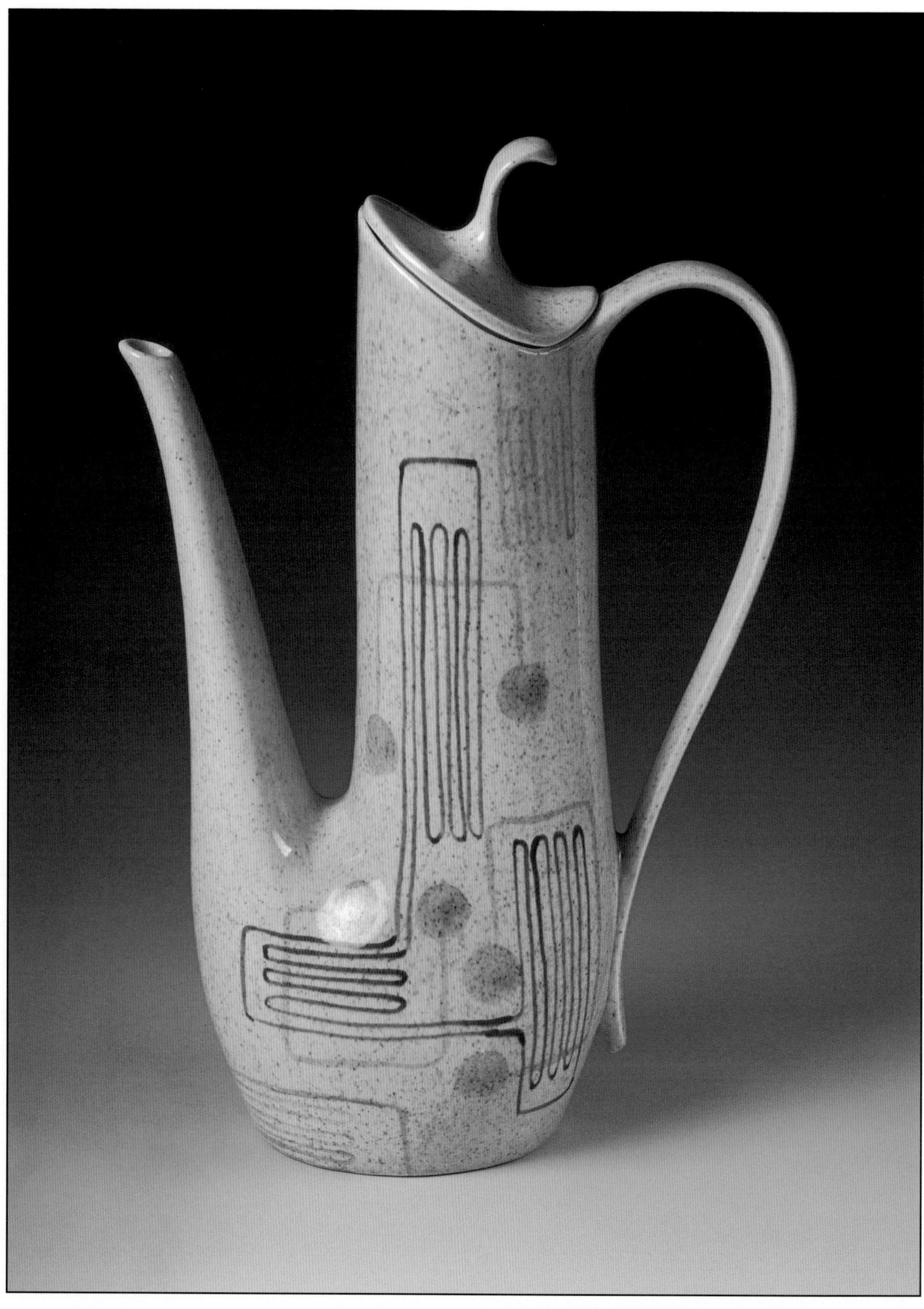

Red Wing.* *Crazy Rhythm.* Beverage server and cover, $90-150.

Red Wing.* *Crazy Rhythm.* Salt & pepper, pair, $25-35; divided vegetable, 10", $25-30; gravy boat with tray, $30-40; sauce or fruit dish, 5 1/8" x 4 3/4" x 1 1/2", $8-12.

Red Wing.* **Futura**. Charles Murphy. *Northern Lights.* 1956. Creamer, $14-22; teapot and cover, $70-125; sugar with cover, $30-40; relish dish, $20-30.

Red Wing.* **Futura**. Charles Murphy. *Golden Viking.* 1956. Cup & saucer, $10-15.

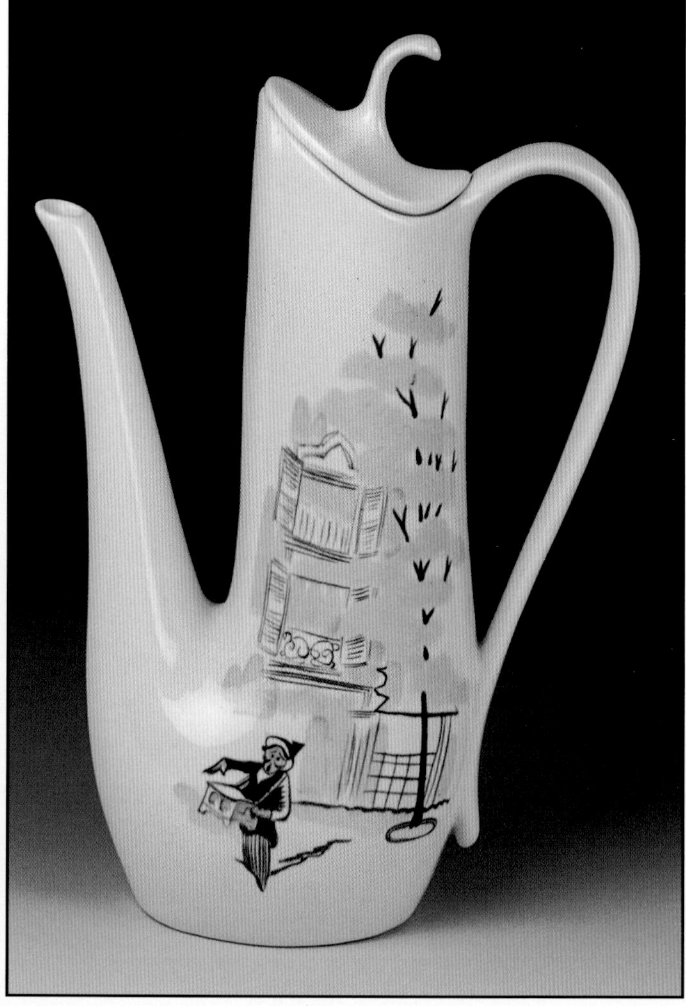

Red Wing.* **Futura**. Charles Murphy. *Montmartre.* 1957. Beverage server and cover, $150-160.

Red Wing.* *Montmartre*. Water pitcher, 2 quart, $140-150; water pitcher, 1 quart, $75-100.

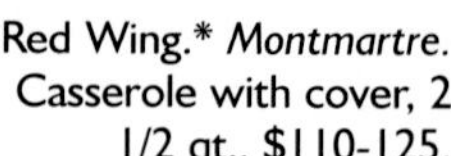

Red Wing.* *Montmartre*. Casserole with cover, 2 1/2 qt., $110-125.

Red Wing.* *Montmartre.* Teapot with cover, $150-160; cup & saucer, $25-35.

Red Wing.* *Montmartre.* Creamer, $30-35; sugar with cover, $45-55.

Red Wing.* *Montmartre.* Salt & pepper, pair, $30-35; salad bowl, 12", $75-85.

Red Wing.* *Montmartre.* Salad bowl, 12", $75-85.

Red Wing.* *Montmartre.* Relish dish, $45-50; divided vegetable, $45-55.

Red Wing.* Charles Murphy (s). *Continental Buffet*. 1957. 2 Qt. casserole with stand, $180-250.

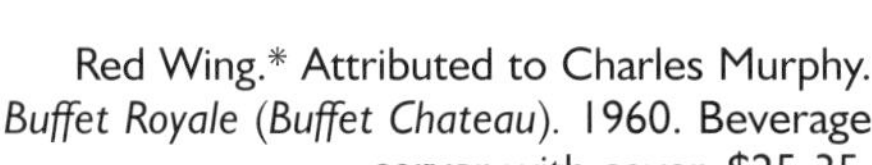

Red Wing.* Attributed to Charles Murphy. *Buffet Royale* (*Buffet Chateau*). 1960. Beverage server with cover, $25-35.

Red Wing.* ***True China***. **True China**. Charles Murphy. *Lute Song*. 1960. Sugar with cover, $15-25; teapot & cover, $75-100; creamer, $10-15.

Red Wing.* *Lute Song*. Gravy boat with cover, $40-45; butter dish with cover, $30-35; vegetable dish, 8 1/4" x 3", $20-25.

Red Wing.* *Lute Song.* Large salad bowl, 11 1/4" x 4 7/8", $30-40; cereal salad soup, 6 1/4" x 2 1/2", $10-15; sauce or fruit, 4 7/8" x 2 1/8", $8-12.

Red Wing.* *Lute Song.* Cup & saucer, $8-15; divided vegetable, 11 3/4", $20-25; bread tray, 19 1/8", $35-45.

Red Wing.* *Lute Song.* Casserole with cover, 2 1/2 qt., $55-75.

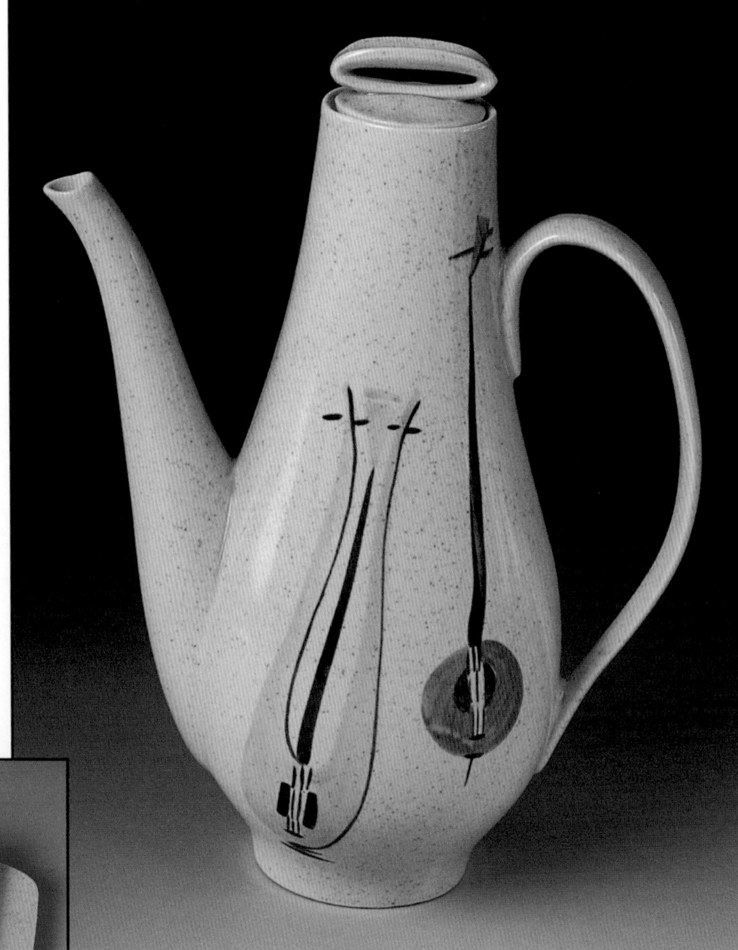

Red Wing.* *Lute Song.* Beverage server with cover, $75-100.

Red Wing.* *Lute Song.* Six piece relish, $200+.

Red Wing.* **Cylinder.** Charles Murphy. *Pompeii.* Dinner plate, 10" [10 1/4"], $10-12; cup & saucer, $8-12.

Red Wing.* *Pompeii.* Salt & pepper, $15-25, per pair. Dinner plate, $10-12; cereal salad soup, 6 1/4" x 1 5/8", $10-15; cup & saucer, $8-12.

Red Wing.* *Pompeii.* Creamer, $10-15; butter dish with cover, $25-35; sugar with cover, $20-25.

Red Wing.* *Pompeii.* 1962. Teapot with cover, $90-125.

Red Wing.* *Pompeii.* Teapot & butter dish.

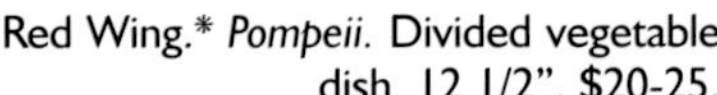

Red Wing.* *Pompeii.* Divided vegetable dish, 12 1/2", $20-25.

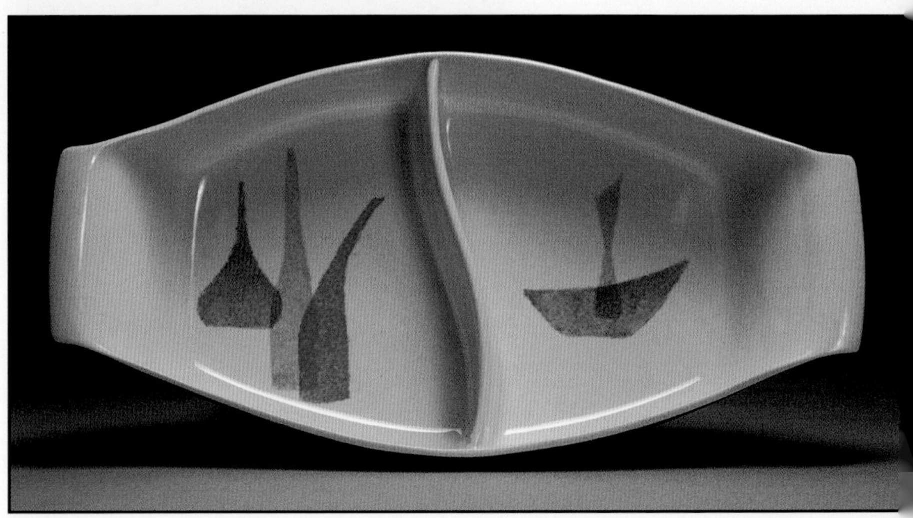

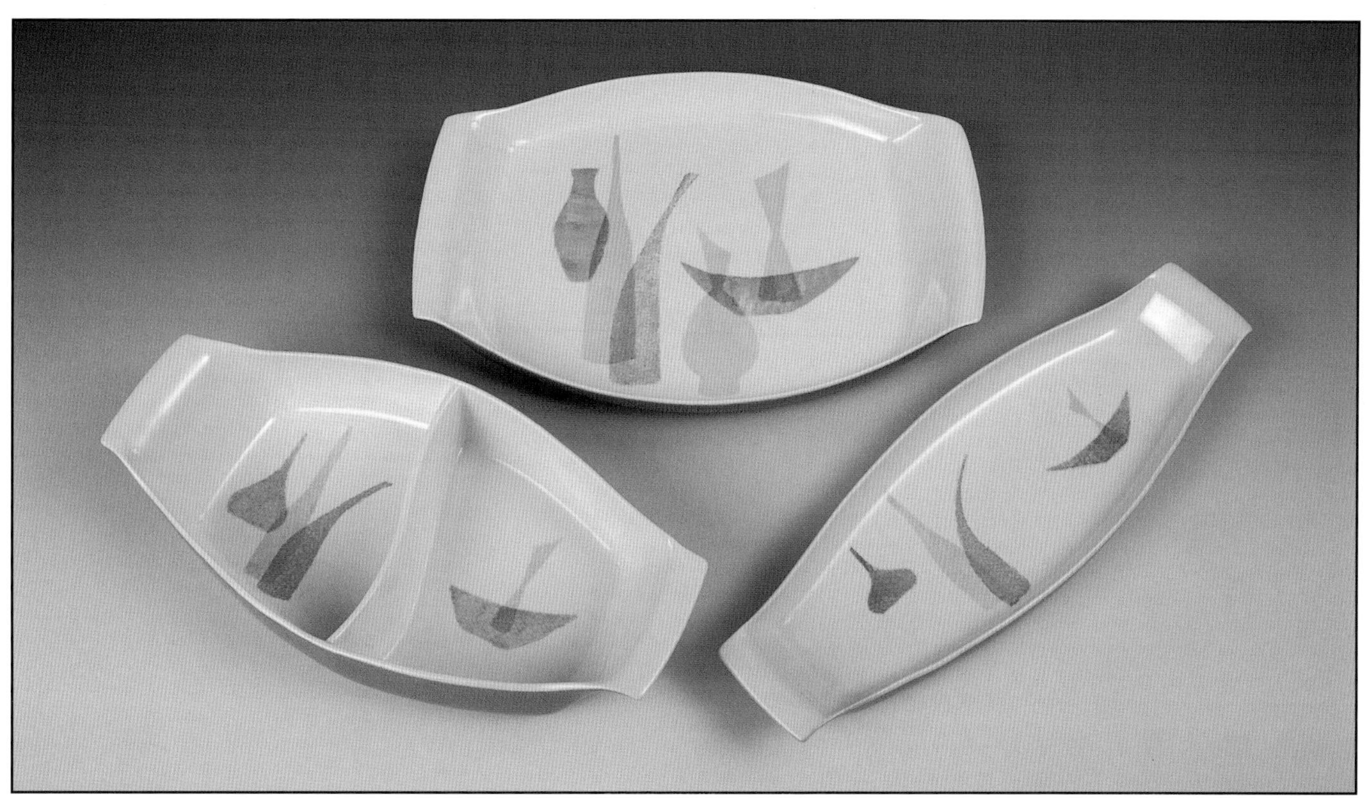

Red Wing.* *Pompeii.* Divided vegetable dish, 12 1/2", $20-25; celery dish, 14" x 4 1/2", $20-25; small platter, 13", $30-35.

Red Wing.* **Cylinder.** Charles Murphy. c.1963. *Pepe.* Cup & saucer, $5-12; beverage server with cover, $75-85; sugar with cover, $18-24; creamer, $12-15.

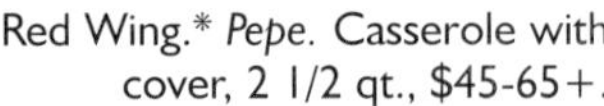
Red Wing.* *Pepe.* Casserole with cover, 2 1/2 qt., $45-65+.

Red Wing.* *Pepe* casserole. Another view.

Red Wing.* *Pepe.* Salt & pepper, $15-25; butter dish with cover, $30-35.

Riverside China™

Riverside Ceramic Company (Riverside, California) for Richards Morgenthau & Co. (Raymor). ***Riverside China***. Eva Zeisel. 1947. Teacup, $50-100. This rare line of fine china was said to feature a unique process that permitted the creation of "iridescent lustre glazes" on china (*Crockery & Glass Journal*, July 1947). The line was referred to as "**Riverside**"..."New Fine China", while the backstamp read, "California Riverside China."

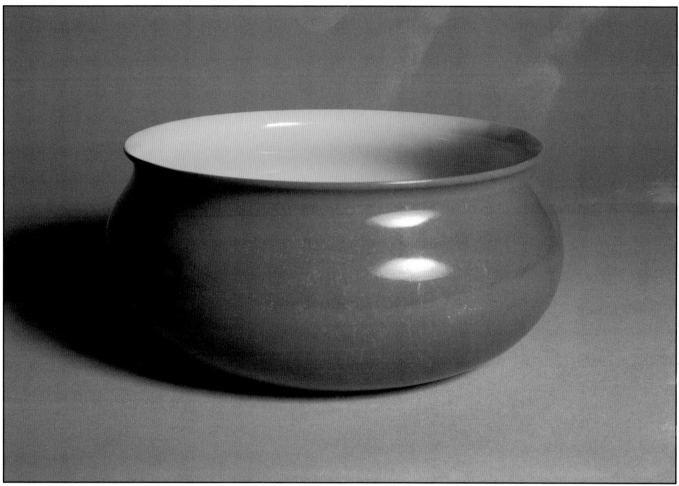

Riverside. ***Riverside China***. Vegetable bowl, 8 1/8", $350-500.

Roselane Pottery™

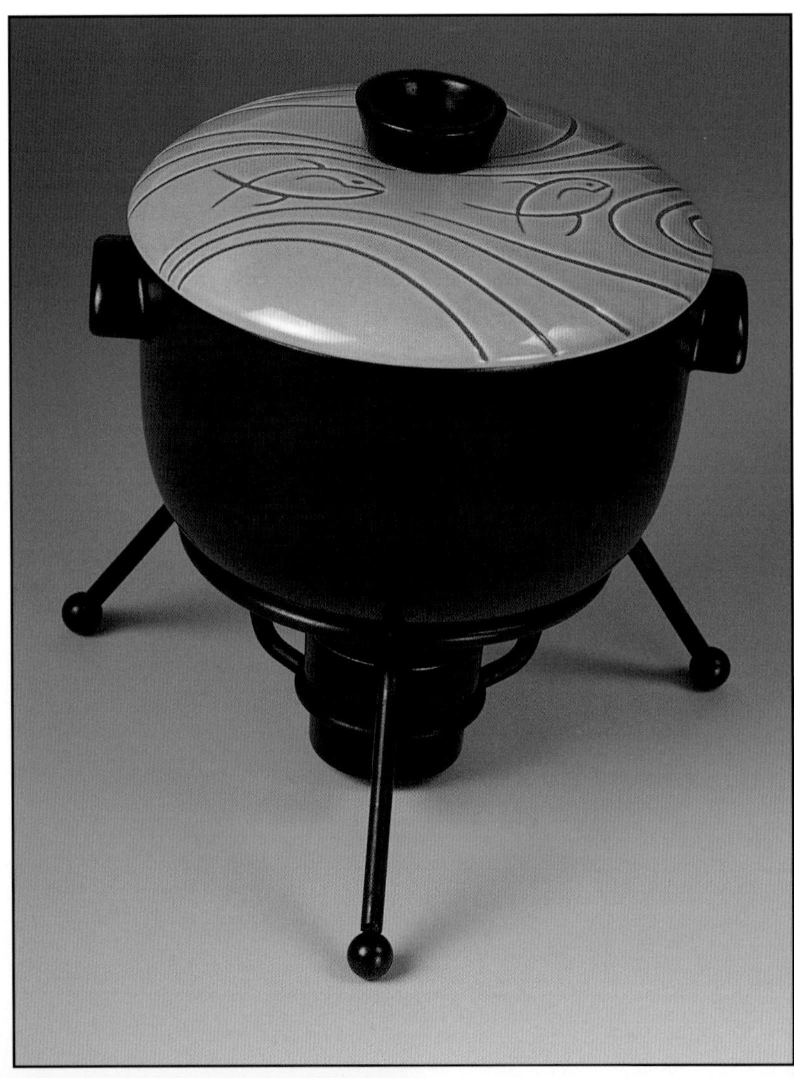

Roselane. *Pink with Black* [*Fish*]. <1955. Covered casserole with stand, $30-50.

Roselane Pottery (Pasadena, California). *Sea Green with Black* [*Fish*]. <1955. Bowl, 13 3/4", $30-55; fork & spoon, $30-45.

Roseville Pottery Company

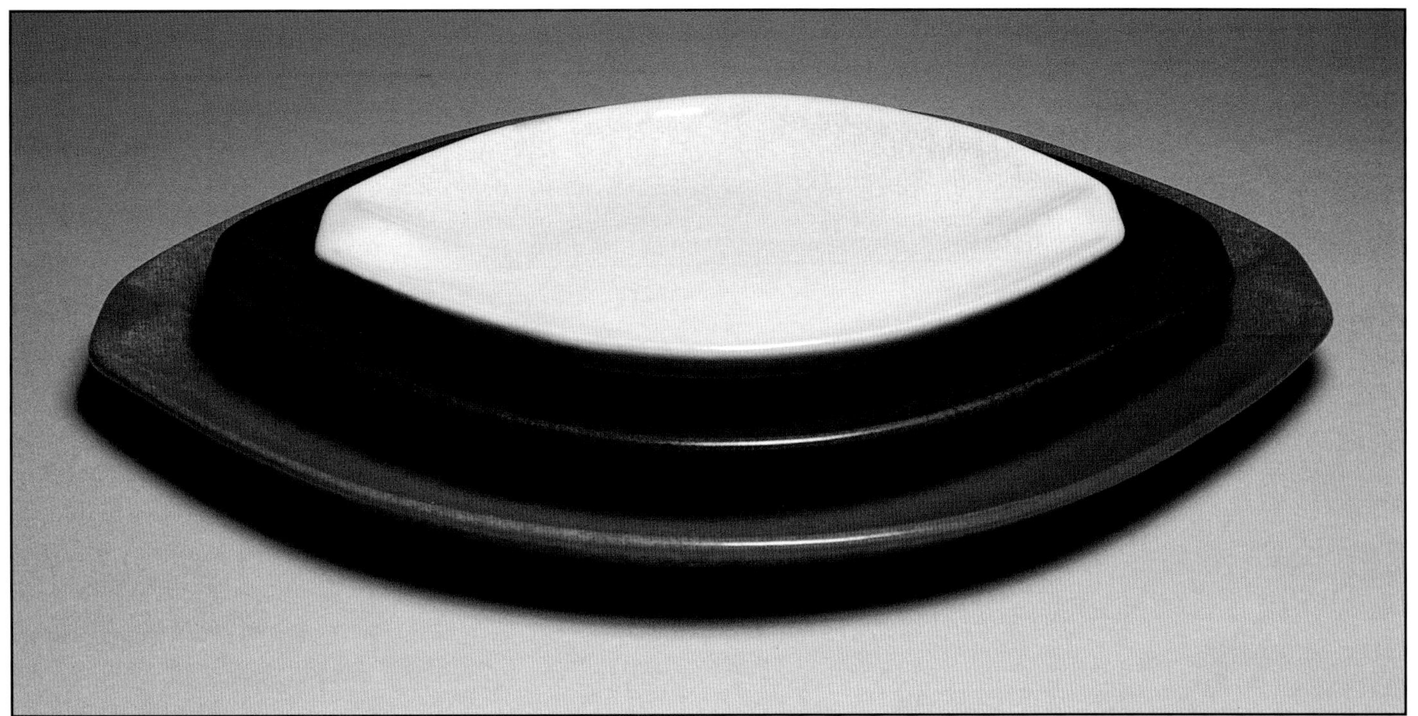

Roseville Pottery Company (Zanesville, Ohio) for Raymor (Richards Morgenthau & Co. New York, New York).* ***Raymor Modern Stoneware***. Ben Seibel. *Terra Cotta*. 1952. 152. Dinner plate, 12", $15-25. *Avocado Green*. 153. Salad plate, 10", $15-25. *Contemporary White*. 154. Bread & butter plate, 7 3/4", $12-15. ***Raymor Modern Stoneware*** was one of the most attractive lines of American mid-century dinnerware ever to grace a table. Each shape is visually spectacular and a sculpted work of art. The line was touted as combining "cook-in, bake-in, [and] serve-in" features. Ben Seibel was a masterful industrial designer whose creations included metal cooking ware, fine china, lamps, clocks, glassware, and furniture. His ceramic designs included lines for Iroquois China Company, Mikasa, and Pfaltzgraff—among others. Seibel's work is gaining in popularity with collectors and design enthusiasts.

Roseville.* ***Raymor Modern Stoneware***. *Beach Gray*. 159. Stand only for sugar & creamer, $35-55. *Autumn Brown* [*Chocolate*]. 157. Covered sugar, $45-55. *Terra Cotta*. 158. Covered cream pitcher, $70-100.

Roseville.* ***Raymor Modern Stoneware***. *Terra Cotta.* 152. Dinner plate, 12", $15-25. 157. Covered sugar, $45-55. 172. Covered jam or relish w/ spoon, $45-85 without spoon. ND with spoon. The spoon is relatively scarce. 203. Ash tray, $45-65. 158. Covered cream pitcher, $70-100.

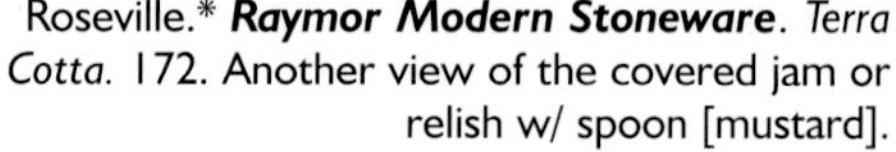
Roseville.* ***Raymor Modern Stoneware***. *Terra Cotta.* 172. Another view of the covered jam or relish w/ spoon [mustard].

Roseville.* ***Raymor Modern Stoneware***. *Avocado Green.* 170, 171. Vinegar & oil cruets, $60-100, each. *Terra Cotta.* 172. Covered jam or relish w/ spoon [mustard], $45-85 without spoon. *Autumn Brown.* 168. Salt shaker, $25-35. 169. Pepper shaker, $25-35.

Roseville.* ***Raymor Modern Stoneware***. *Avocado Green [Frogskin]*. 156. Individual covered ramekin, $40-50. 162. Individual corn server, $50-75. 160. Vegetable bowl, $60-100. 181. Covered butter dish, $200-350+.

Roseville.* ***Raymor Modern Stoneware***. *Avocado Green [Frogskin]*. 158. Covered cream pitcher, $100-150.

Roseville.* ***Raymor Modern Stoneware***. *Avocado Green.* 157. Covered sugar, $45-55. 200. Shirred egg, $45-75. 195. Individual bean pot, $55-80. 156. Individual covered ramekin, $35-40.

Roseville.* ***Raymor Modern Stoneware***. *Avocado Green.* 170, 171. Vinegar & oil cruets, $60-100, each. 154. Bread & butter plate, 7 3/4", $12-15. 191. Pickle dish, 9 5/8", $50-95. 150, 151. Cup & saucer, $15-25.

Roseville.* ***Raymor Modern Stoneware***. *Avocado Green.* 177. Celery & olive dish, 15 1/2", $65-130. 198. 1 1/2 Qt. handled casserole, $60-125. 163. Platter, 14", $65-100. 198.

Roseville.* ***Raymor Modern Stoneware***. *Avocado Green.* 198. 1 1/2 Qt. handled casserole, $60-125. 184/188. Medium casserole trivet/bean pot trivet, $70-90. 187. 4 Qt. bean pot, $120-150. 199. Individual casserole, $45-50.

Roseville.* ***Raymor Modern Stoneware***. *Avocado Green.* 181. Covered butter dish, $175-225. 192. Lug fruit, 5 3/4", $12-30. 155. Lug soup, 6 3/4", $20-30. 174. Teapot, $225-295. 175. Teapot trivet, $70-85.

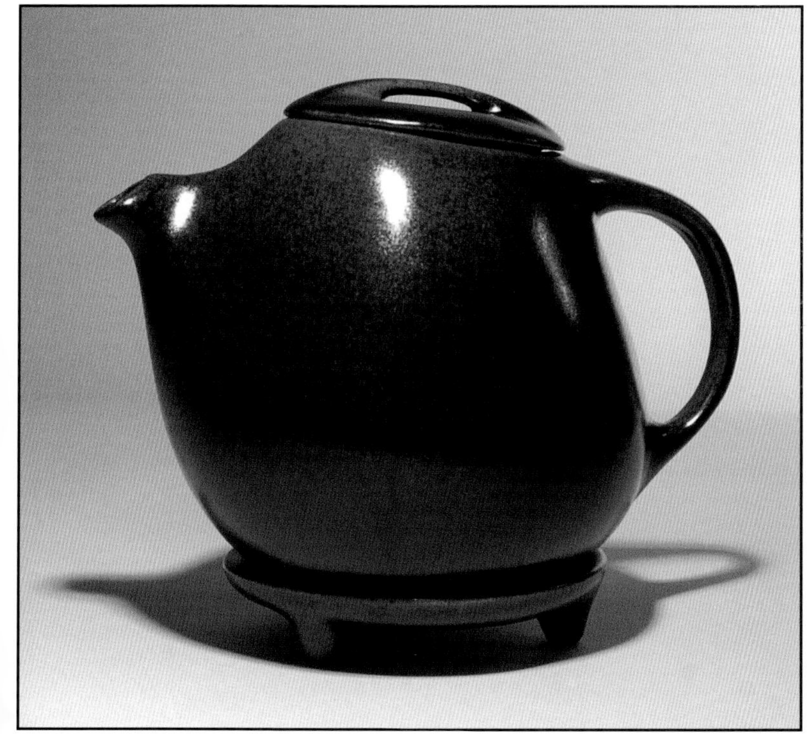

Roseville.* ***Raymor Modern Stoneware***. *Avocado Green.* Teapot and trivet, another view.

Roseville.* ***Raymor Modern Stoneware***. *Avocado Green.* 185. Large casserole, $200-250.

Roseville.* ***Raymor Modern Stoneware***. *Avocado Green.* 168, 169. Salt shaker & pepper shaker, $60-80, pair. 189. Water pitcher, $100-200. 179. Handled coffee tumbler [long handle], $50-100.

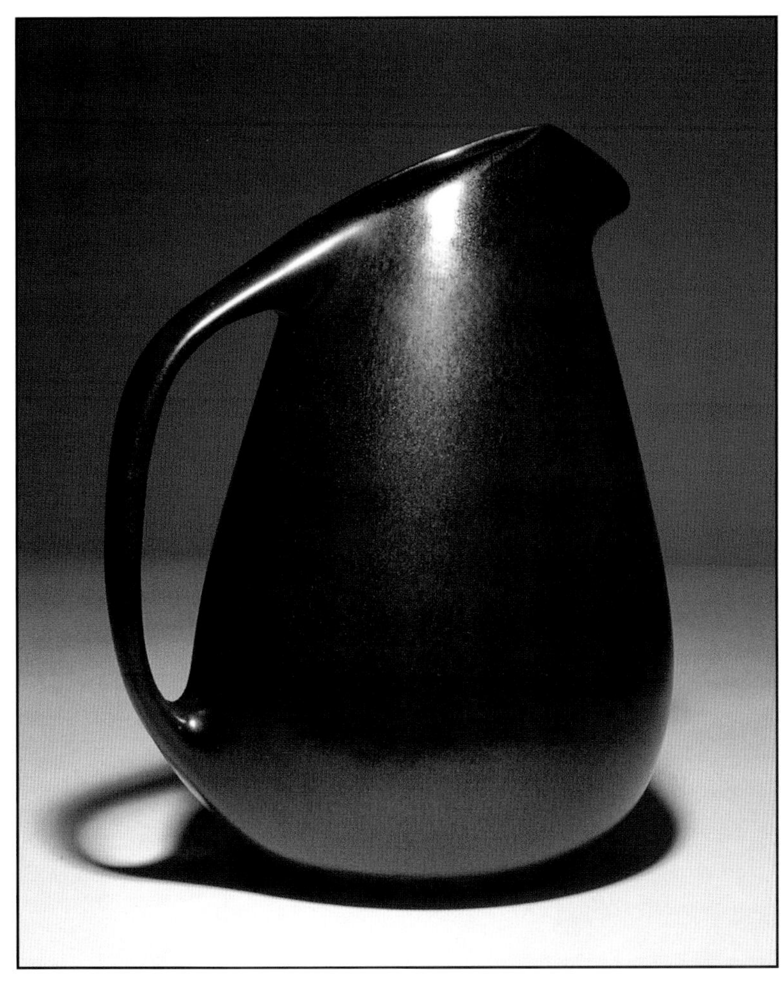

Roseville.* ***Raymor Modern Stoneware***. *Avocado Green.* 189. Water pitcher, another view. $100-200.

Roseville.* ***Raymor Modern Stoneware***. *Autumn Brown [Chocolate]*. 201. Double stacked warmer, $150-200. *Avocado Green.* 187. 4 Qt. bean pot, $120-150.

Roseville.* ***Raymor Modern Stoneware***. *Autumn Brown.* 168, 169. Salt shaker & pepper shaker, $60-75; 162. Individual corn server, 12 1/2", $50-75. 192. Lug fruit, 5 7/8", $12-30. 172. Covered jam or relish w/ spoon, $45-85 without spoon. The glass spoon is very hard to find.

Roseville.* ***Raymor Modern Stoneware***. *Autumn Brown* [*Chocolate*]. 158. Covered cream pitcher, $70-120. 250R-251R. Cup & saucer [redesigned/round], ND. 201. Double stacked warmer, $150-200. 157. Covered sugar, $45-55.

Roseville.* ***Raymor Modern Stoneware***. *Autumn Brown*. 177. Celery & olive dish, $65-130. 156. Individual covered ramekin, $25-40. 150, 151. Cup & saucer, $15-25. 252R. Dinner plate, 10 7/8" [redesigned/oval], $30-40.

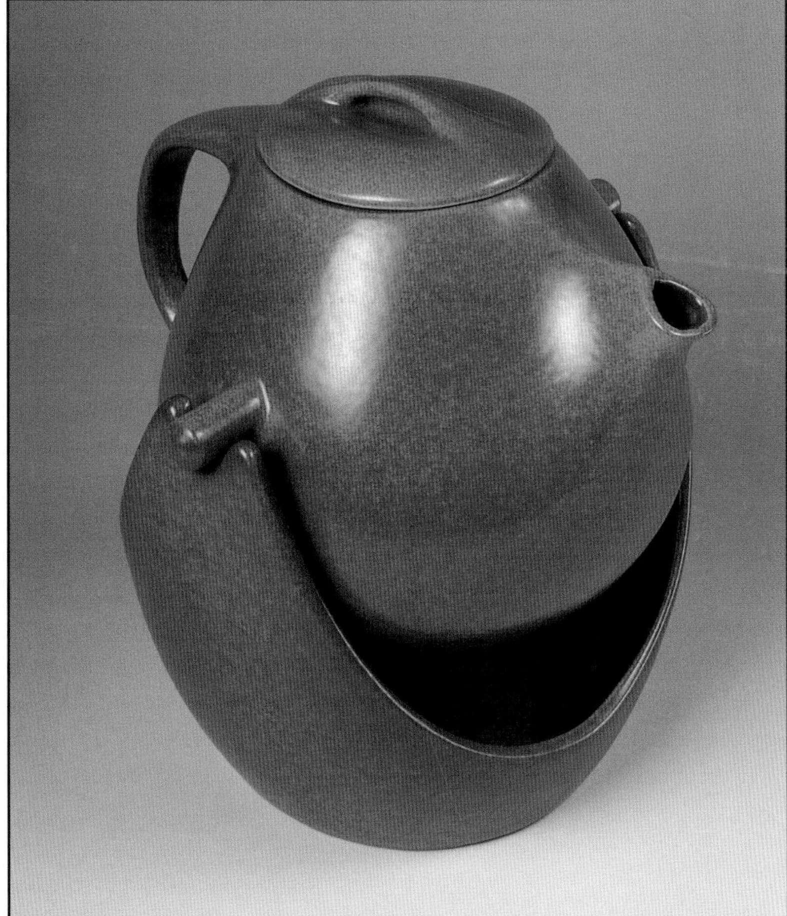

Roseville.* ***Raymor Modern Stoneware***. *Terra Cotta*. 176. Large coffee pot & stand, $350-550.

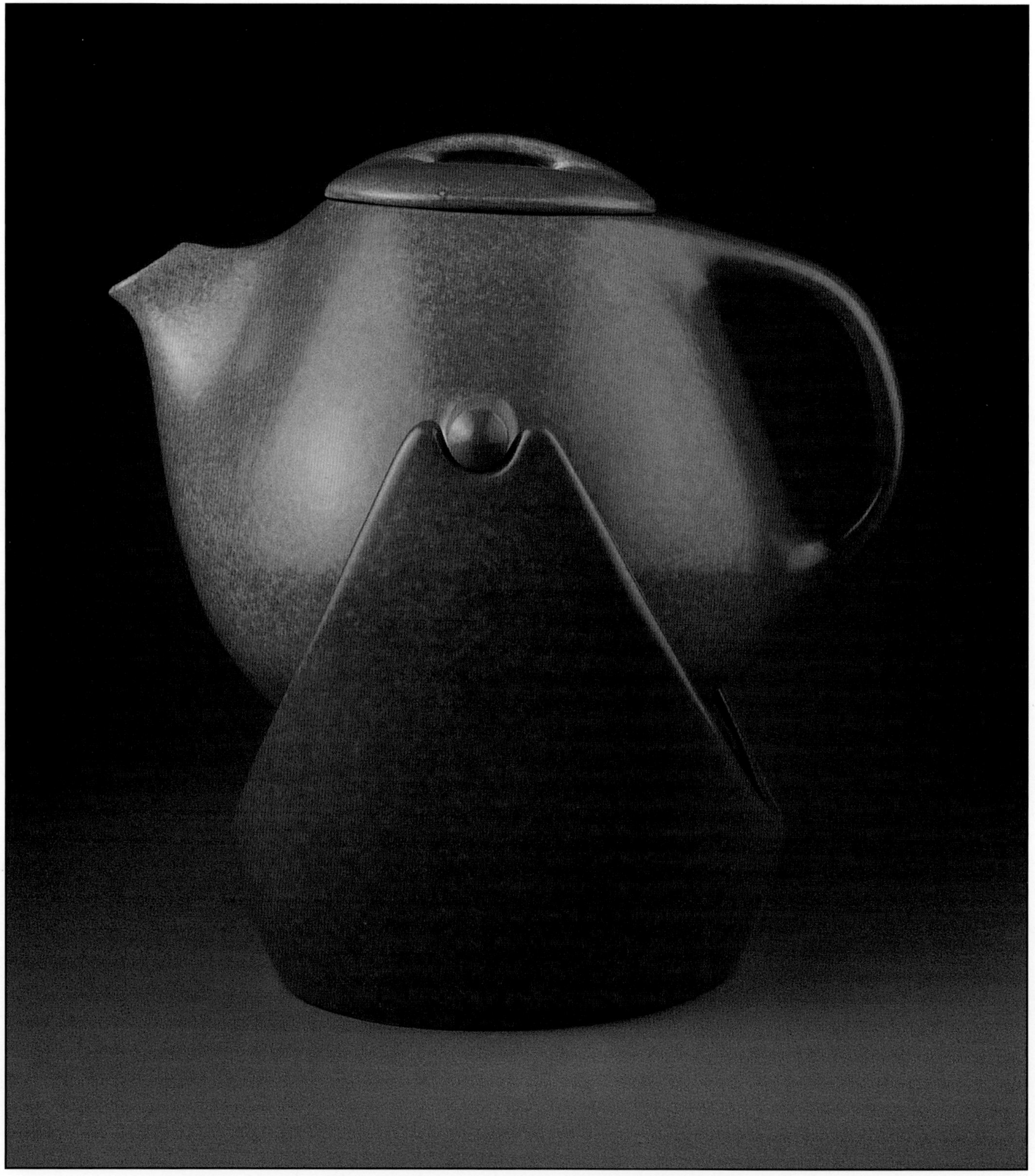

Roseville.* ***Raymor Modern Stoneware***. *Terra Cotta.* 176. Large coffee pot & stand, $350-550.

Roseville.* ***Raymor Modern Stoneware***. *Autumn Brown, Beach Gray, Contemporary White, Terra Cotta.* A parade of coffee pots, $350-550, each.

Roseville.* ***Raymor Modern Stoneware***. *Avocado Green.* 175. Teapot trivet, $70-85. *Contemporary White.* 159. Stand only for sugar & creamer, $35-55. *Autumn Brown.* 184/188. Medium casserole trivet/ bean pot trivet, $70-90.

Roseville.* ***Raymor Modern Stoneware***. Bowls posing for the camera.

Roseville.* ***Raymor Modern Stoneware***. *Terra Cotta.* 194. 2 Qt. bean pot, $100-125. *Avocado Green.* 195 Individual bean pot, $55-80. *Contemporary White.* 193. 3 Qt. bean pot, $100-140. *Autumn Brown.* 187. 4 Qt. bean pot, $120-150.

Roseville.* ***Raymor Modern Stoneware***. *Avocado Green.* 199. Individual casserole, $45-50. *Autumn Brown.* 179. Handled coffee tumbler [short handle], $50-100. *Terra Cotta.* 250R. Cup [redesigned, round], N.D., *Autumn Brown.* 251R. Saucer [redesigned/round], N.D., *Contemporary White.* 181. Covered butter dish, $160-200.

Roseville.* ***Raymor Modern Stoneware***. Comparison of short and long handled coffee tumblers.

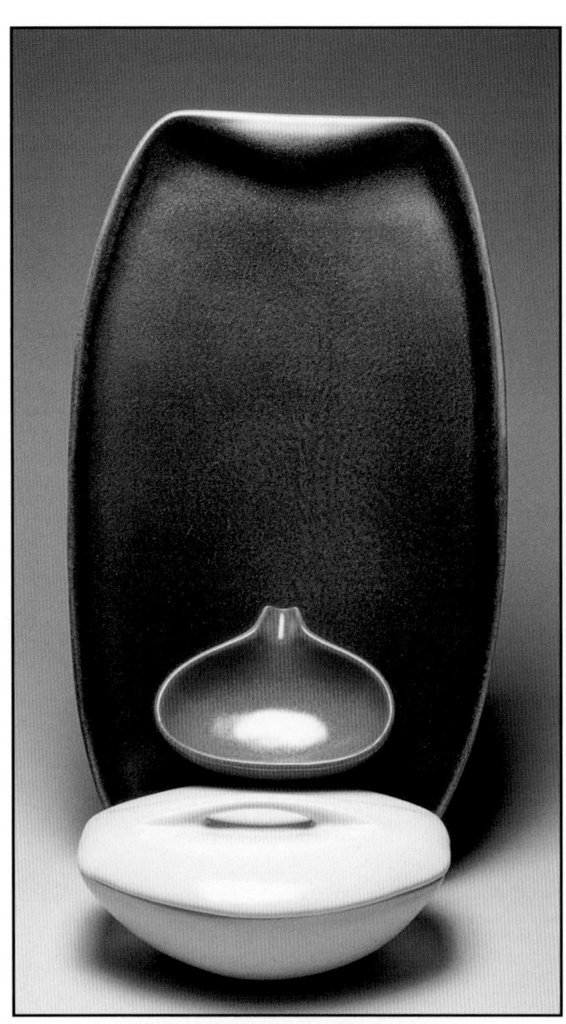

Roseville.* ***Raymor Modern Stoneware***. Another pose.

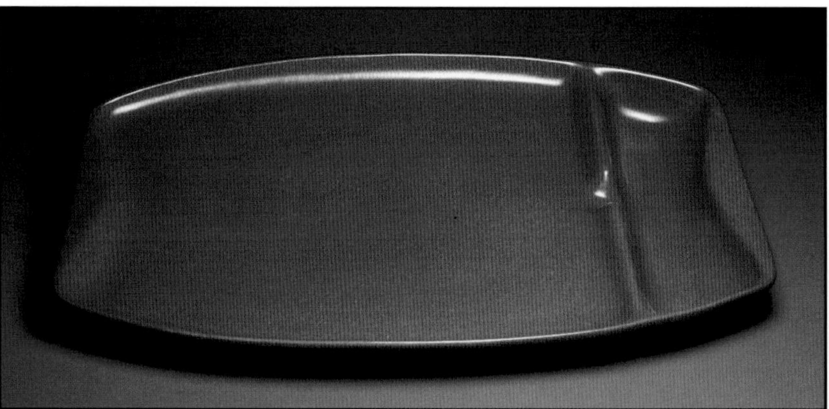

Roseville.* ***Raymor Modern Stoneware***. *Terra Cotta.* 178. Steak platter with well, $150-225.

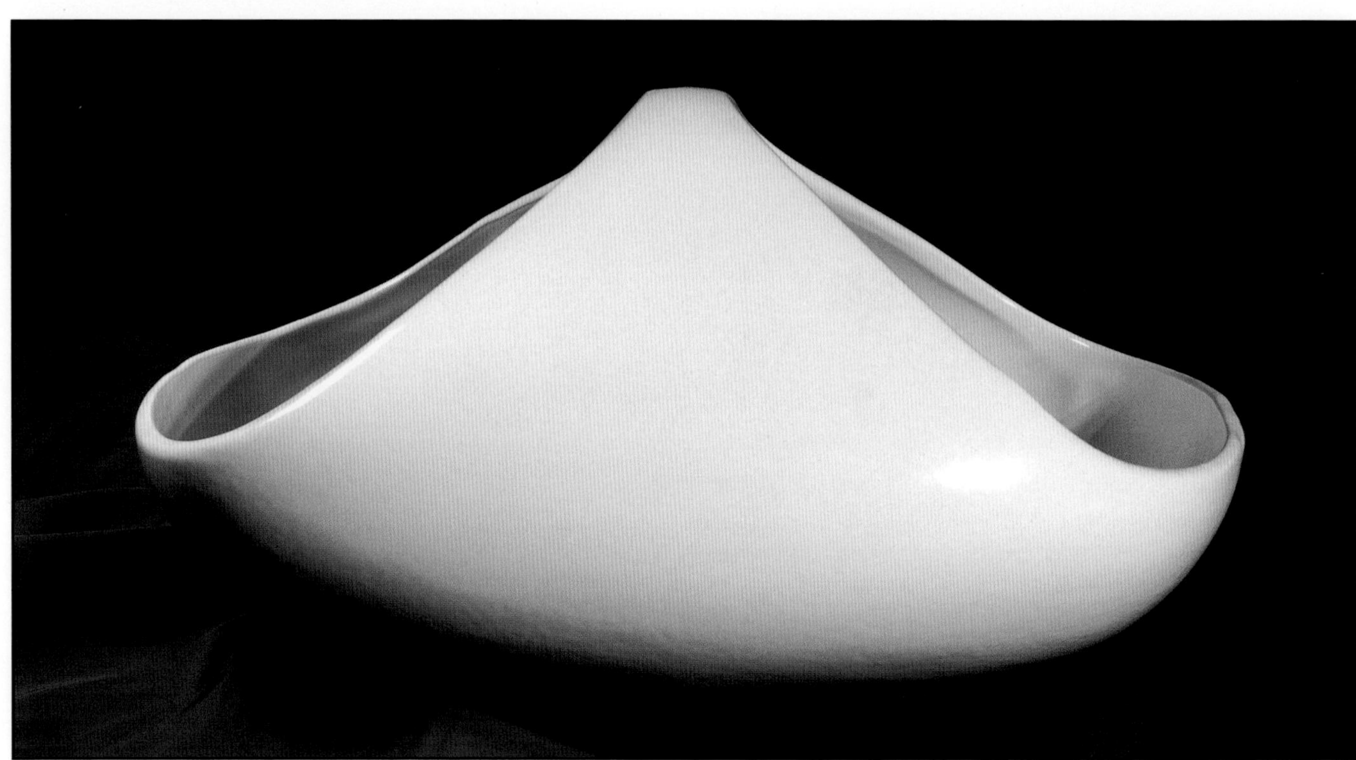

Roseville.* ***Raymor Modern Stoneware***. *Contemporary White.* 166. Handled fruit bowl, $250-450.

Roseville.* ***Raymor Modern Stoneware***. *Contemporary White*. 166. Handled fruit bowl, another view.

Roseville.* ***Raymor Modern Stoneware***. *Robins Egg Blue*. 254R. Bread & butter plate, [redesigned/round], ND. 250R, 251R. Cup & saucer [redesigned/round], ND. 163. Platter, 13 7/8", $100-130. 151L. Saucer [redesigned, oval], ND.

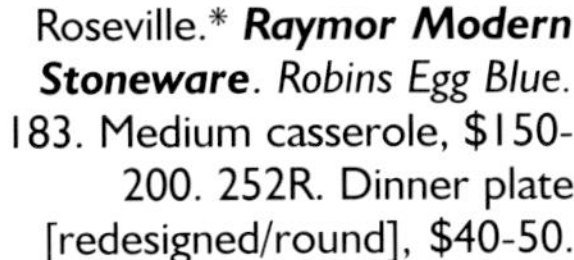

Roseville.* ***Raymor Modern Stoneware***. *Robins Egg Blue*. 183. Medium casserole, $150-200. 252R. Dinner plate [redesigned/round], $40-50.

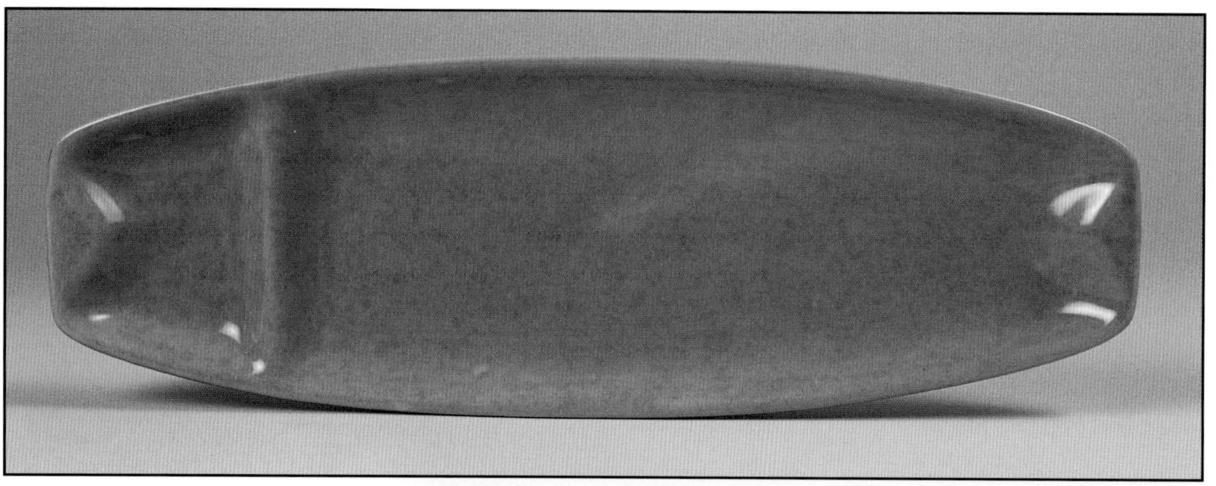

Roseville.* ***Raymor Modern Stoneware***. [*Chartreuse*]. 162. Individual corn server, 12 1/2", ND. This rare color may have been experimental.

Morgantown Glassware Guild for Raymor. ***Raymor Modern Glassware***. Ben Seibel. [*Honey.*] 1952. Dessert bowl, $45-75. [*Green.*], Tumbler, 8 oz., 5", $45-75. Juice, $45-75. This line was designed to accompany ***Raymor Modern Stoneware***. Other colors available included [*Gray*] and [*Crystal*].

Roseville. ***Raymor Two-Tone Casual***. 1954. 2-Pt. covered casserole, $40-50.

Royal China, Inc.

Royal China. **Suburban**. *Tweed.* Gene Patterson (p). 1955. Coffee pot, $25-35; wing-handled bowl, 7", $1-5; platter, $8-15; sugar, $12-20; creamer, $6-10; cup & saucer, $3-8; covered casserole, $25-35.

Royal China, Inc. (Sebring, Ohio). **Suburban**. *Seafare*. Gene Patterson (p). 1955. Creamer, $15-18; sugar, $20-25.

Royal China. *Farmer in the Dell*. 1957. Bowl, 7", $5-8.

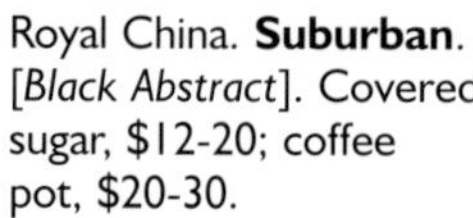

Royal China. **Suburban**. [*Black Abstract*]. Covered sugar, $12-20; coffee pot, $20-30.

Royal China for Mar-crest. **Prestige**. *Terrace.* Plate, 9 1/2", $1-3; cup & saucer, $2-5. *Patio* was a blue on white version of this pattern by Royal China.

Royal China. **Prestige**. *Jester* (*Harlequin* when on **Futura**, c.1962). Plate, 10 1/8", $4-6; cup & saucer, $5-8.

Royal China. **Prestige**. *Deer Me.* Dinner plate, 10 1/8", $4-6.

Royal China. **Prestige**. *Navajo*. <1962. Coffee pot, $25-35.

Royal China. **Prestige**. *Navajo*. <1962. Salt & pepper shakers, $10-15 pair.

Royal China. **Prestige**. Creamer, $3-8.

Royal China. **Prestige**. *Star-Glow.* Gene Patterson (p). <1962. Covered sugar, $6-12; creamer, $5-10; covered butter dish, $10-14.

Royal China.* **Futura**. Arthur Kendricks (s). *Star-Glow.* Ashtray, 5 3/8", $6-8; [plates], 6 1/2", $1-3, each; large vegetable, 9 5/8" x 2 3/8", $2-8. [bowls], 6 1/4" x 1 3/4", $1-3, each; **Prestige**. Gravy, $4-8. **Futura**. Teapot, $15-25; salt & pepper, $5-8, pair.

Royal China.* **Futura**. *Star-Glow.* Tab platter, 11 1/2", $4-8; cup & saucer, $2-5; pie baker, 9 7/8", $15-18; covered casserole, $12-15; plate [dinner], 10 1/8", $1-3; bowls [gravy], $4-8, each; ladles, $15-18, each.

Royal China.* **Futura**. *Star-Glow.* Sugar bowl with lid, $4-6; creamer, $2-5; 13" oval platter, [13 1/8"], $4-8; coffee pot, $15-25.

Royal China.* **Futura**. *Star-Glow.* Three different sized glasses, $6-10, each; [tab plate], 7 1/2", $10-13; pitcher, $15-25.

Royal China.* **Futura**. *Blue Heaven.* Gene Patterson (p). c.1961. Plate, 10 1/8", $1-4; glass, $6-10.

Royal China.* **Futura**. *Mojave.* Gene Patterson (p). c.1961. Chop plate, 12", $15-20.

Royal China.* **Futura**. *Fall Accent.* c.1962. Cup & saucer, $3-6; [plate], 6 1/2", $1-3; bowl, 6 1/4", $1-3.

Royal China.* **Futura**. *Sante Fe.* Curtis Fahnert (p). c.1966. Plate, 10", $4-8; cup & saucer, $3-6.

Royal China.* ***Royal Stone***. Don Schreckengost (s). [***Accent*** in *Sky Blue*]. Don Schreckengost/Charles Henderson (p). c.1966. Covered coffee pot, 8 cup, $25-35. While *Caribe Blue* is a known ***Royal Stone*** color, the color of this lid and ceramic body remain unidentified. The ***Accent*** line featured ***Royal Stone*** with different colored body and lid. This pot is attributed to that line.

Royal China.* ***Royal Stone***. ***Carioca Series***. Don Schreckengost (s). *Tangerine*. Don Schreckengost/Charles Henderson (p). 1966. Covered teapot, 6 cup, $25-35; salt & pepper, $15-20.

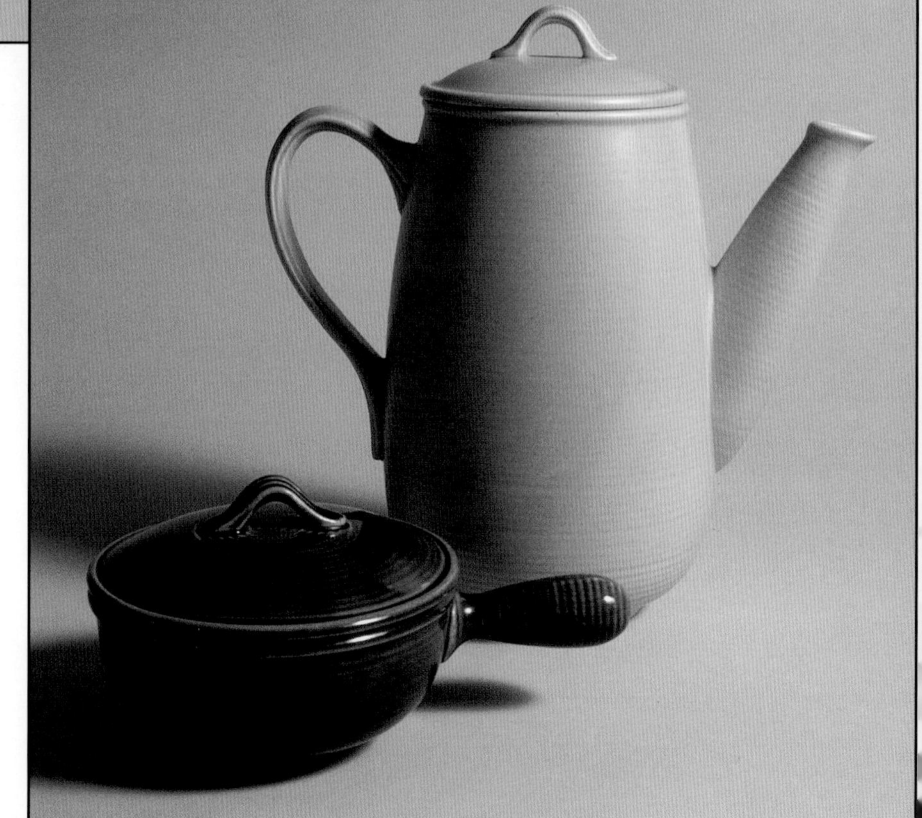

Royal China.* ***Royal Stone***. ***Carioca Series***. *Lime*. Don Schreckengost/Charles Henderson (p). 1966. Covered coffee pot, 8 cup, $25-35; *Aztec Green*. (Not part of ***Carioca Series***). 1966. Ramekin (individual casserole), $12-20.

Rubel & Company Decorative Accessories™

Rubel & Company Decorative Accessories, Inc. (New York, New York).* Fred Press (s). *Contemporary Provincial.* 1952. Individual handled casserole with lid, $15-20.

Saar Ceramics™

Saar Ceramics (California). Attributed to Richard Saar. [*White Bird on Gray-Brown*]. c.1953. Demitasse cup & saucer, $25-40.

The Salem China Company™

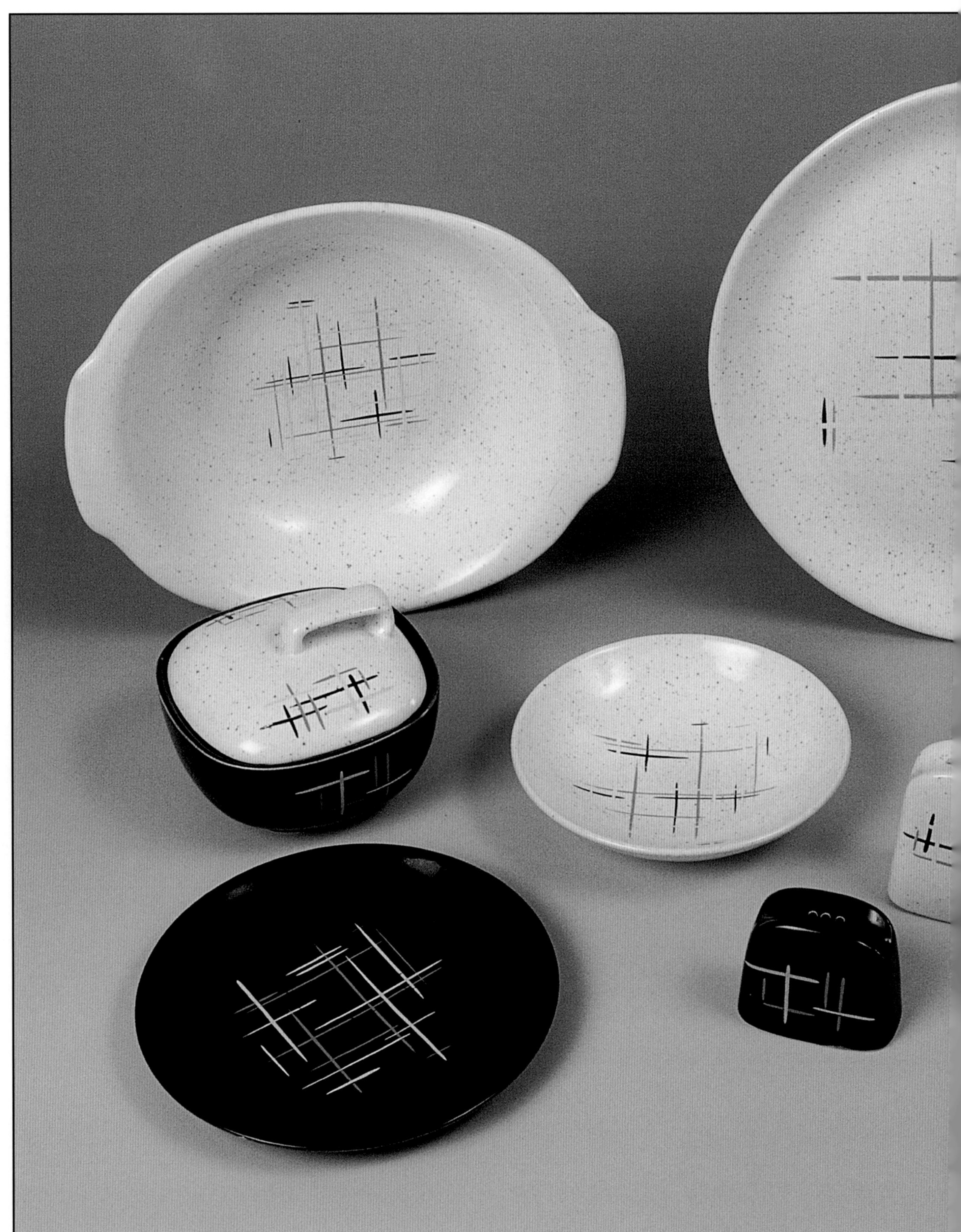

The Salem China Company (Salem, Ohio).* ***Constellation***. Viktor Schreckengost. *Jack Straw Constellation.* 1953-1954. Oblong vegetable dish, 9 1/4", $14-20; covered sugar bowl, $14-20; bread & butter plate, 6", [6 1/8"], $8-10; fruit dish, 5 3/8" x 1 1/8", $6-8; hi-lo salt & pepper shaker, $35-45, pair; dinner plate, 10" [9 7/8"], $10-14; cream pitcher, $10-15. A variety of patterns were available in *Jackstraws*. One pattern, *Jackstraw Red,* featured this pattern in *Flame Red*, *Ebony,* and *Smoke Gray* on the **Ranch Style** coupe shape. Another decoration, *Jackstraw Accent,* displayed this pattern in *Chalk White*, *Canary Yellow*, and *Chocolate Brown* on the boxy **Flair** shape. The trade journal description of *Jackstraw Blue* appears to be similar to or identical to *Jackstraw Constellation*.

Salem.* *Jack Straw Constellation.* Onion soup, 6" x 2 1/4", $10-15; coffee server (lid not shown), $40-55; $60-80 w/lid. Gravy boat, $25-35.

Salem.* *Jack Straw Constellation.* Round vegetable dish, 9" x 2 1/4", $10-15; chop plate, 13" [12 7/8"], $20-30; hors d'oeuvre [plate], 8", $8-14. The 9-piece hors d'oeuvre set featured a wire stand holder for stacks of these plates.

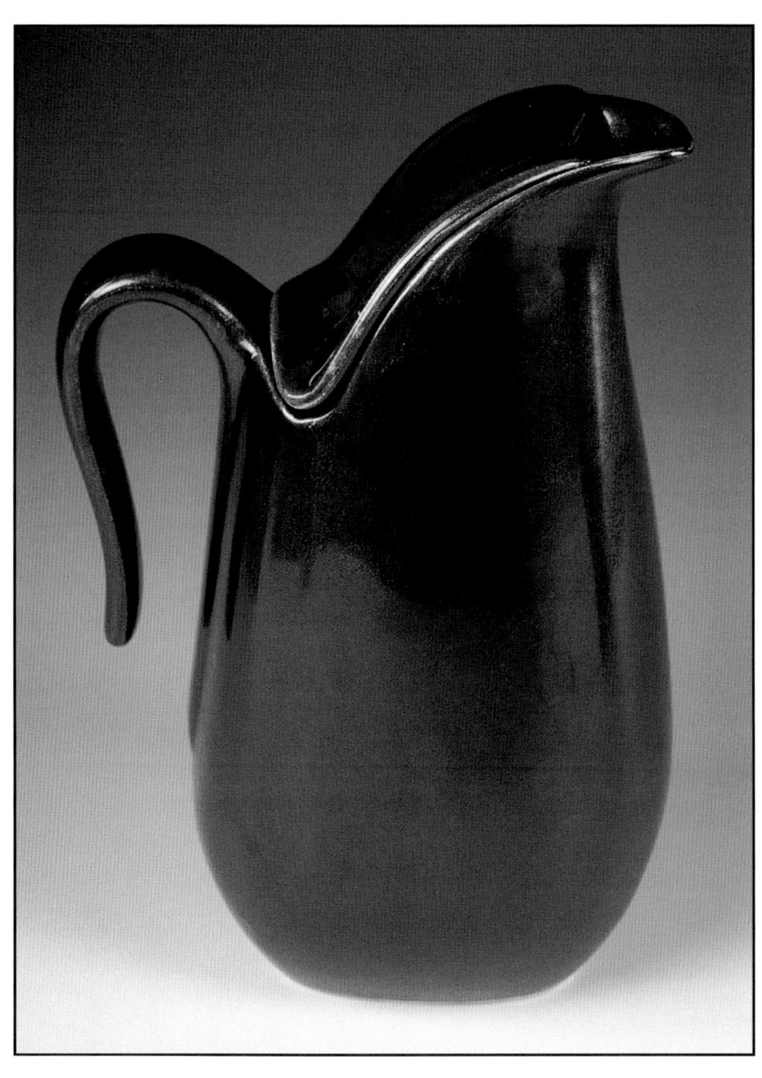

Salem.* ***Constellation***. Viktor Schreckengost. [*Ebony*]. 1953. Covered batter pitcher, $60-75.

Salem for Sears (Harmony House). ***Main Street***. **Flair**. Viktor Schreckengost. *Mint Green, Chartreuse, Jubilee Peach, & Parchment Brown.* 1953. Bowls: 10 1/2" x 8 3/4" x 2", 5 1/4" x 1 1/4", $8-15; plates: 6 3/8", 7 1/8", 10 1/4", $3-8; platter, 13 1/2" x 11 1/4", $10-15; cup & saucers, $8-12; creamers (open handle is **Fortune** shape), $6-12; sugar w/ lid, $10-15.

Salem for Sears (Harmony House). ***Main Street***. Another view. Lighting significantly affects the colors, drama, and mood of many mid-century dinnerware lines.

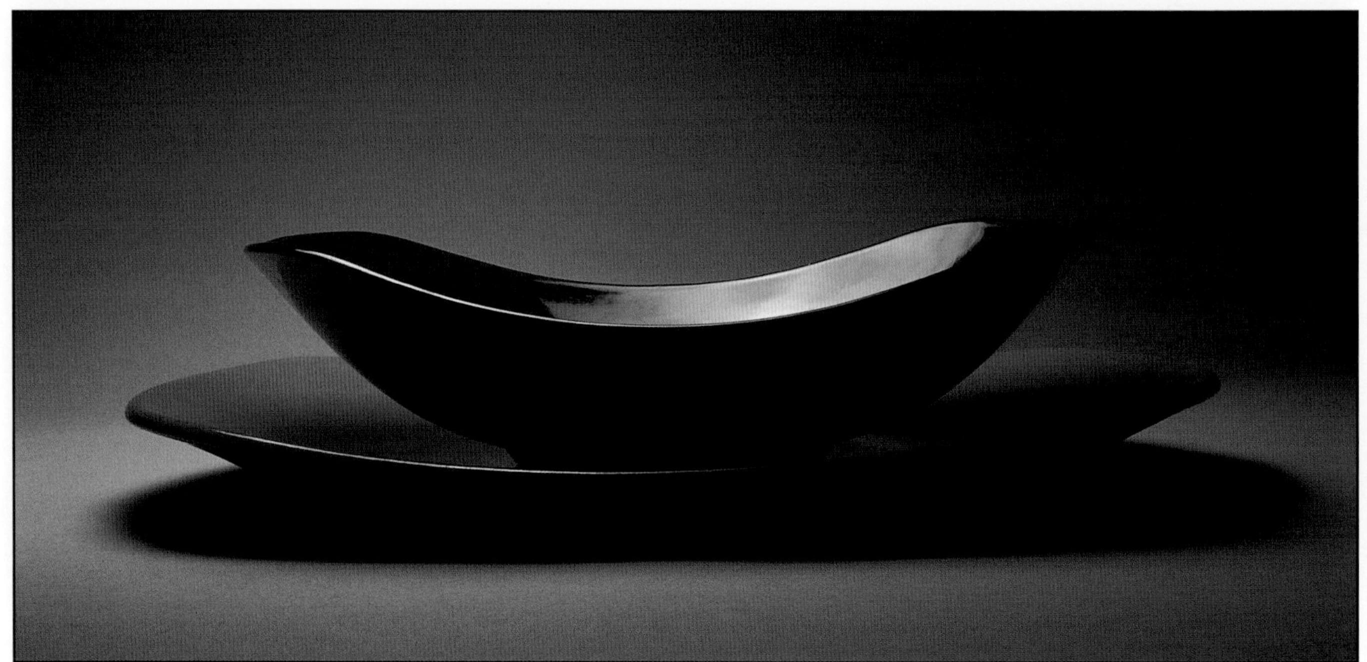

Salem for Sears (Harmony House). ***Main Street***. *Mint Green.* Salad bowl, $6-10; *Jubilee Peach.* Platter, $8-12.

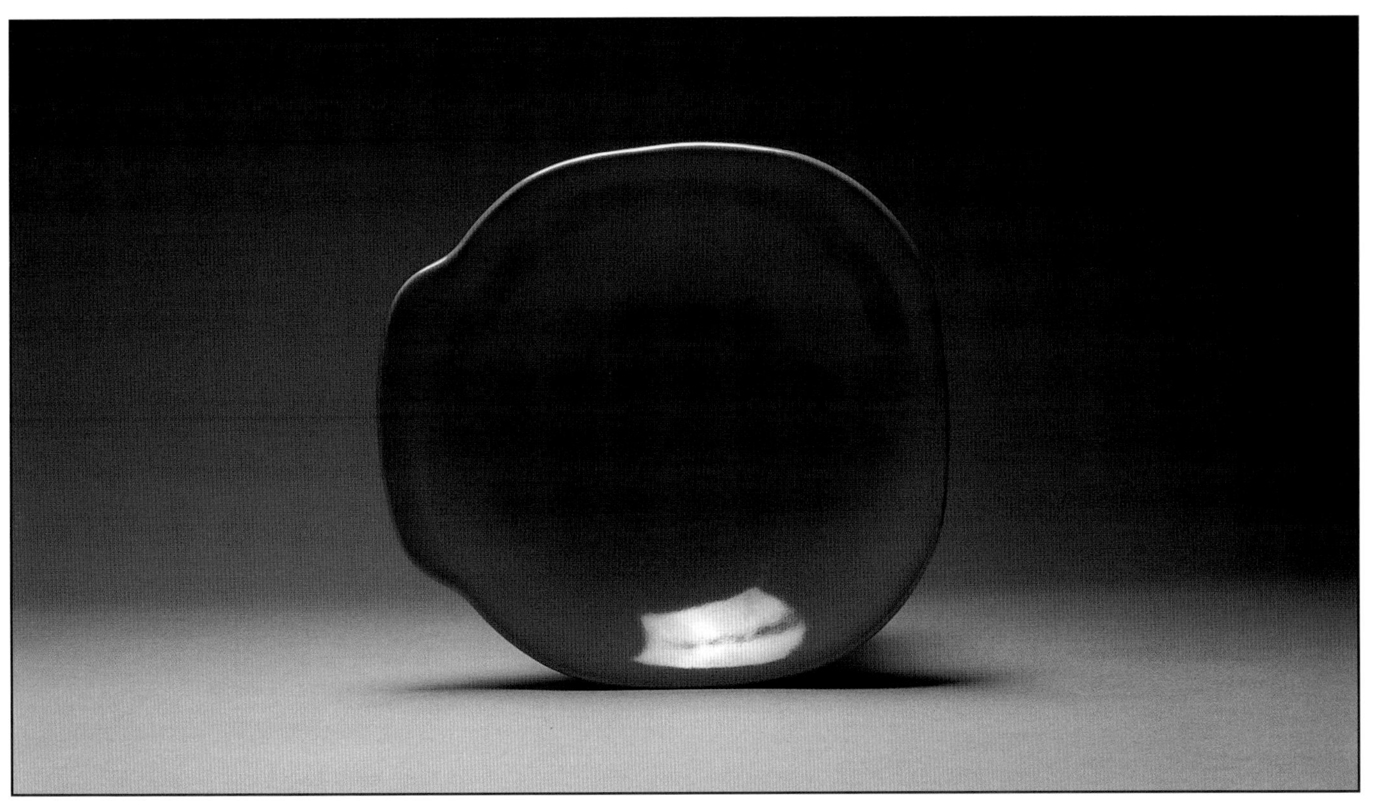

Salem for Sears (Harmony House). ***Main Street***. *Jubilee Peach.* Cereal bowl, $3-5.

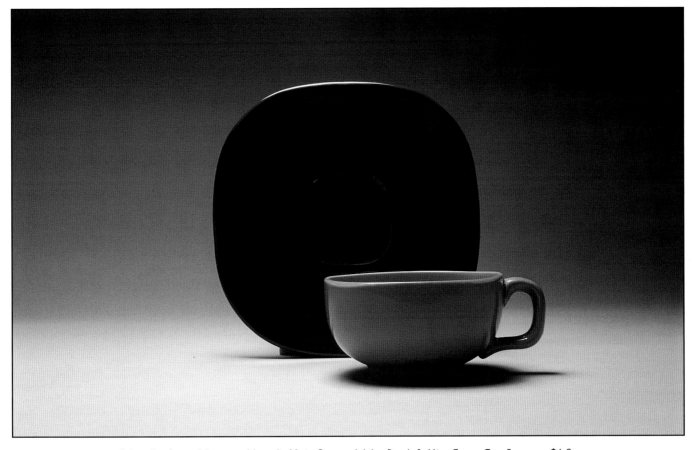

Salem for Sears (Harmony House). ***Main Street***. *Jubilee Peach & Mint Green.* Cup & saucer, $4-8.

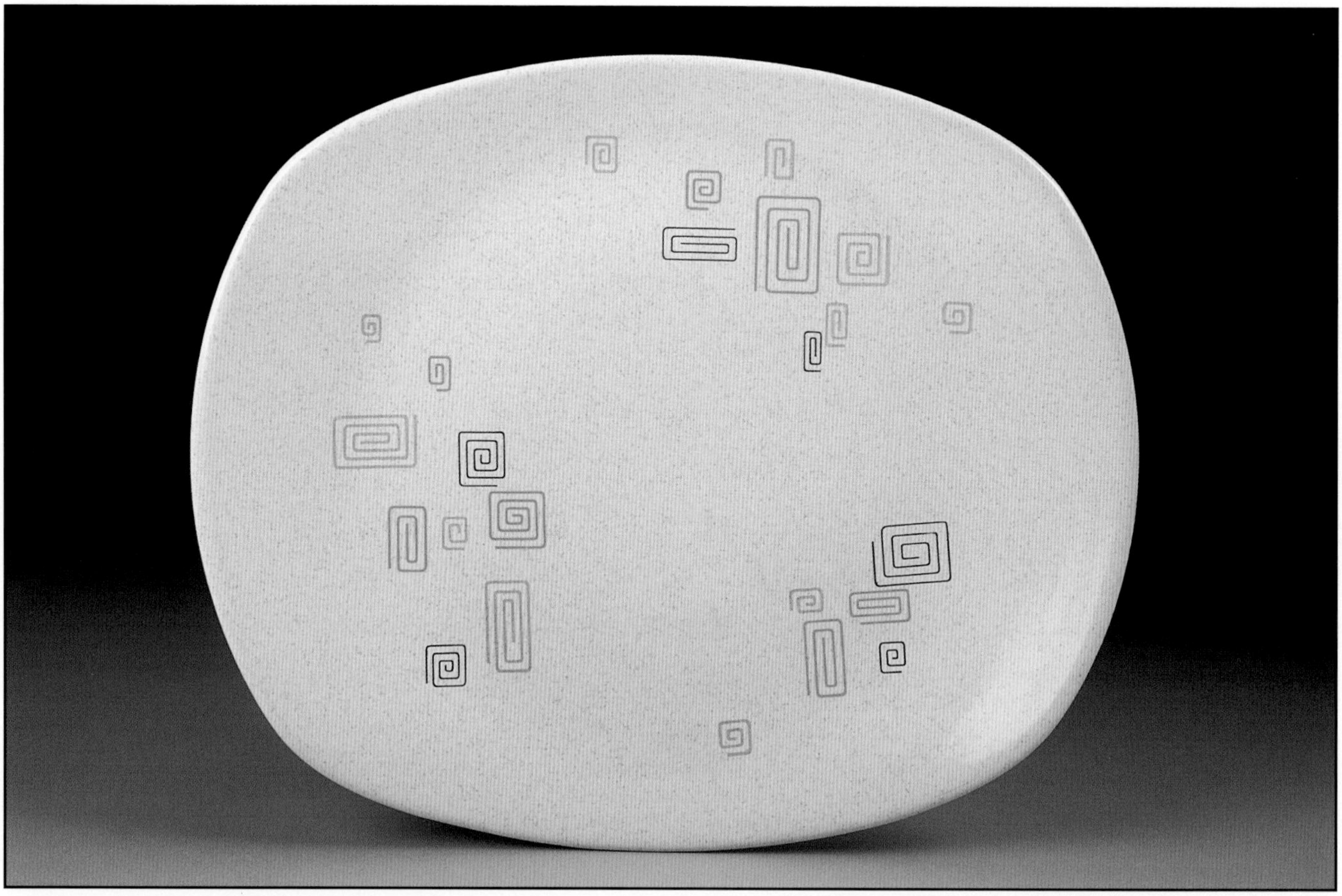

Salem for Sears (Harmony House). **Flair**. *Grecian Keys.* <1956. Plate, 13 3/4" x 11 1/4", $12-25.

Salem.* ***Free·Form***. **Free·Form (Free Form, Free-Form)**. Viktor Schreckengost. *Primitive.* 1955. Platter, 13", $60-85; special footed cup & saucer, $20-30. This patented cup & saucer was hailed as "dripless." ***Free·Form*** is one of the mid-century's highly celebrated modern ceramic tableware lines. It was created by one of America's most award-winning "creatives," Viktor Schreckengost. His achievements span the world of art, sculpture, and industrial design. He was awarded the coveted Binns Medal in 1938.

Salem.* *Primitive.* Covered sugar, $50-65; creamer (3/4 pt.) $45-55.

Salem.* *Primitive.* Onion soup, $20-30; plate, 10" (large dinner), $15-25.

Salem.* *Primitive*. Serving dish (left), $55-125; decorative bowl (right), $55-125.

Salem.* *Primitive*. Teapot, $350-500.

Salem.* *Primitive*. Teapot, another view.

Salem.* *Primitive.* Cruet set (5 pcs), $385-475.

Salem. *Primitive.* Vinegar & oil cruets [with rubber stoppers], $100-125, each. Salt & pepper shakers, $60-75, pair. Cruet set stand, $125-150.

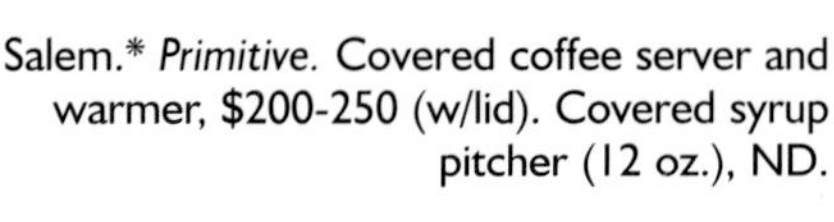

Salem.* *Primitive.* Covered coffee server and warmer, $200-250 (w/lid). Covered syrup pitcher (12 oz.), ND.

Salem.* *Primitive.* Tumbler, ND. This was likely a special order item only. Plate, 7" (pie or salad), $10-15; coupe soup, $10-15.

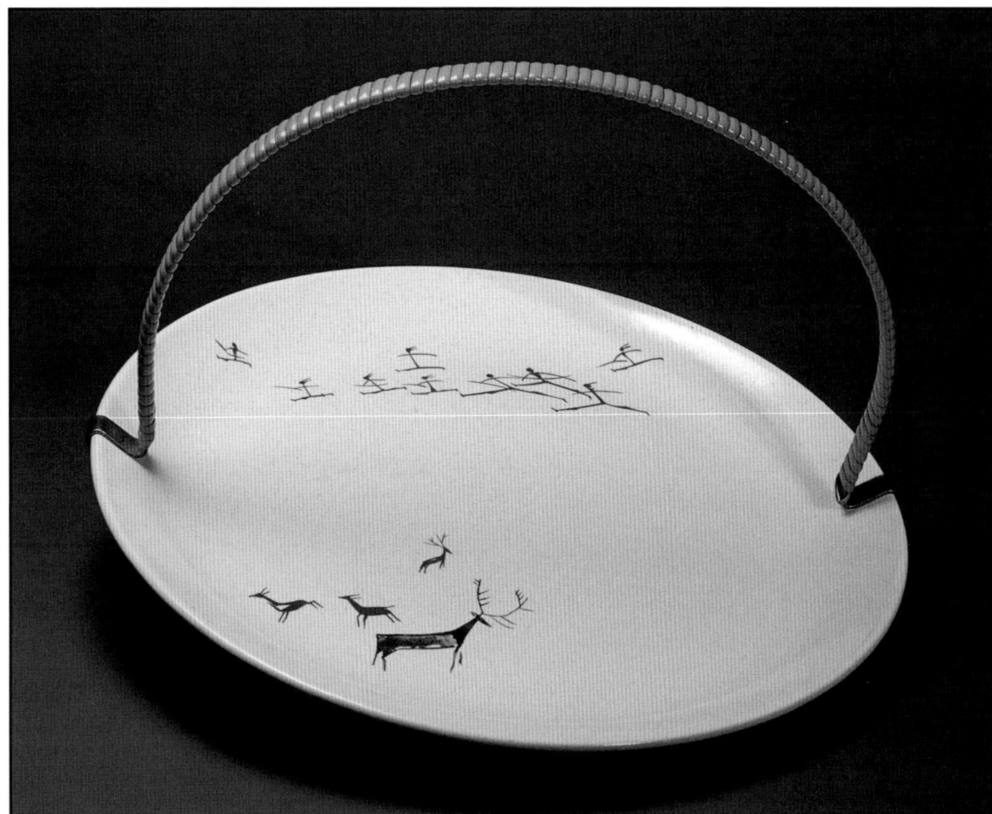

Salem. *Primitive.* Cake dish: dinner plate, 10" [with rattan handle], ND.

Salem.* *Primitive.* Tumblers.

Salem.* *Primitive.* Covered syrup pitcher (12 oz.), ND. Hors d'oeurve [plate], ND. Cup & saucer. ND. This is an unknown shape and was likely special order only.

Salem.* *Primitive.* Three tier tidbit tray, ND. This was likely a special order item only. This center post is typical of other Salem tidbits. Salt (right) and pepper shakers, $60-75, pair.

Salem.* **Free·Form**. Viktor Schreckengost. *Hopscotch Turquoise.* c.1956. Teapot, $250-350.

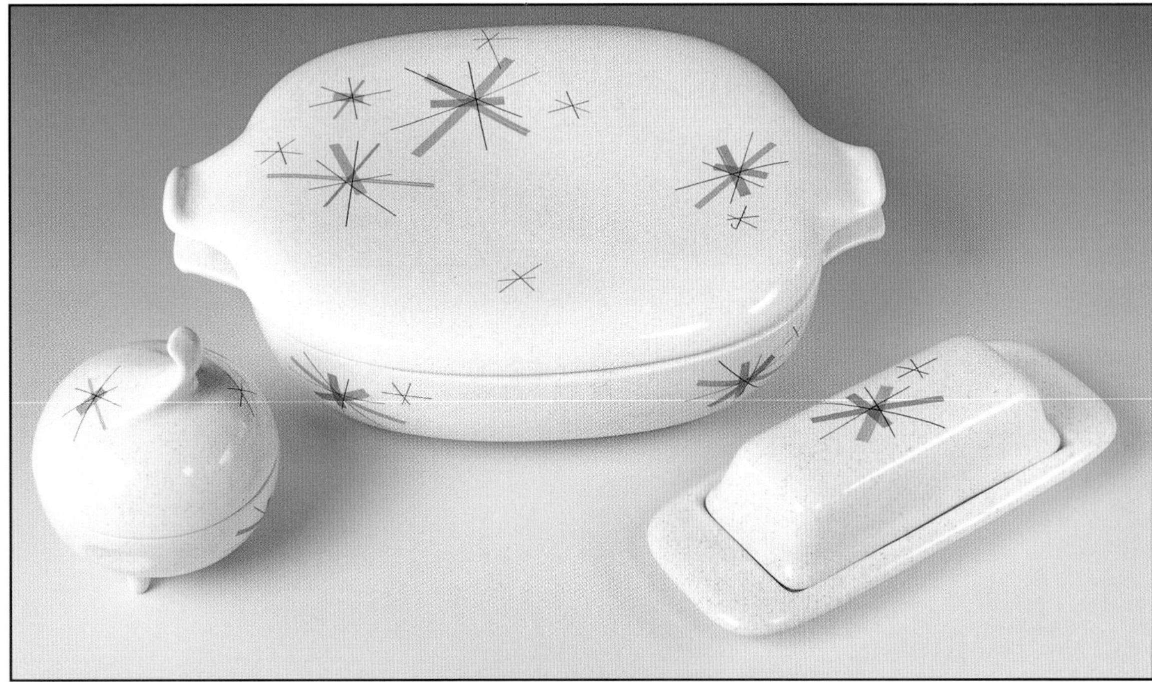

Salem.* *Hopscotch Turquoise.* Covered sugar, $35-50; covered casserole (2 qt.), $75-125; covered butter, $50-60.

Salem.* *Hopscotch Turquoise.* Salad bowl, 10 5/8", $35-45; large dinner plate, 10", $18-22; onion soup, 6" x 2 1/4", $15-25; pickle, 8" (open butter), $20-25.

Salem.* *Hopscotch Turquoise.* Salt & pepper shakers, $35-45.

Salem. *North Star.* c.1958. Glass (unknown manufacturer), $10-20; cream, $6-12; plate, 10 1/8", $4-10; cup & saucer, $4-10; coffee pot, $25-35; sugar, $8-15. Archival information suggests that both decorated and undecorated holloware may exist.

Salem.* **Free·Form**. Viktor Schreckengost. *Hopscotch Pink.* 1955. Coupe soup, 10 1/2", $35-45; fruit, 5 3/8" x 1 1/4", $14-18; plate, 10" (large dinner), $18-22; decorative bowl, $40-55; plate, 6" [6 1/8"] (bread & butter), $6-12; special footed cup & saucer, $18-25.

Salem.* *Hopscotch Pink.* Covered coffee server, \$100-150+; cup & saucer, \$18-25.

Salem.* *Hopscotch Pink.* Covered coffee server, another view.

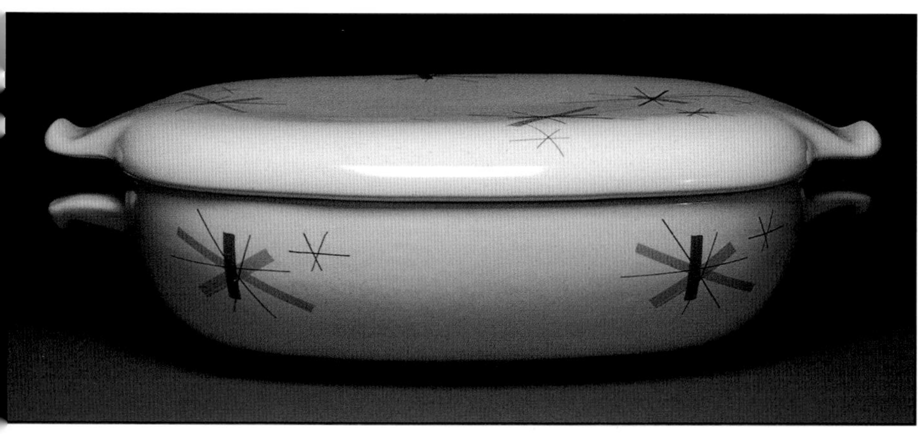

Salem.* *Hopscotch Pink.* Covered casserole (2 qt.), \$60-100.

Salem.* *Hopscotch Pink.* The lid could serve as a tray.

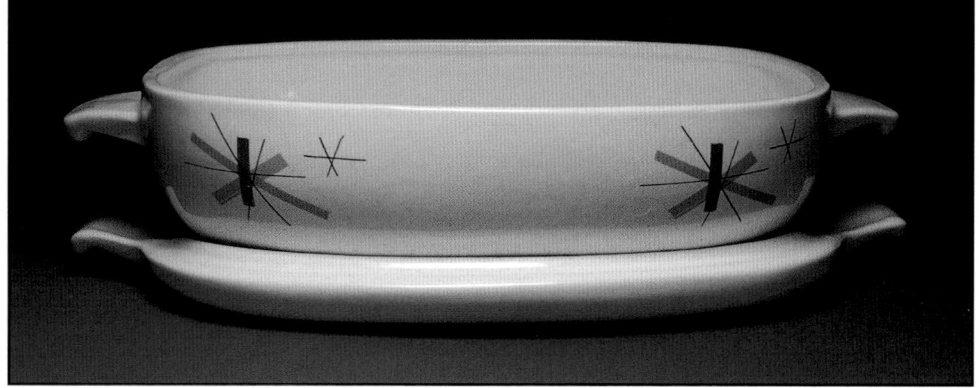

Salem for Sears (Harmony House). *Celeste.* 1956. Plate, dinner, ND. Cup & saucer, ND.

Salem. *Martinique.* <1958. Sugar, $15-25.

Salem.* **Free·Form**. Viktor Schreckengost. *Aquaria.* <1956. Creamer (3/4 pt.), $150-200+; fruit [bowl, 5 3/8" x 1 1/4"], $35-45+.

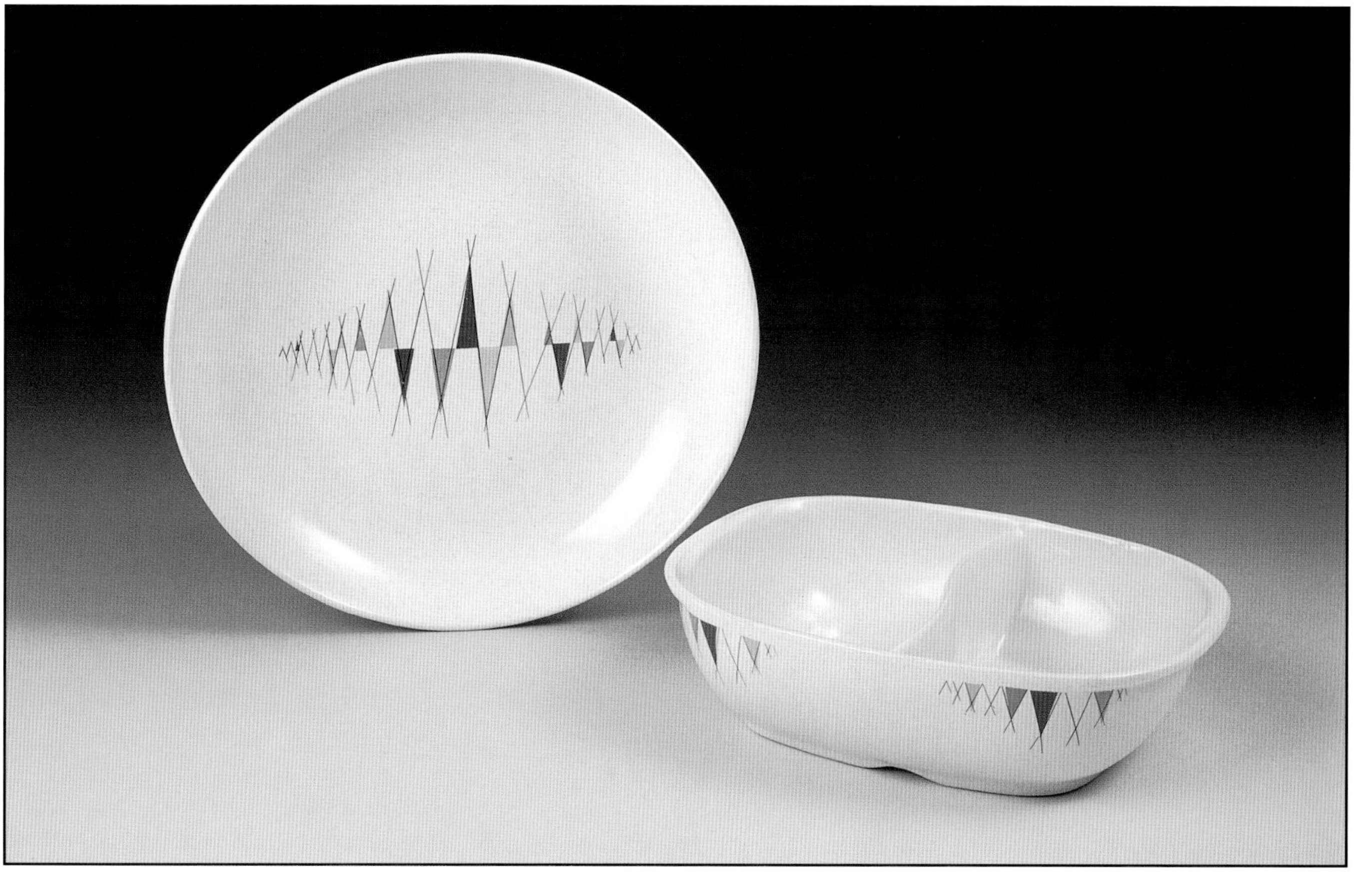

Salem.* **Free·Form**. Viktor Schreckengost. *Tepee.* 1956. Vegetable dish, 10 5/8" x 1 1/2", $65-75+; divided vegetable dish, 9 3/8" x 7 1/2", $60-75+.

Salem.* ***Nostalgic Old America*. Free·Form**. Viktor Schreckengost (s). *Comstock*. Pat Prichard (p). 1956. Creamer, $25-30; *Gloucester*. Pat Prichard (p). 1956. Serving dish, $18-25.

Salem *Old Gloucester*. Plate, 9 1/4", $6-12. This plate is not part of the ***Free-Form*** line.

Salem.* ***Nostalgic Old America*. Free·Form**. Viktor Schreckengost (s). *Showboat*. Pat Prichard (p). 1956. Teapot, $125-250+.

Salem.* ***Nostalgic Old America***. **Free·Form**. *Showboat*. Pat Prichard (p). 1956. Opposite side view.

Salem.* **Free·Form**. [*Festive Botanicals*]. Salt & pepper shakers, $25-40.

Salem.* **Free·Form**. *Aquaria, Comstock, [Spencerian] (Pen & Pencil* on **Flair**), *Southwind.* Creamers. *Aquaria*, $150-200+; *Southwind*, $15-25; *Comstock*, $25-35; *[Spencerian]*, $35-45+.

Salem for W. T. Grant. ***Grant Crest***. **Contour**. *Tempo.* 1961. Covered sugar with closed loop finial, $14-20; 1958. Covered sugar with open finial (shape not identified), $12-22; <1956. Bowl, 9" x 2 3/8", $12-15; platter 13", $35-55. **Flair**. Gravy, $25-35. Salem lines frequently borrowed pieces from other shape lines. The dates used here are from the dates printed on the bottom of the pieces.

Salem for W. T. Grant. ***Grant Crest***. **Constellation**. *Tempo.* Cream pitcher [w/o lid], $14-18.

Salem for W. T. Grant. ***Grant Crest***. *Tempo*. Salt & pepper, $10-15; plate, 10", $5-14; **Contour**. Cup & saucer, $8-15. The salt & pepper shape has not been identified and was likely adopted from an earlier line of shapes.

Salem. *Mardi Gras*. Plate, 7 1/4", $8-12.

Salem. *Mardi Gras.* Plate, 7 1/4", $8-12; cup & saucer, $12-18; bread & butter, $4-8; gravy, $12-18+.

Salem. *Mardi Gras.* Tab bowl, 9 1/4" x 2 1/4", $12-18.

Santa Anita Potteries™

Santa Anita Potteries (former Division of National Silver Company. Los Angeles, California). ***California Modern***. [**California Modern**]. *Dubonnet*. 1949. Coffee pot, $28-35; sugar with cover, $10-15; creamer, $8-12. This line was available in at least eleven colors: *Dubonnet*, *Siesta Yellow*, *Mist Grey*, *Mission Ivory*, *Cedar Brown*, *California Lime*, [*Mat Charcoal* or *Charcoal Gray*], *Sandlewood Grey*, *Lakewood Blue*, *Stark White*, and *Satin Pink*.

Santa Anita. ***Santa Anita Ware***. [**California Modern**]. Vreni Wawra. *California Fantasy.* 1953. Bowl, 8 7/8" x 2 1/2", $14-20.

Santa Anita. ***Santa Anita Ware***. *Cosmopolitan.* Charles Cobelle (p). 1952. Cup & saucer, $15-20. The *Crockery & Glass Journal* (Aug. 1952) introduced this pattern with a black trimmed rim.

Santa Anita. ***Santa Anita Ware***. *Cosmo-politan.* Bread & butter plate, 6 5/8", $12-18.

Santa Anita. ***Vreniware***. Vreni Wawra. *Stylized Spirals* [*Pink*], *Stylized Spirals* [*Chartreuse*]. 1951. Coffee pots, $45-65, each. This pattern of Vreni dinnerware was actually first introduced in 1949 in blue-green, chartreuse, or pink, by Maggie of California and distributed by Dick Knox. It was not until 1951 that Santa Anita picked up the Vreni lines.

Santa Anita. Vreni Wawra. *Stylized Spirals* [*Blue*]. 1951. Covered casserole. $35-50.

Santa Anita. Vreni Wawra. *Stylized Spirals* [*Chartreuse*]. 1951. Deep covered bowl, $35-50.

Santa Anita. ***Santa Anita Ware***. *Pom Pom.* Plate, 10 3/8", $5-10.

Santa Anita. ***Santa Anita Ware***. *Button Button.* Plate, 6 3/4", $3-5.

Santa Anita. ***Santa Anita Ware***. [**Pompeii**]. *Flagstone*. c.1955. Plate, 8 1/8", $3-6.

Santa Anita. [**Pompeii**]. *Hi-Fi* [*Cantaloupe* holloware]. 1956. Covered beverage, $30-45; bowl, 10 3/4" x 2 1/8", $5-10; bowl, 5 1/8" x 1 1/2", $3-5; salt & pepper, $5-10.

Santa Anita. *Mist* [*Platinum/ White*]. Covered dishes with warming stand, $75-85.

Sascha Brastoff Products, Inc.™

Sascha Brastoff Products, Inc. (Los Angeles, California). ***Surf Ballet***. Sascha Brastoff. [*Deep Green*]. 1952. Covered sugar, $16-25; cup & saucer, $12-25; creamer, $14-20.

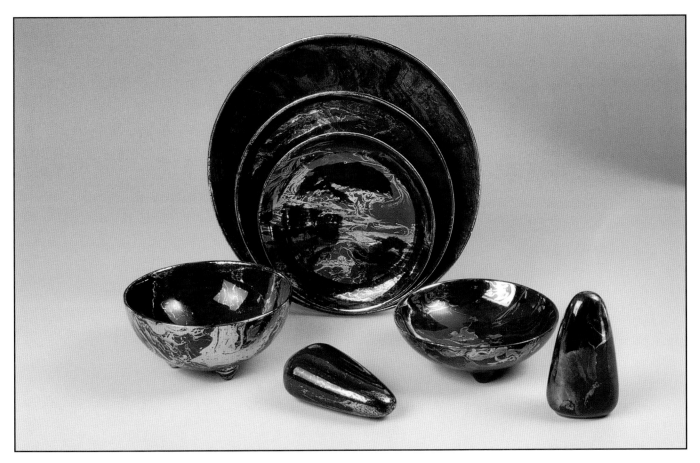

Sascha Brastoff. ***Surf Ballet***. [*Deep Green*]. Salt & pepper, $15-20; plates, 6 1/2", 8", 10", $8-25; footed bowls, 5 1/2" x 2 1/2"; 5 1/2" x 1 3/4", $8-25.

Sascha Brastoff. ***Surf Ballet***. [*Chartreuse*]. Footed bowl, 5 1/2" x 1 3/4", $8-25; [*Turquoise*]. Large divided bowl, 14" x 2 1/2", $15-30.

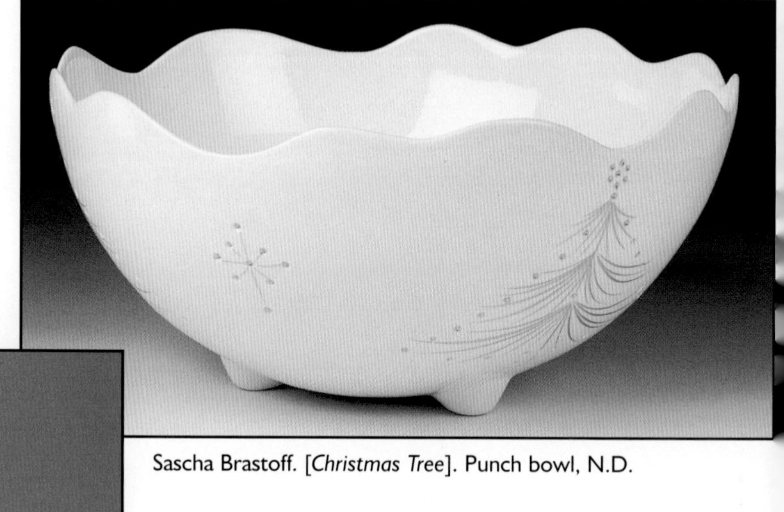

Sascha Brastoff. [*Christmas Tree*]. Punch bowl, N.D.

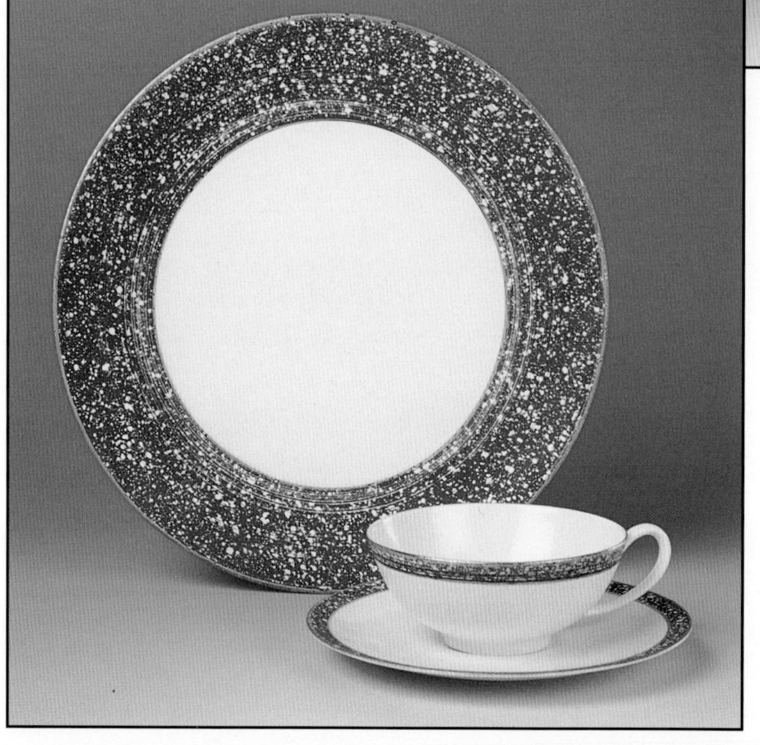

Sascha Brastoff. *Night Song*. Dinner plate, $18-28; cup & saucer, $18-28.

Scammell China Company™

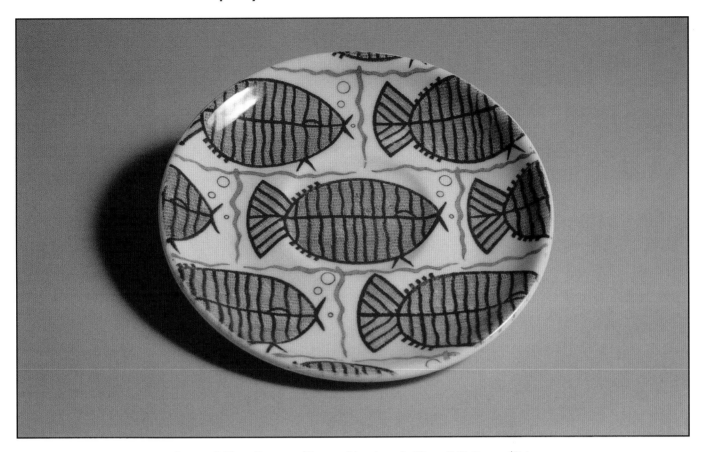

Scammell China Company (Trenton, New Jersey). [*Green Fish*]. Saucer, $3-6.

Scammell. [*Red Fish*]. Bowl, $5-10.

Senegal China™

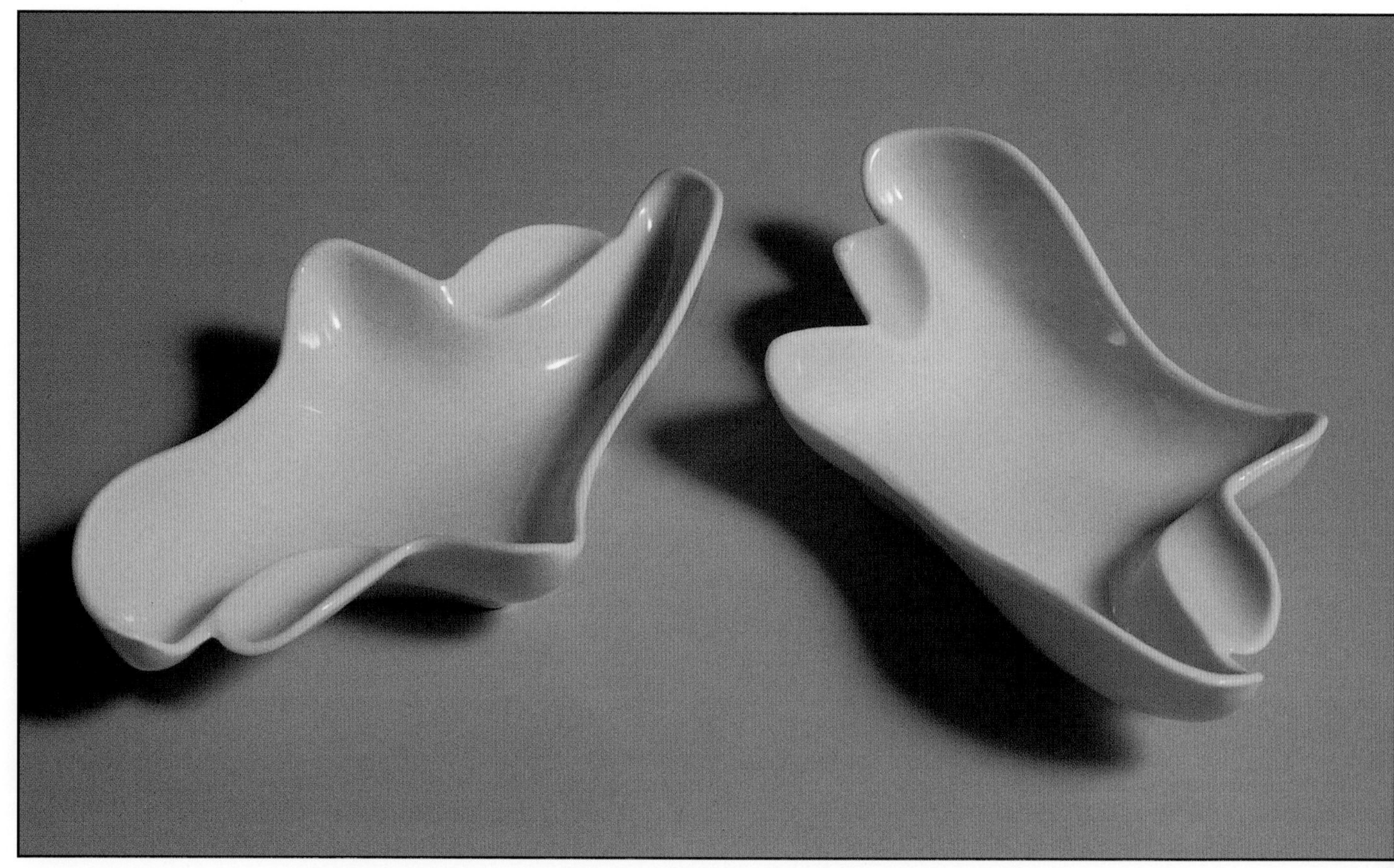

Senegal China (Pelham, New York). ***Senegal Fine China***. Attributed to Simon Slobodkin (s). Ashtray, 5 7/8", $10-15, each.

Shenango China, Inc.™ (Shenango Pottery Company™)

Shenango China, Inc. (Shenango Pottery Company. New Castle, Pennsylvania). ***Peter Terris China Originals***. William Craig McBurney (s). *Terris White*. 1954. Cream, $12-18; sugar, $14-22; coffee pot, $25-40; cup & saucer, $4-10. Peter Terris China Originals was a division of Shenango China, Inc. While this line was the backdrop for many stylized florals, of most interest to the modernist is *Bali*, a geometric pattern, and *Terris White*.

Shenango. *Terris White.* Coffee pot with cup & saucer, another view.

Shenango. *Terris White.* Cream & sugar, a closer view.

Shenango. Restaurant China. [*Flamingo in Pink & Green*]. <1957. Plate, 8", $15-30.

Shenango.* Restaurant China. [*Abstract Black Fish*]. **Boston** teacup & **Colonnade** tea saucer RE [Rolled Edge], $8-15.

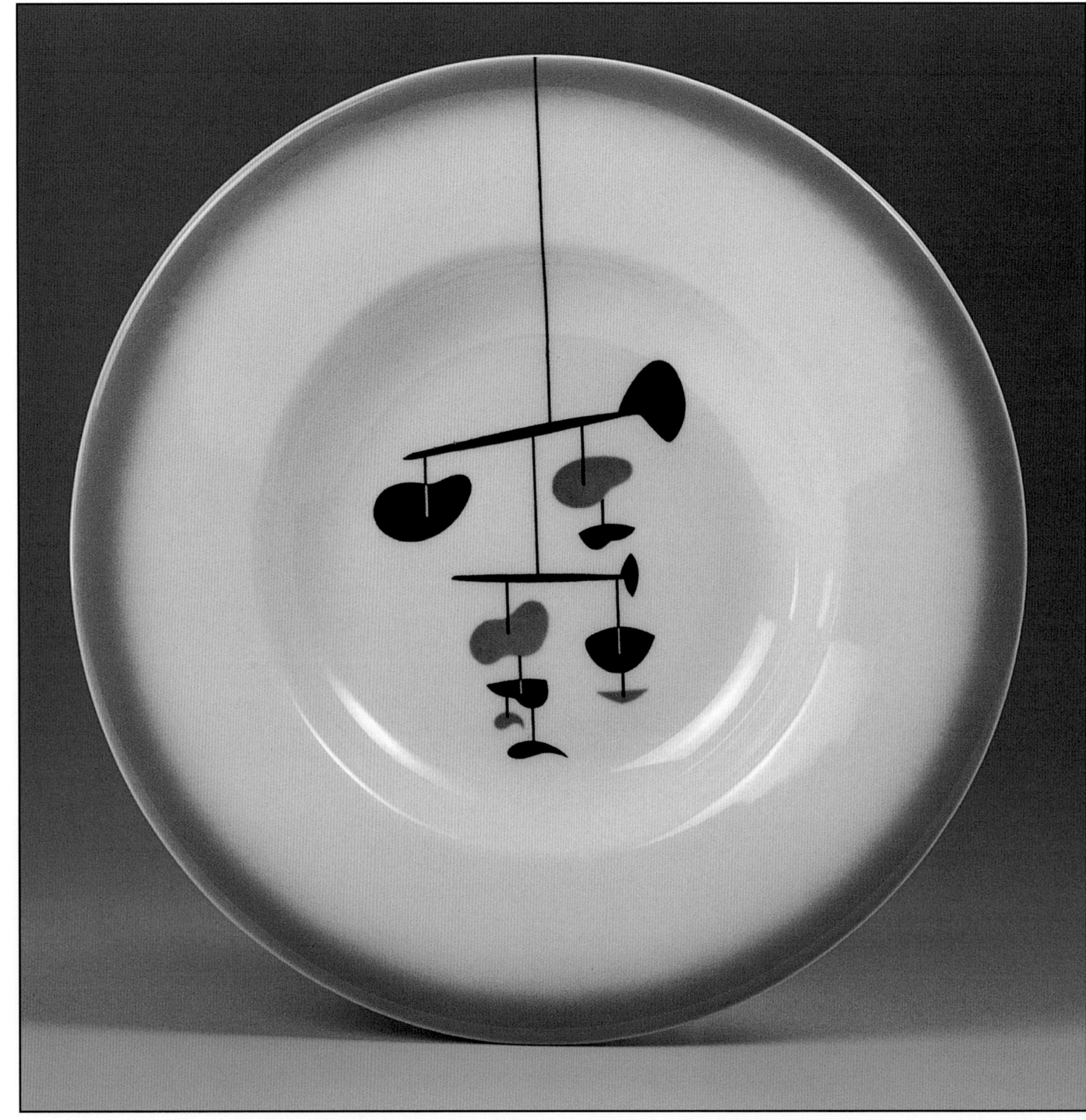

Shenango.* **Continental**. Restaurant China. *Mobile.* Paul Cook (p). 1952. **Royal Rim** deep soup RE, 9 1/4", $20-35. *Mobile* was designed specifically for the Kellogg Center for Continuing Education at Michigan State College. The facility was designed to be a working laboratory for hotel and restaurant management studies.

Shenango.* **Continental**. Restaurant China. *Well of the Sea.* Paul Cook (p). **Continental** plate WE, 9", $20-40. This pattern was originally designed for the Sherman Hotel in Chicago.

Shenango.* **FöRM** [Logotype as shown]. William McBurney (s). [*Blue*] *Accent Color.* Solid accent colors were designed to mix and match with patterns that were available in the **FöRM** dinnerware line. All the following geometric patterns were arranged or drawn as one or two large circles: *NöT* (green & blue bowties), *TUö* (blue & green thin circles), *SVäR* (blue & purple blocks), *KöNE* (thick blue circle with solid purple center), *SOM* (thick brown circle & white center), *GILD* (thin circles in gold & orange), *TRIA* (solid color triangles), and *STRä* (tightly packed straw). 1962. Individual ash tray, 3 3/4" [3 5/8"], $2-5.

Ernest Sohn Creations™

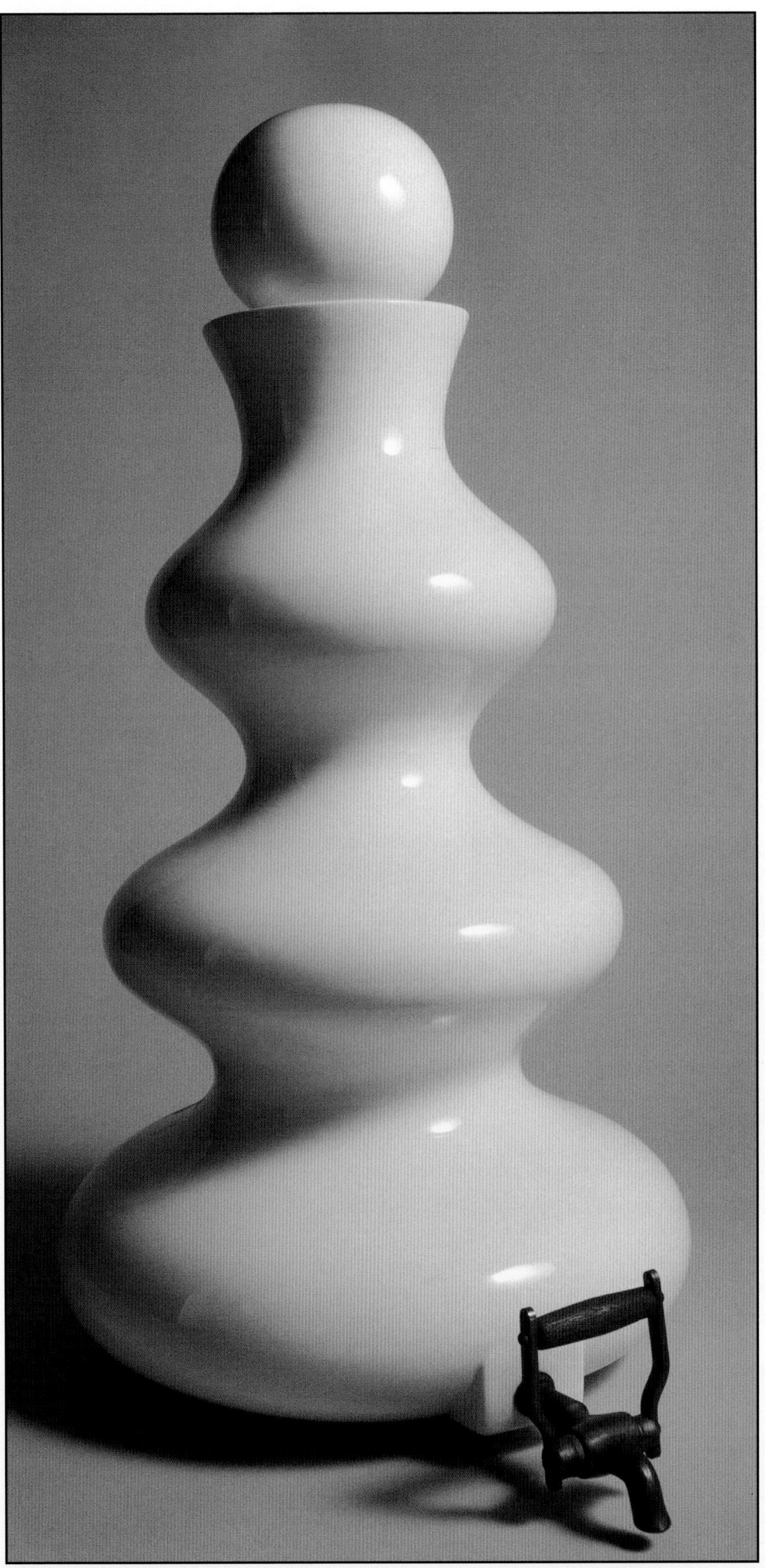

Ernest Sohn Creations (for Jack Orenstein Associates, Inc., New York). Ernest Sohn. 1958. Samovar, 19", $100-150. Ernest Sohn's ceramic ware was manufactured by Hall China. Ernest Sohn was a prolific mid-century industrial designer who designed primarily for the house and giftwares industry. His designs were widely popular and brought a touch of class and drama to the mid-century table. His designs are also featured in the Hall China section of *Mid-Century Modern Dinnerware: Ak-Sar-Ben to Pope Gosser*.

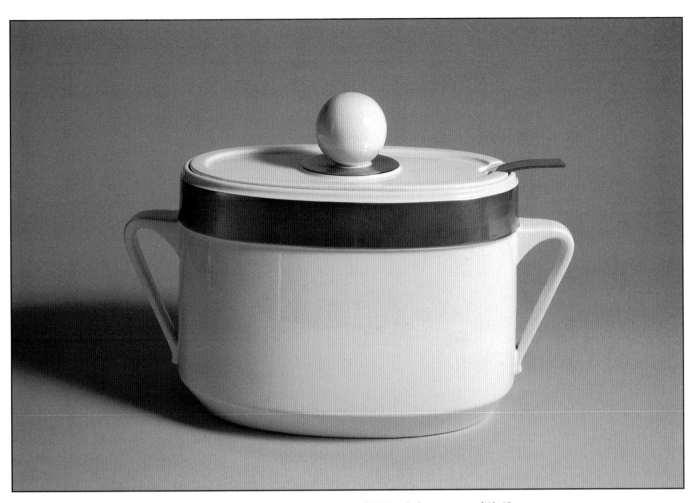

Ernest Sohn Creations. Ernest Sohn. [*Gold Band*]. Soup tureen, $40-60.

Ernest Sohn Creations. Ernest Sohn. [*White Ribbed*]. Covered casserole, $20-35.

Southern Potteries, Inc.™ (Blue Ridge™)

Southern Potteries, Inc. (Blue Ridge. Erwin, Tennessee). **Skyline**. *Ribbon* (*No. 4181 Skyline*) [*Streamers*]. 1951. Plate, 10 1/4", $8-12. This was one of at least six *Ribbon* patterns introduced in 1951 on the **Skyline** shape. The author has found no company brochure information to assist in the identification of the many ***Blue Ridge*** patterns, although one salesman has noted that such information did exist. Southern Potteries advertised extensively, both in trade and consumer magazines. Names have been primarily gleaned from these sources. Despite frequent advertisement by Southern Potteries in the trades, patterns were typically referred to by their factory numbers, rather than by name.

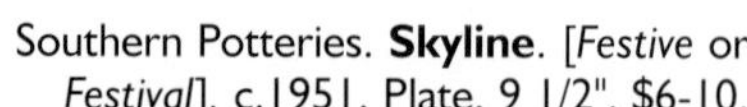

Southern Potteries. **Skyline**. [*Festive* or *Festival*]. c.1951. Plate, 9 1/2", $6-10.

Southern Potteries. **Woodcrest**. *Ming Tree*. c.1953. Sugar, $15-22. [*Stencil*]. Cream, $12-15.

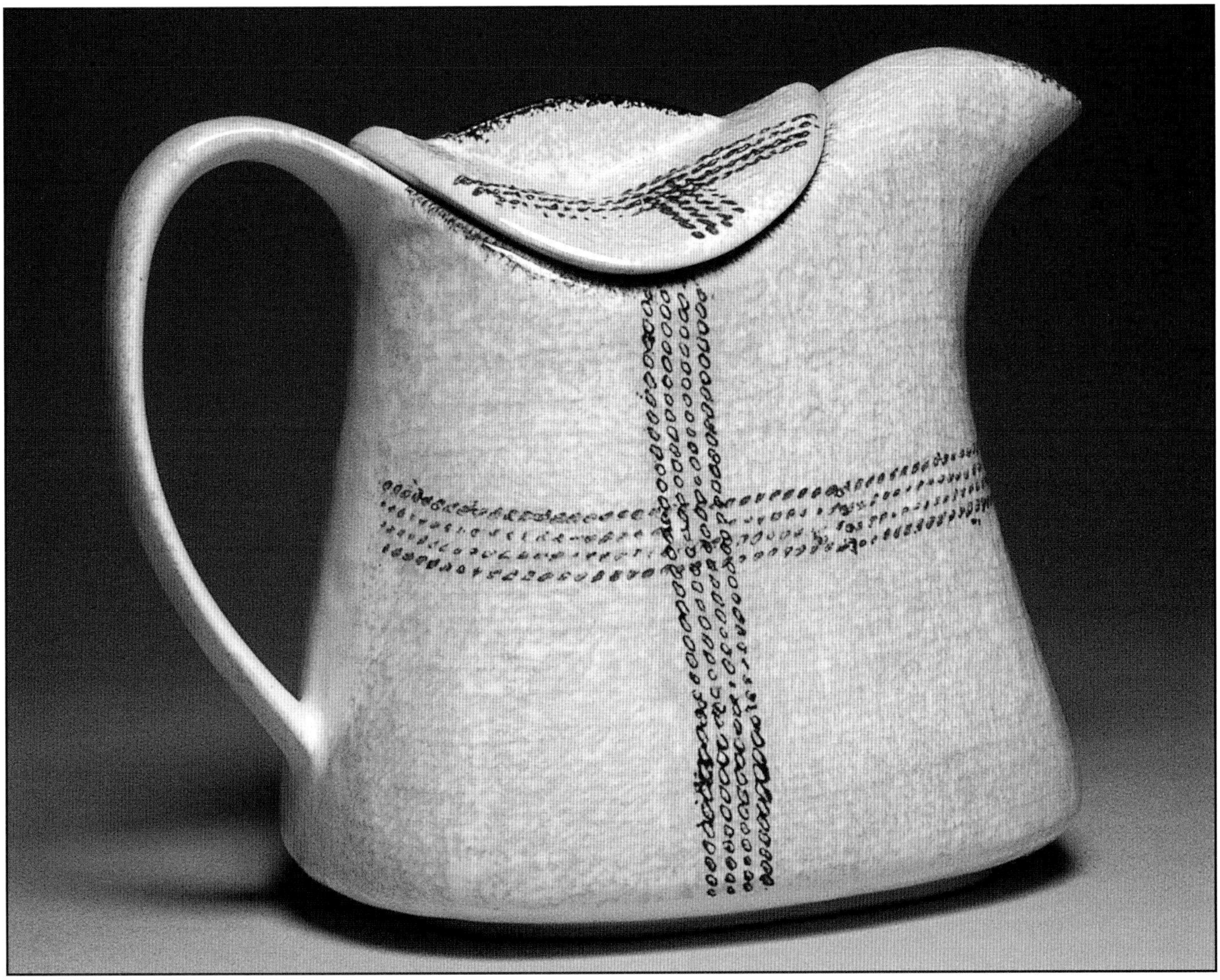

Southern Potteries. **Woodcrest**. [*Stencil*]. c.1953. Teapot, ND.

Southern Potteries. **Woodcrest**. [*Jungle Grass*]. c.1953. Teapot, ND.

Southern Potteries. ***Marbella* [*Spiderweb*]. Palisades**. *Turquoise Blue, Onyx Black*. c.1955. Sugar, $15-22; creamer, $8-10.

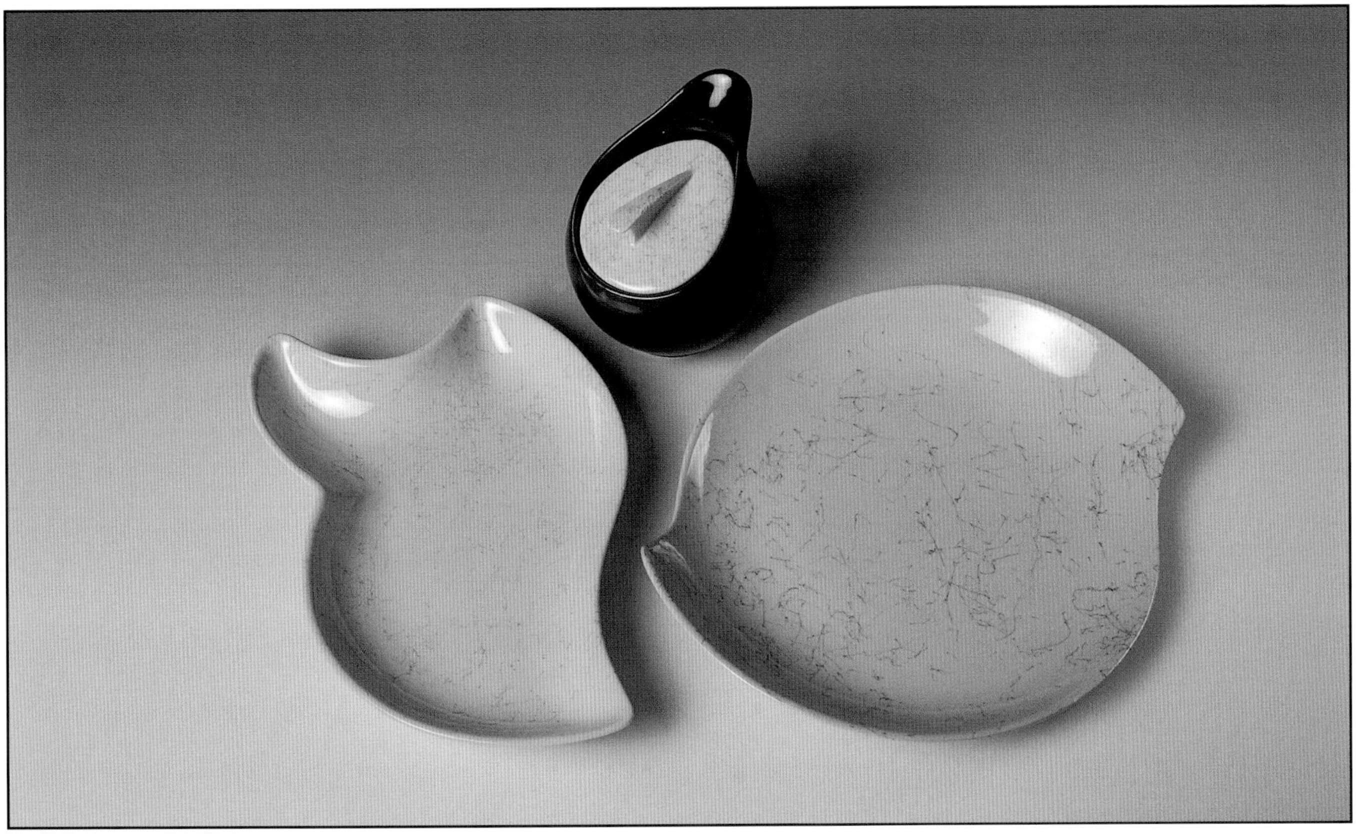

Southern Potteries. ***Marbella* [*Spiderweb*]. Palisades**. *Citron, Charcoal Gray.* 1955>. Sugar, $18-25; plate, 12 1/8", $8-15. [*Beige*]. Plate, 11 1/2", $10-15.

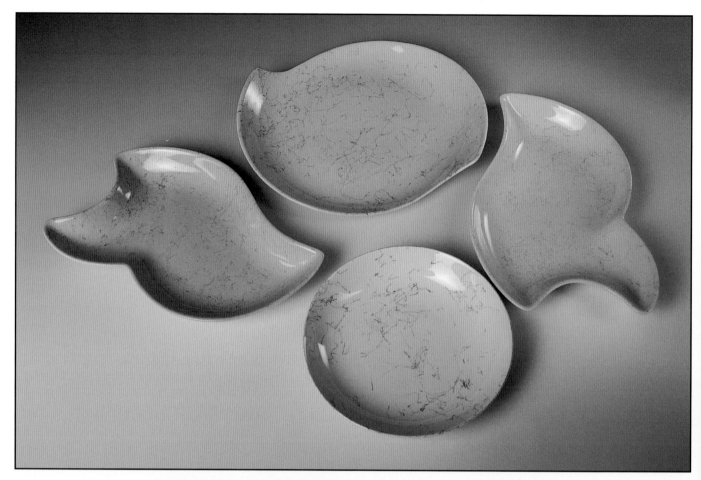

Southern Potteries. ***Marbella*** [***Spiderweb***]. *Citron, Coral Pink, Snowy White,* [*Beige*]. c.1955. Various items, $12-20.

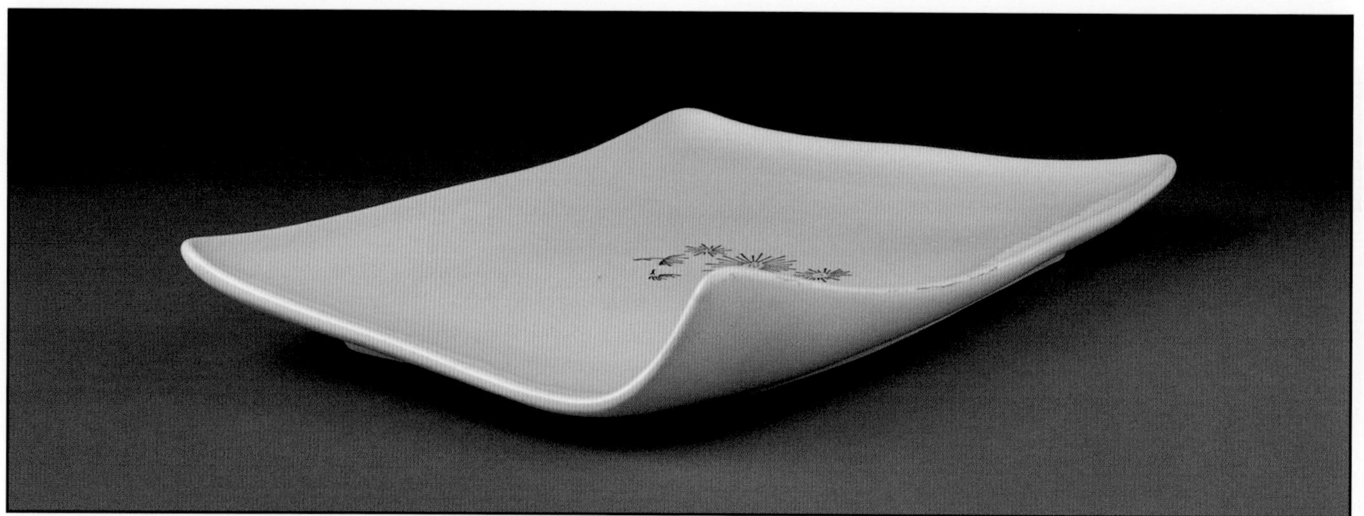

Southern Potteries. **Palisades**. There appear to have been two **Palisades** shapes. The difference is readily apparent in the holloware. The least common **Palisades** shape is asymmetrical & freeform, with a shark fin-like finial. The tray, shown here, is known to have accompanied this **Palisades** design that was called the **New Trends** shape prior to its introduction to the consumer. The more common **Palisades** shape features a lid with a finial that resembles a shortened sundial, as featured in this book. The author strongly suspects Simon Slobodkin as the designer of Southern Potteries' **Skyline**, **Woodcrest,** and **Palisades** shapes. While there is no trade journal proof that this is the case, interviews reveal that Slobodkin did freelance design for the company. The freeform shapes are suggestive of Slobodkin's design style. 1956. Tray, 13 3/4", $15-25.

Southern Potteries. ***Marbella* [*Spiderweb*]**. **Skyline**. *Coral Pink.* 1955. Bowl, 8 3/4" x 2 1/2", $3-10; plate, 10 1/2", $3-12; bowl, 5 1/2" x 1 3/8", $3-6. *Coral Pink, Onyx Black.* Covered casserole, $25-35+.

Southern Potteries. ***Marbella* [*Spiderweb*]**. **Skyline**. *Coral Pink, Turquoise Blue, Onyx Black.* 1955. Butter dishes, $35-45+.

Southern Potteries. ***Marbella*** [***Spiderweb***]. **Skyline**. *Turquoise Blue, Onyx Black.* 1955. Covered casserole, $18-25. Two ***Marbella*** colors not shown here are *Willow* (spring green) and *Sandstone Gray*.

Southern Potteries. ***Marbella*** [***Spiderweb***]. **Skyline**. *Coral Pink, Charcoal Gray.* 1955. Cup & saucer, $5-15; Teapot, $50-65.

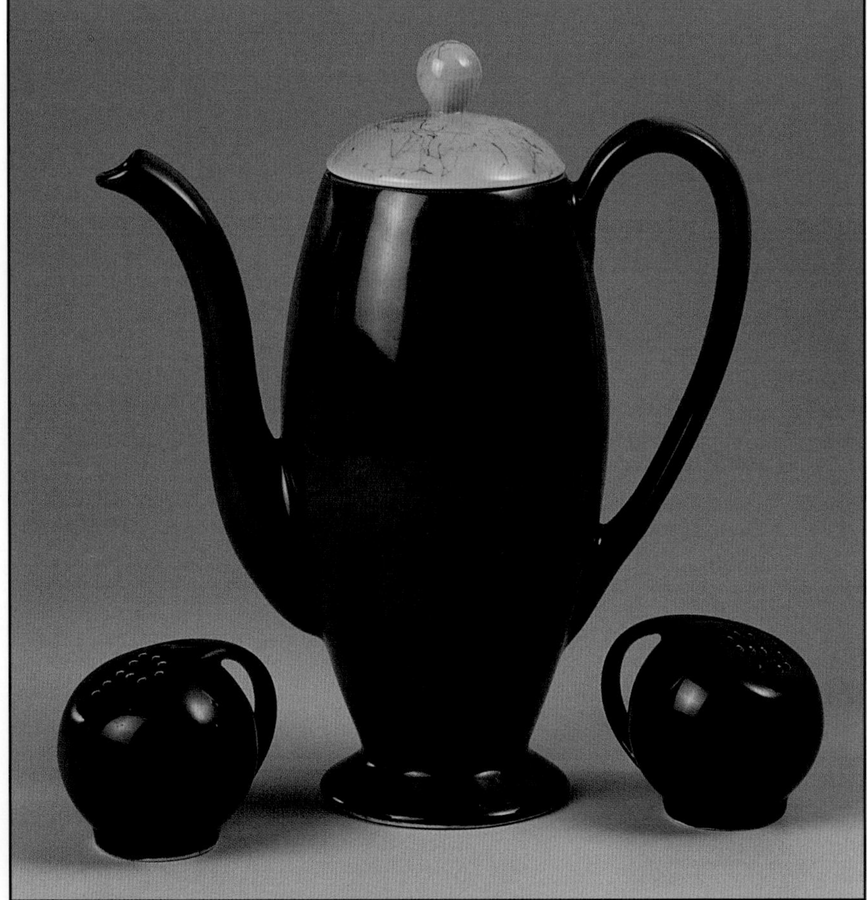

Southern Potteries. ***Marbella*** [***Spiderweb***]. **Skyline**. *Coral Pink, Onyx Black, Charcoal Gray.* 1955. Coffee pot (**Colonial** shape), $40-65+. **Skyline**. Salt & pepper, $8-15.

Southern Potteries. ***Studio Ware***. **Skyline** (**Studio Ware**). *Southern Rustic* [*Roundelay*]. 1955. Cream, $8-15; sugar, $14-20.

Southern Potteries. **Skyline**. [*Squares & Ribbon*]. Plate, 10 1/4", $4-10.

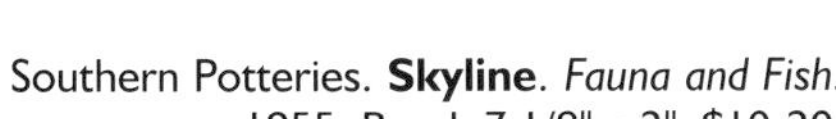

Southern Potteries. **Skyline**. *Fauna and Fish*. 1955. Bowl, 7 1/8" x 2", $10-20.

Southern Potteries. **Skyline**. *Cascade* or *Plaid* [*Brown or Yellow*], [*Rustic Plaid*]. <1951. Sugars, $10-15; creamers, $8-10. Trade journals refer to both names for the brown & green plaid on brown.

Southern Potteries. **Skyline**. *Cascade* or *Plaid.* Creamer and sugar, another view.

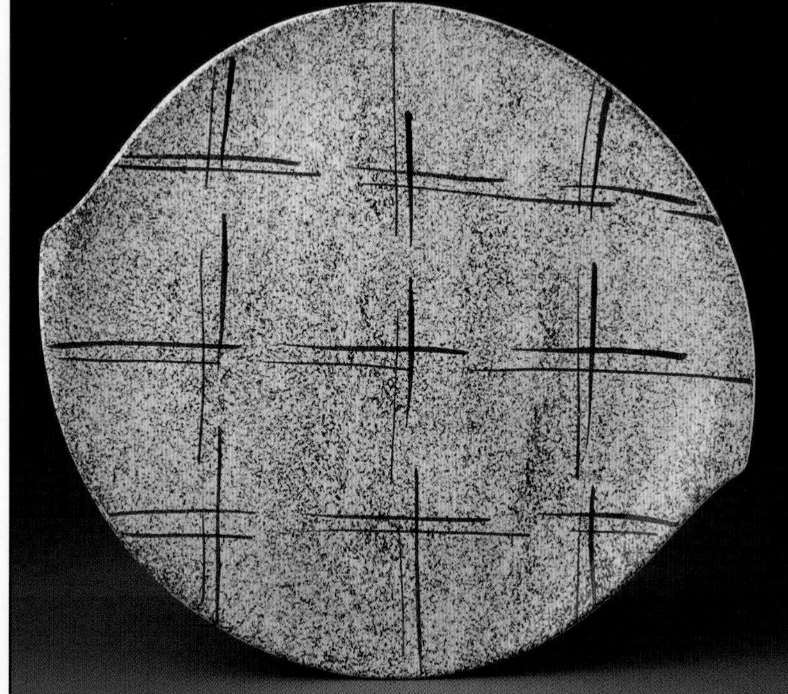

Southern Potteries. **Palisades**. [**Palisades** *Tweed*]. Platter, 12 1/2" x 11 1/4", $10-20. A similar, if not identical pattern, was available in 1951 on the **Skyline** shape and was referred to as No. 4153 **Skyline** "*Tweed*." This pattern, like *Plaid*, was available in several colors.

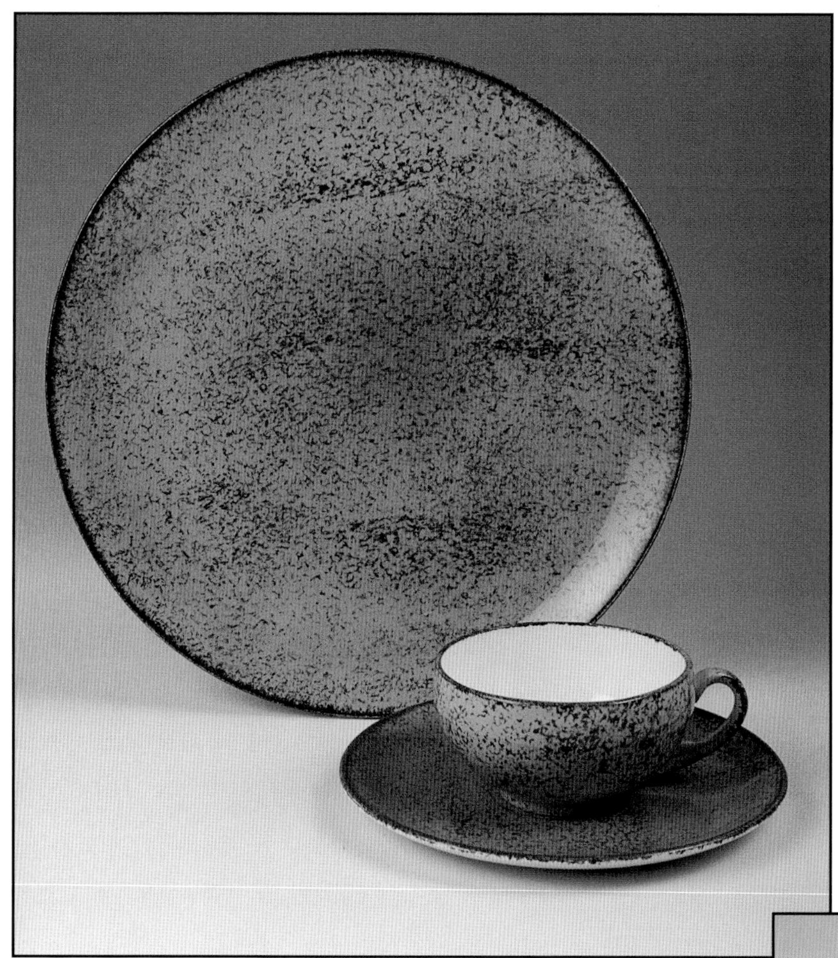

Southern Potteries. **Skyline**. [*Orange Sherbet*]. Plate, 10", $3-10; cup & saucer, $5-10.

Southern Potteries. [*Pineapple Sherbet*]. Divided bowl, $12-18.

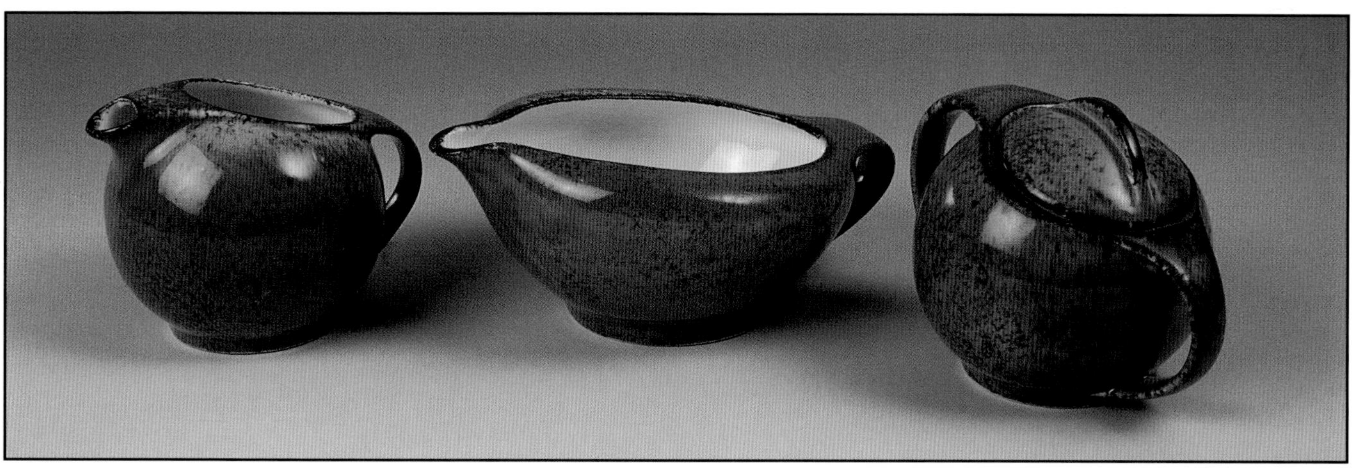

Southern Potteries. **Skyline**. [*Orange Sherbet*]. Creamer, $8-10; gravy, $10-14; sugar, $10-15.

Stangl Pottery™

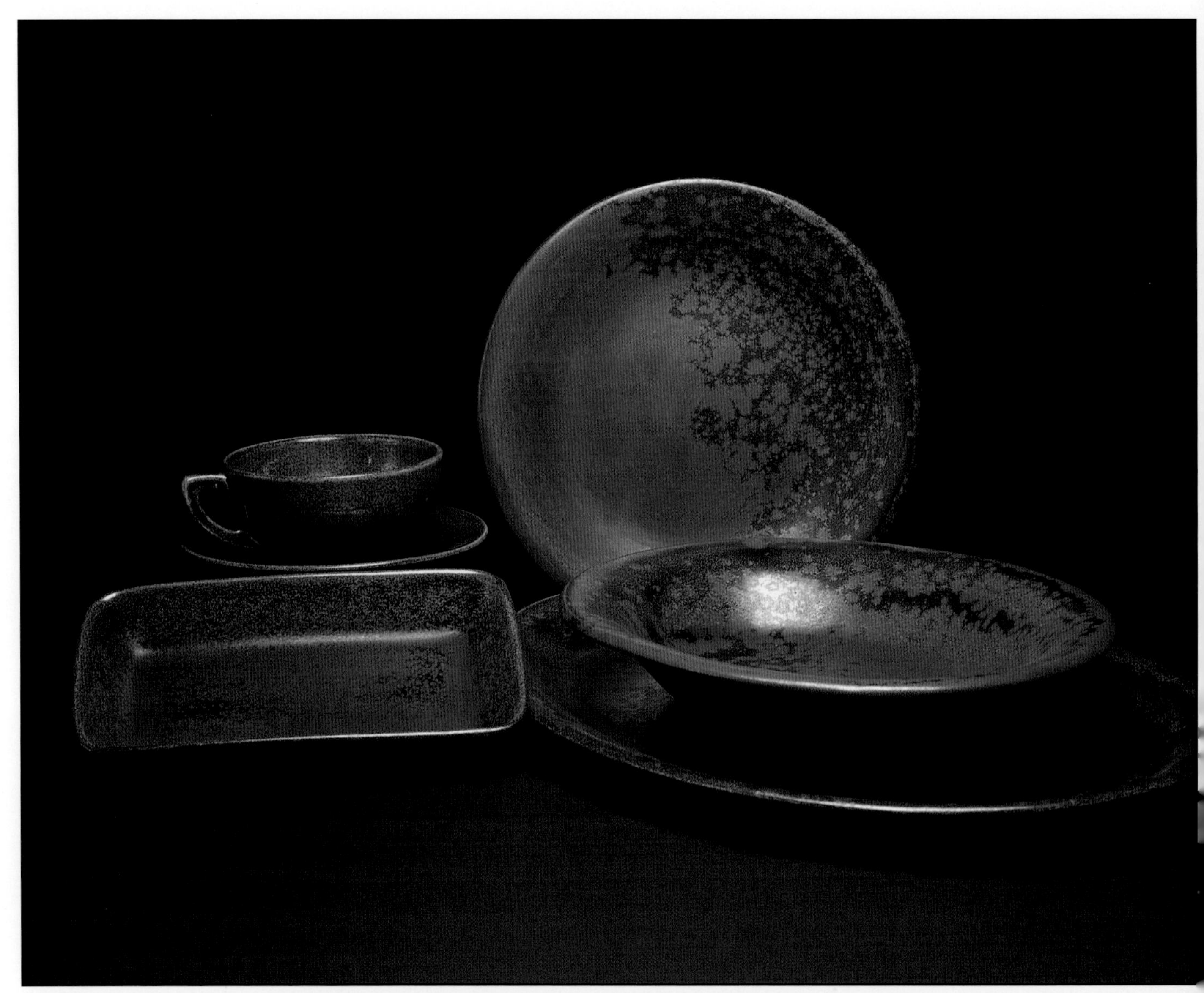

Stangl Pottery. ***Americana***. **Americana**. *Variegated Rust*. Cup & saucer, $14-20. 1937. ***Toastmaster***. Tray. $13-16. ***Americana***. Plate, 8 7/8" $25-30; bowl, 10 3/4" x 1 3/4", $30-50; platter, 14" $30-40.

Stangl Pottery (Trenton, New Jersey). ***Americana***. *Tangerine*. c.1936. Teapot, $75-100+; sugar, $15-22.

Stangl Pottery. **Americana**. *Ranger.* Gerald Ewing (p). 1939. Chop plate, 14 1/2", $450-550+; sugar, $150-160+; creamer, $125-130.

Stangl Pottery.* **Coupe**. John Tierney (s). *Lyric.* Mug, $30-40; plate, 10", $50-60.

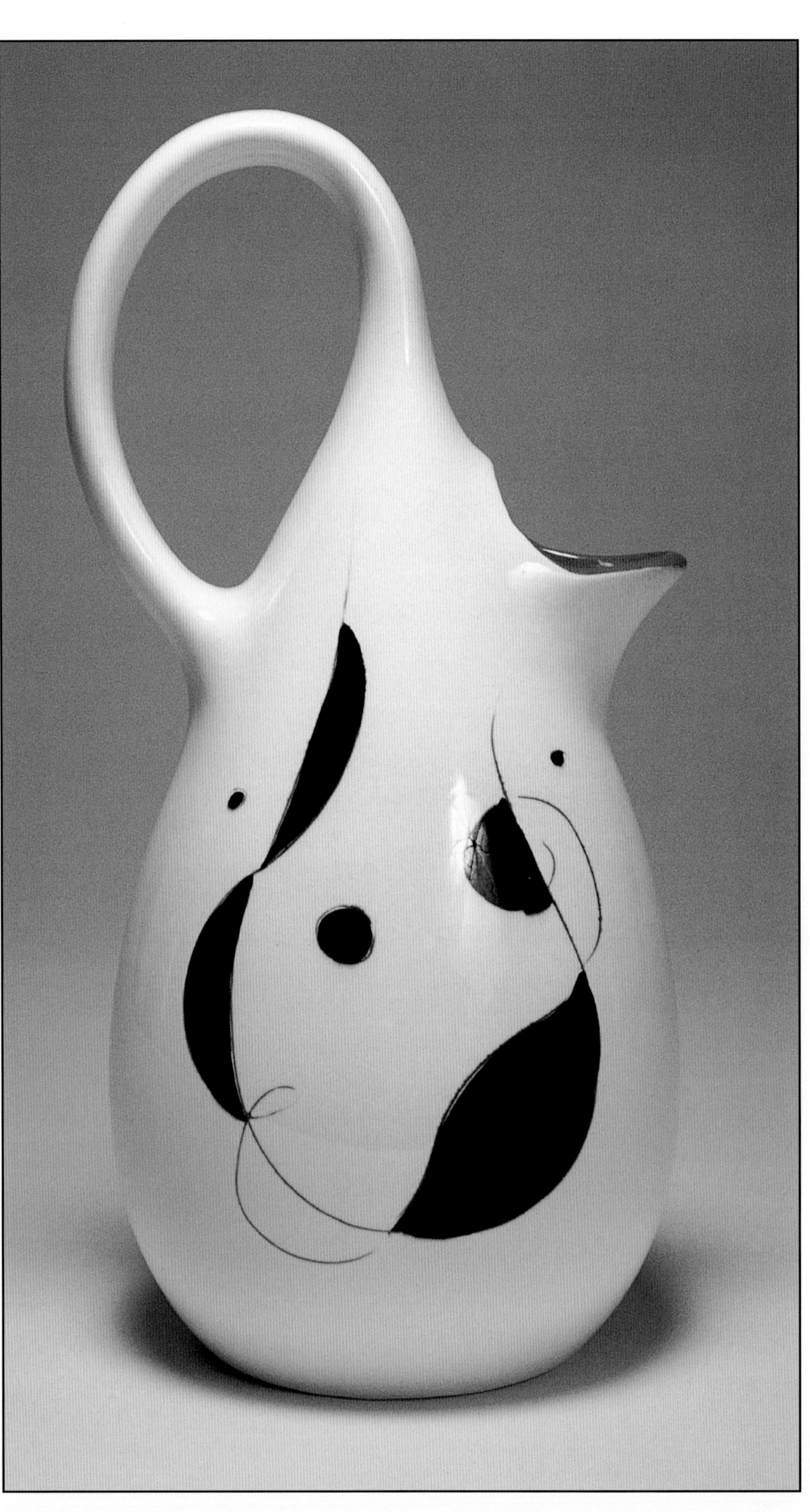

Stangl Pottery.* **Casual**. Ed Pettingil (s). *Lyric.* Kay Hackett (p). 1954. Coffee server (**Casual**), $95-185+. A regular shape coffee pot was not available in *Lyric,* which featured an abbreviated selection of items. A **Casual** shaped creamer and sugar would accompany this modern coffee pot. Trade advertisements pictured this line as early as 1953 (see *Crockery & Glass Journal*, Sept. 1953). Other information suggests the line may have been introduced to consumers in 1954.

Stangl Pottery.* *Lyric.* Divided vegetable, 10 3/4", $50-65; 4" individual casserole with cover, $60-70.

Stangl Pottery.* *Lyric.* Cup & saucer. $25-30. Mug, $30-40. Decorated saucers were also available.

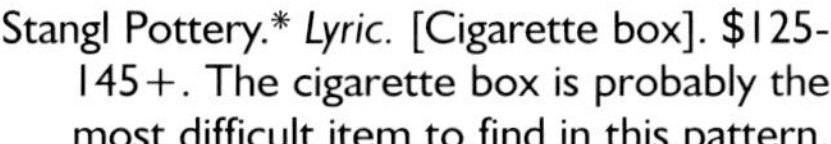

Stangl Pottery.* *Lyric.* [Cigarette box]. $125-145+. The cigarette box is probably the most difficult item to find in this pattern.

Stangl Pottery. Tierney (s). *Carnival.* Kay Hackett (p). 1954. Chop plate, 12 1/2", $25-35.

Stangl Pottery. [*Veiled Dinnerware*]. Dave Thomas (p). 1954. Plate, 10", ND. Robert Runge, Jr. reports, in the *Collector's Encyclopedia of Stangl Dinnerware*, that this line is considered "very scarce." According to Runge, only a small quantity was produced. These did not sell well and so the remaining pieces were destroyed.

Stangl Pottery.* **Coupe**. *Amber-Glo.* Kay Hackett (p). 1954. Coffee mug, $18-22; plate, 8", $10-12; regular sugar & cover, $12-18. A **Casual** shape sugar & creamer were also made to accompany the Casual shape coffee pot.

Sterling China Company™

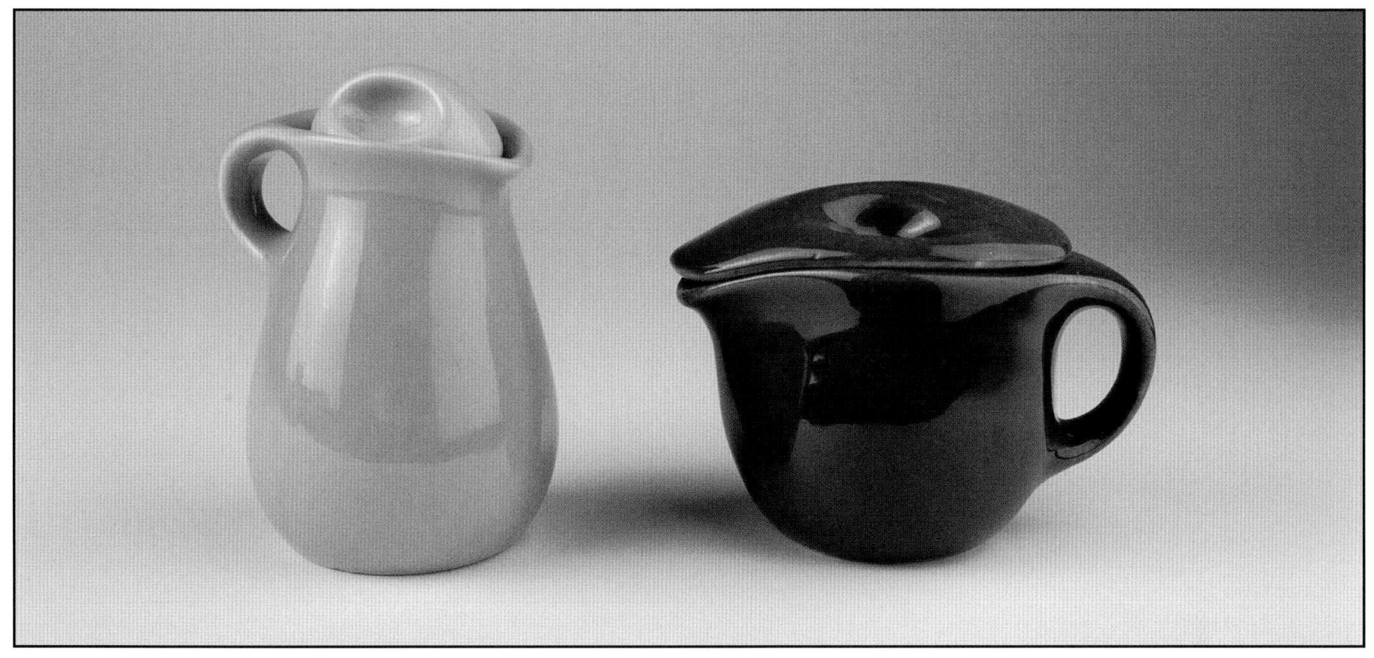

Sterling China Company (Wellsville, Ohio).* ***Vitrified China***. Russel Wright. *Suede Gray.* 1949. Coffee bottle, $200-225. *Ivy Green.* Teapot, $200-225.

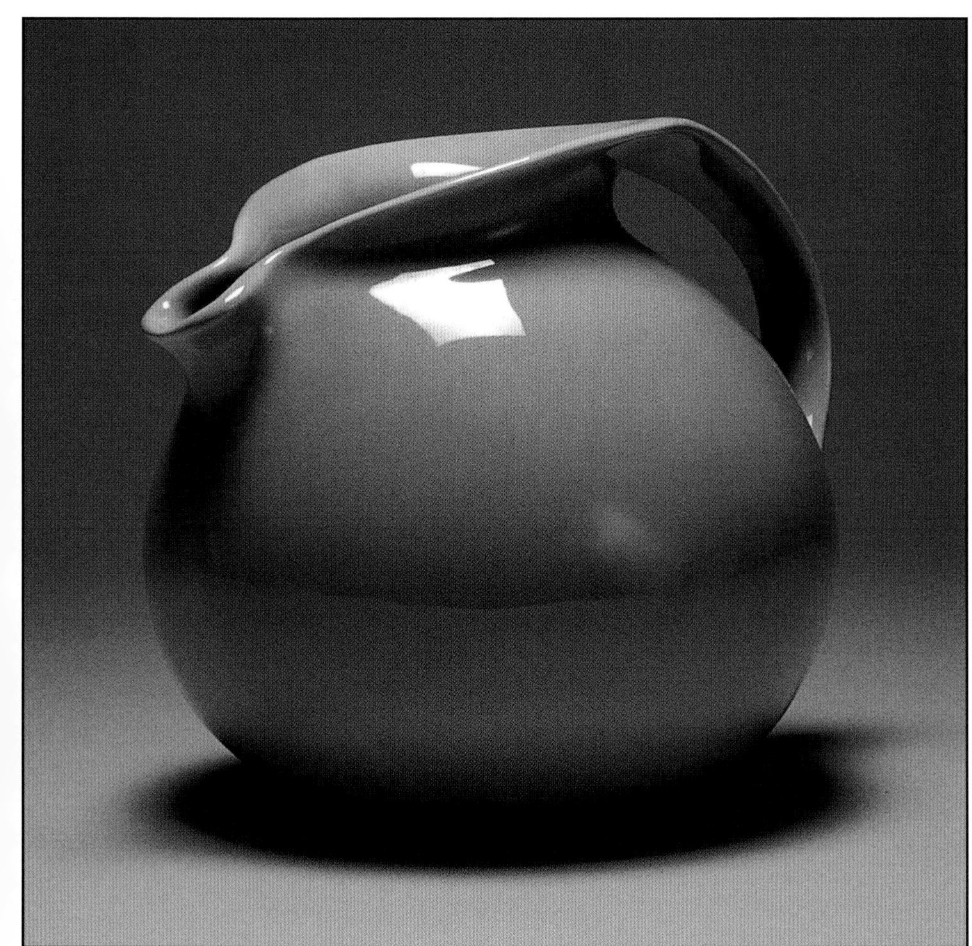

Sterling China.* *Suede Gray.* Water pitcher [restyled], $275-300.

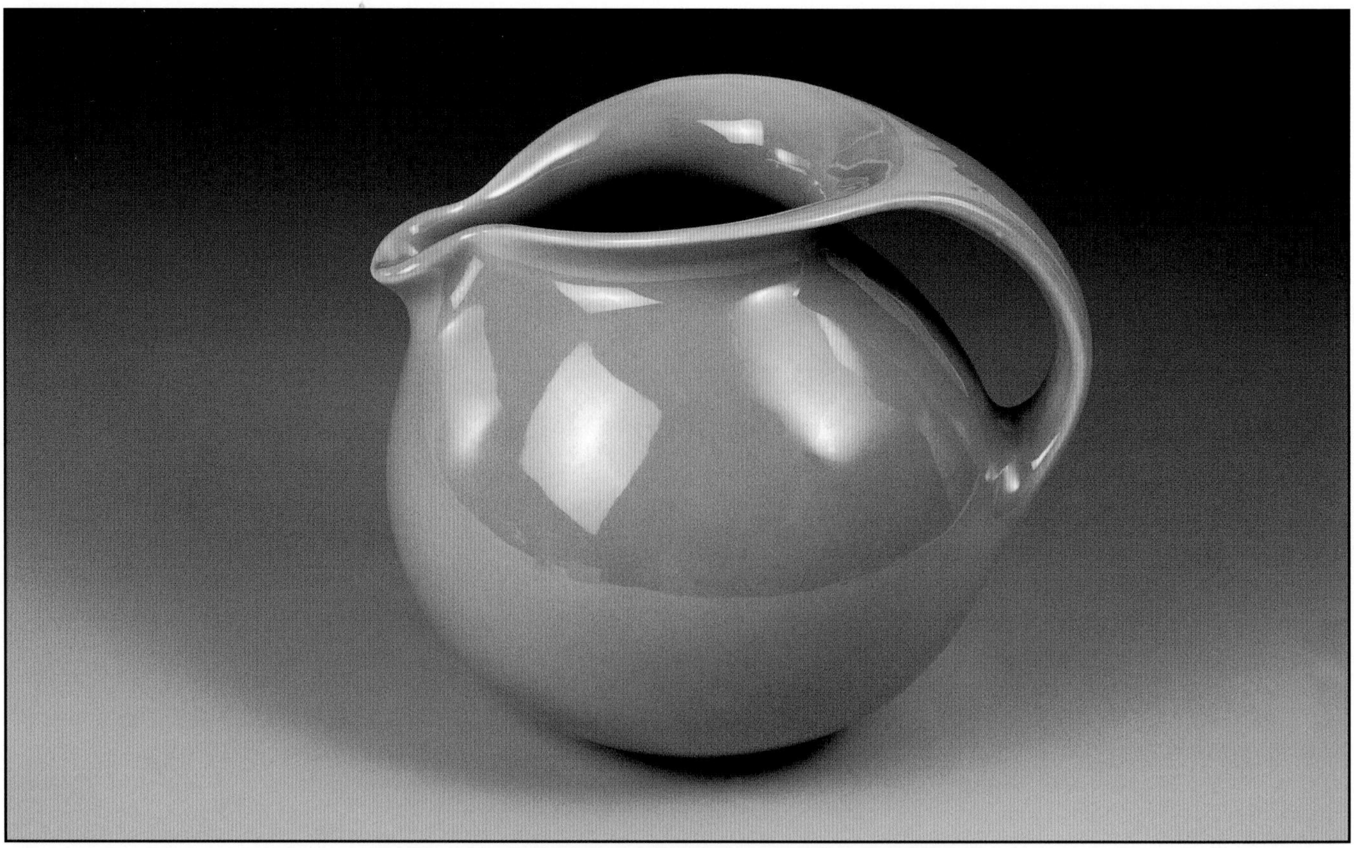

Sterling China.* *Suede Gray*. Water pitcher [restyled], another view.

Sterling China.* ***Vitrified China.*** *Ivy Green.* Oval platter, 13 1/2", $30-40; *Straw Yellow.* Covered sugar, $65-85. *Cedar Brown.* Onion soup, $25-35. *Straw Yellow.* Plate, 10 1/4", $20-28. [*White*]. Individual creamer, 1 oz., $50-60+. *Suede Gray.* Bouillon, $26-40. *Cedar Brown.* Handled cream pitcher, $45-60+. *Cedar Brown/Straw Yellow.* Cup & saucer, $17-35. *Cedar Brown.* Ash tray, $90-125.

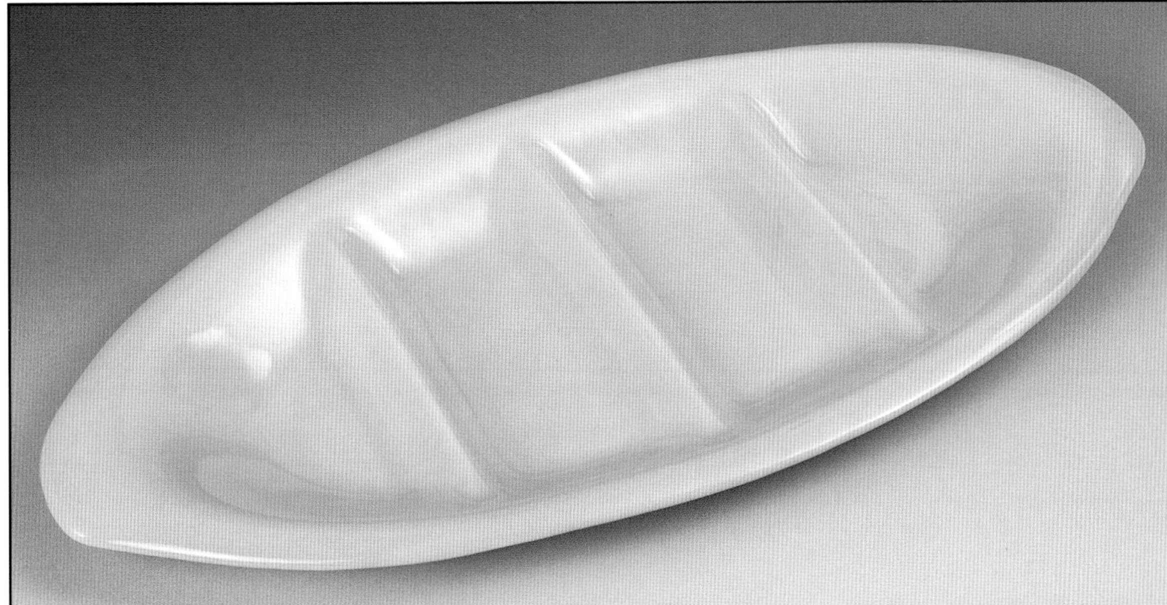

Sterling China.* *Straw Yellow.* Four compartment relish server, 16 3/4", $175-200.

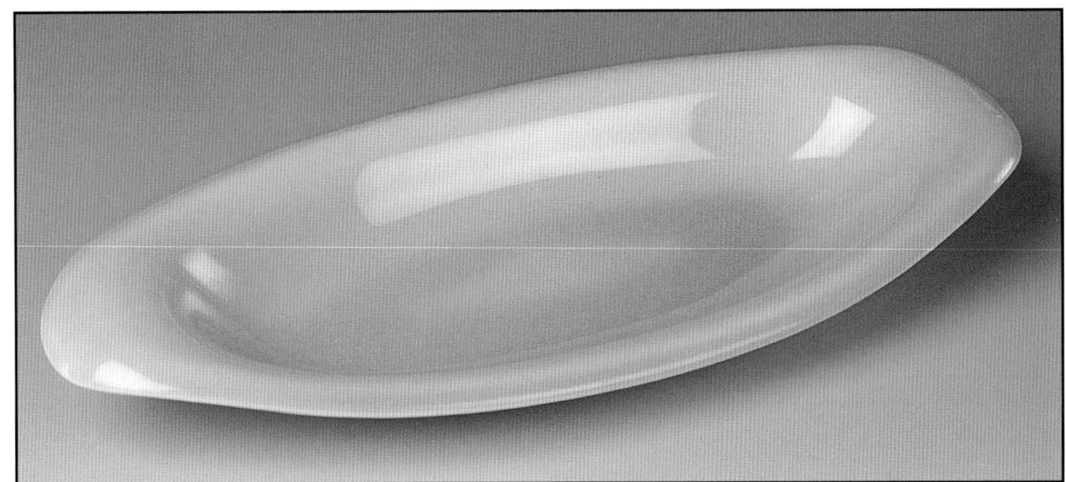

Sterling China.* *Straw Yellow.* Celery server, $100-125.

Sterling China. [*Space Traveler*]. Plate, 8", ND.

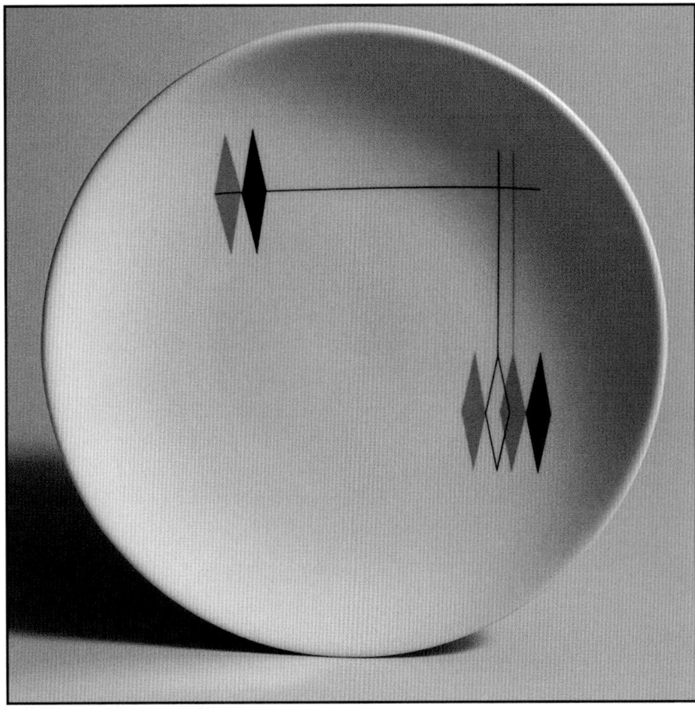

Sterling China. ***Lamberton Sterling***. [*Blue & Black Diamonds*]. <1961. Plate, 9 3/8", $5-8.

Stetson China Company™

Stetson China Company (Lincoln, Illinois). **Catalina**. Charles Murphy (s). 1949>. Covered sugar, $25-35; covered casserole, $50-75+; creamer, $25-35. The shape of Charles Murphy's line for Stetson is of more interest to the modernist than the floral decoration. Charles Murphy created most of his ceramic lines for Red Wing Potteries. He worked for Stetson China from 1949-1953.

Stetson. **Rio**. Charles Murphy (s). *Scots Clan, Pink and Charcoal.* <1952>. Creamer, $12-15; sugar, $15-20.

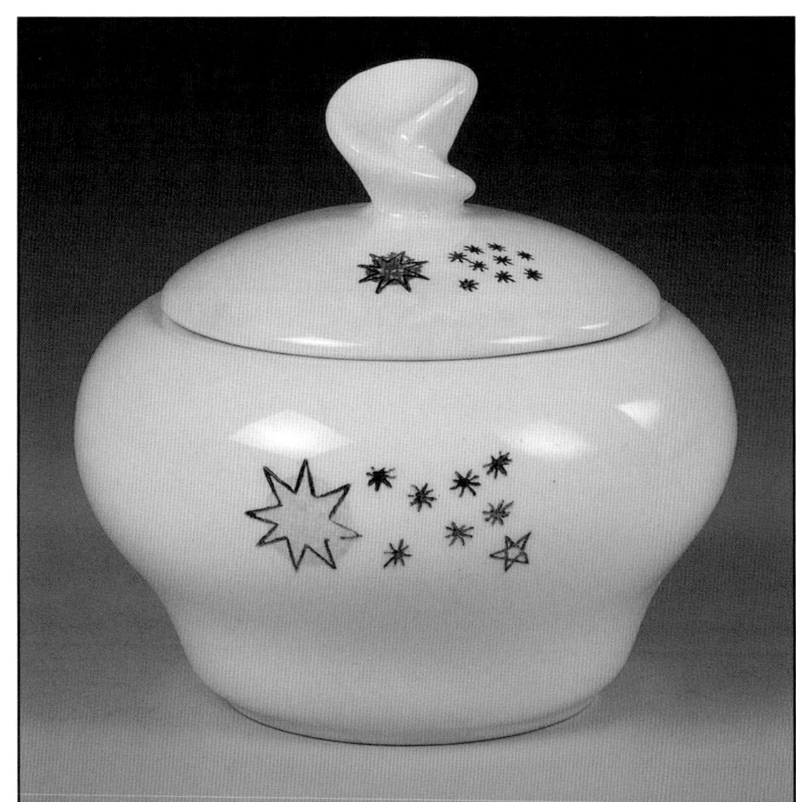

Stetson. **Rio**. [*Stars*]. <1952>. Covered sugar, $20-35.

Stetson. **Holiday**. Alfred Dube. [*Pink Fantasy Flake*]. <1953>. Creamer, $10-12; sugar, $12-22. [*Pink Swirl and Gray.*] Sugar, $12-22. [*Jungle Thicket*]. Sugar, $12-22.

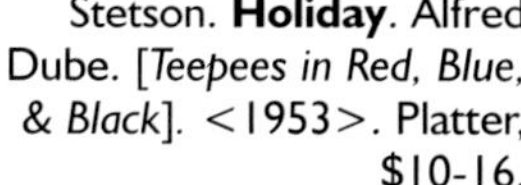

Stetson. **Holiday**. Alfred Dube. [*Teepees in Red, Blue, & Black*]. <1953>. Platter, $10-16.

Stetson. **Holiday**. Alfred Dube. [*Holiday Tiara*]. <1953>. Bowl, 8" x 1 1/2", $8-12; plate, 10 3/8", $5-10; cup & saucer, $5-12.

Stetson. **Holiday**. Alfred Dube. *Hiawatha.* 1953. Teapot, $45-100; plate, 9 1/2", $5-10; salt & pepper, $15-30; cup & saucer, $5-12.

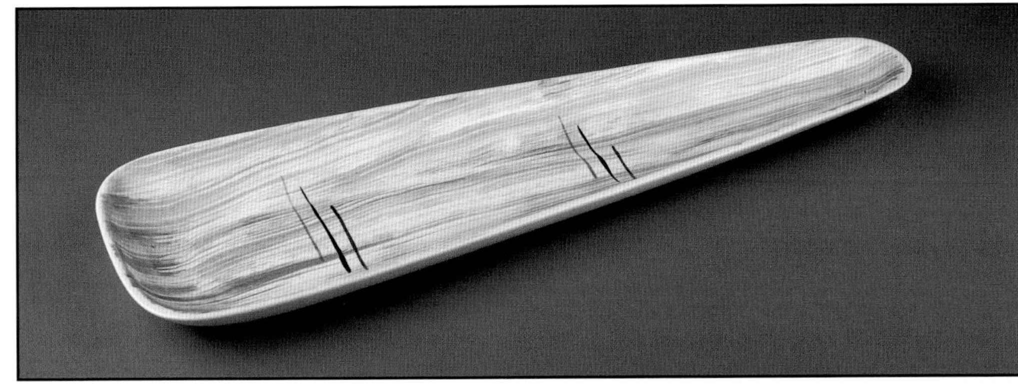

Stetson. **Holiday**. *Hiawatha.* Tray, $35-55. Two variations of this pattern exist. One with an extra set of three stripes carries the *Hiawatha*/Stetson China backstamp. The other has the primrose china backstamp.

Stetson. **Holiday**. Alfred Dube. [*Arrowheads*]. 1954. Buffet plate & cup, 9 5/8", $14-22.

Stetson. **Holiday**. Alfred Dube. *Country Casual.* 1955. Bowl, 8 1/8" x 1 3/8", $8-12; bowl, 5 1/4" x 1 3/8", $4-6; platter, 13 1/2", $12-16; cup & saucer, $5-12; cream, $10-12; sugar, $12-22.

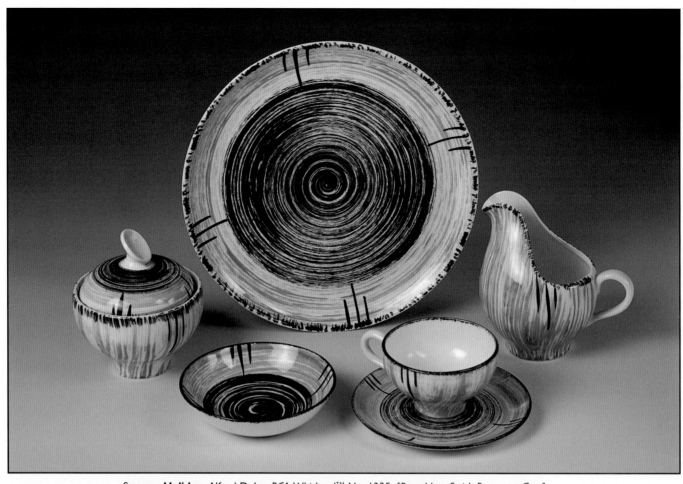

Stetson. **Holiday**. Alfred Dube. *RCA Whirlpool™ No. 1235*. [*Breathless Swirl, Brown on Gray*]. 1955. Sugar, $12-22; plate, 10 1/2", $5-12; bowl, '5 1/4" x 1 3/8", $4-6; cream, $10-12.

Stetson. (McCoy Pottery for Stetson).* **Table to Terrace**. Esta Brody (s). [*Gold Hi-Lights*]. Alfred Dube (p). 1963. Covered coffee server, ND. Meat platter, ND. Cream, ND.

Steubenville Pottery Company™

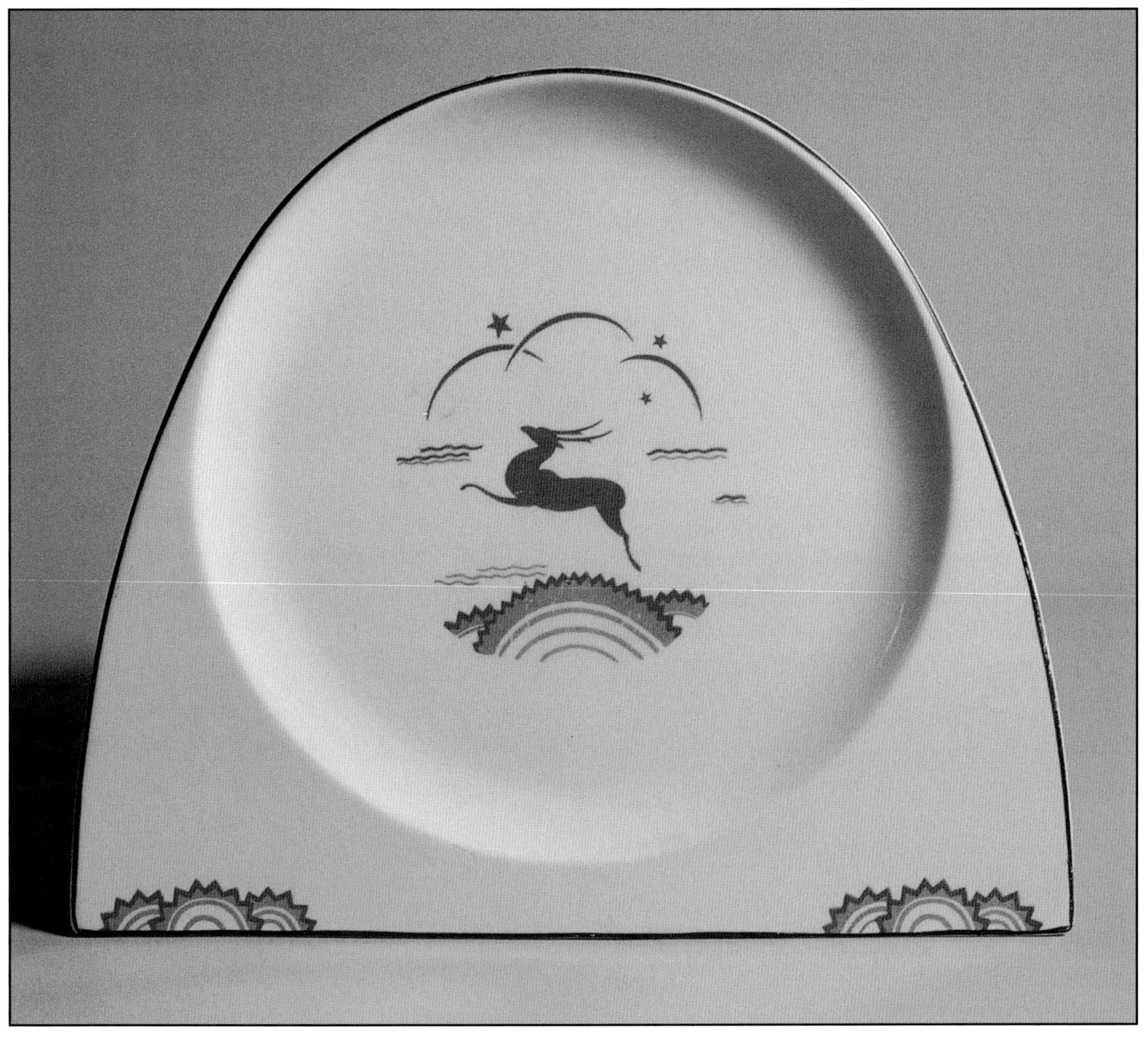

Steubenville Pottery Company (Steubenville, Ohio). **Normandie**. [*Jumping Deer*]. 1935. Plate, $25-35. While the pattern is art deco, the shape is on the cusp of mid-century modern. The trades show this piece in all-white, dramatizing its simple, graceful form.

Steubenville.* ***American Modern***. Russel Wright. *White.* 1939. [Coffee pot], $350-400+; [teapot], $250-300; sugar, $65-75.

Steubenville.* ***American Modern***. *White.* Covered pitcher, $425-500+; divided vegetable dish, $150-200; double stack server, $400-500+.

Steubenville.* ***American Modern***. *White*. Covered pitcher, another view. Salad bowl, 11" x 4 1/2", $100-200; covered vegetable bowl, $125-150.

Steubenville.* ***American Modern***. *White*. Celery dish, 13" x 3 1/2", $65-80; salt & pepper, $30-55, pair; water pitcher, $200-250+.

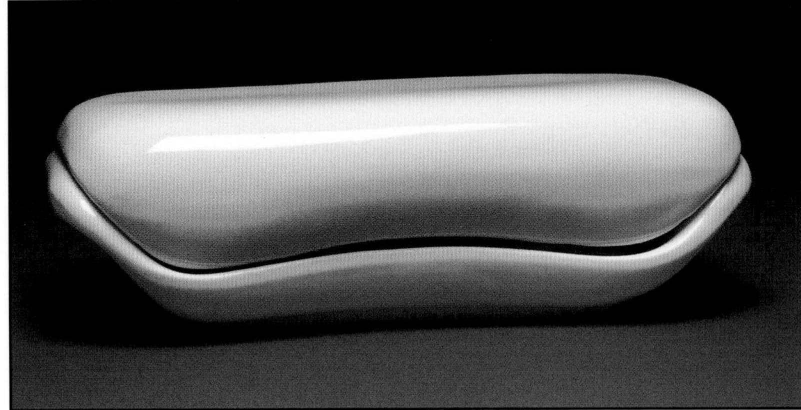

Steubenville.* ***American Modern***. *White*. Covered butter dish, $500-600+.

Steubenville.* ***American Modern***. *White*. Stoppered carafe, $800-1200.

Steubenville.* ***American Modern***. *Granite Grey*. [Unstoppered] carafe, $225-275; *Coral*. Relish rosette, $300-350.

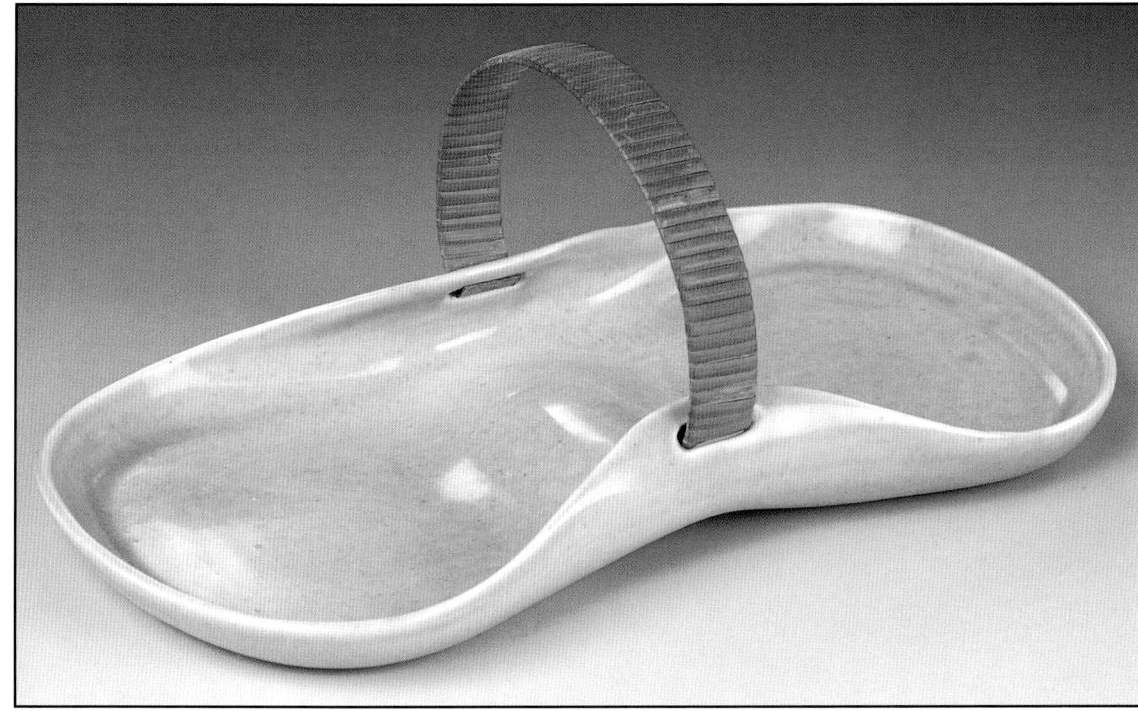

Steubenville.* ***American Modern***. *Coral.* Divided handled relish [rattan covered handle], $250-300.

Steubenville.* ***American Modern***. *Bean Brown.* Sugar, $50-60; *Chartreuse Curry.* Cup & saucer, $12-18; *Cedar.* Divided vegetable dish, $100-150. *Granite Grey.* Hostess party plate & cup, $65-90. *Seafoam.* Celery dish, $35-55.

Steubenville.* ***American Modern***. *Coral.* Cup & saucer, $12-18. *Granite Grey.* After dinner (A.D.) cup & saucer, $20-30.

Steubenville.* ***American Modern***. [*Steubenville Blue*]. Cup & saucer, $350-450.

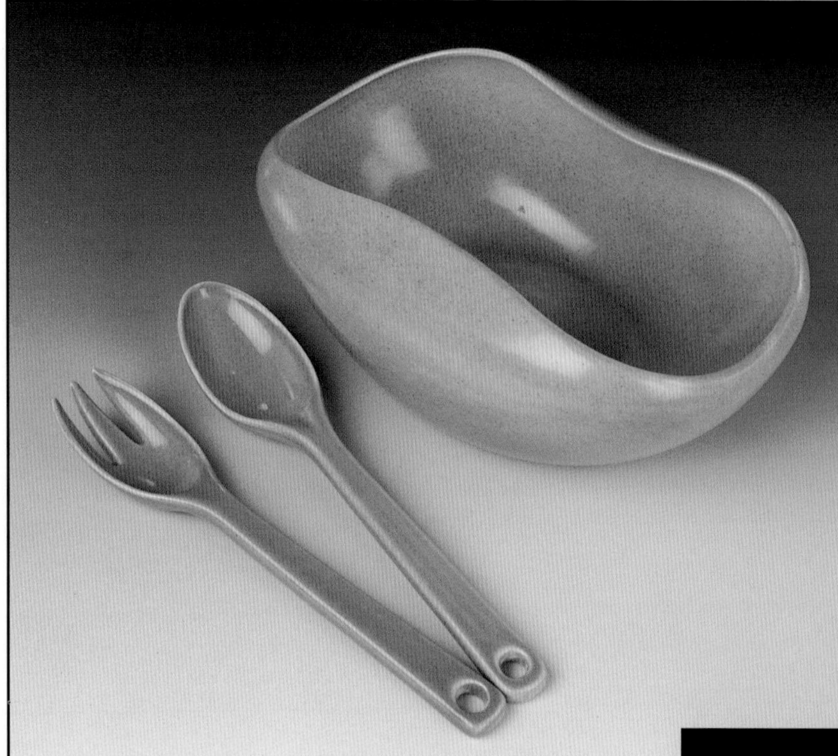

Steubenville.* ***American Modern***. *Coral*. Fork & spoon [***Woodfield***], $50-100, each. Salad Bowl, $60-80.

Steubenville.* ***American Modern***. *Coral*. Water mug, $65-90; covered pitcher, $425-500.

Steubenville.* ***American Modern***. *Gray.* [Teapot], $90-125. *Coral.* Water pitcher, $60-130.

Steubenville.* ***American Modern***. *Coral.* Covered butter dish, $250-350+.

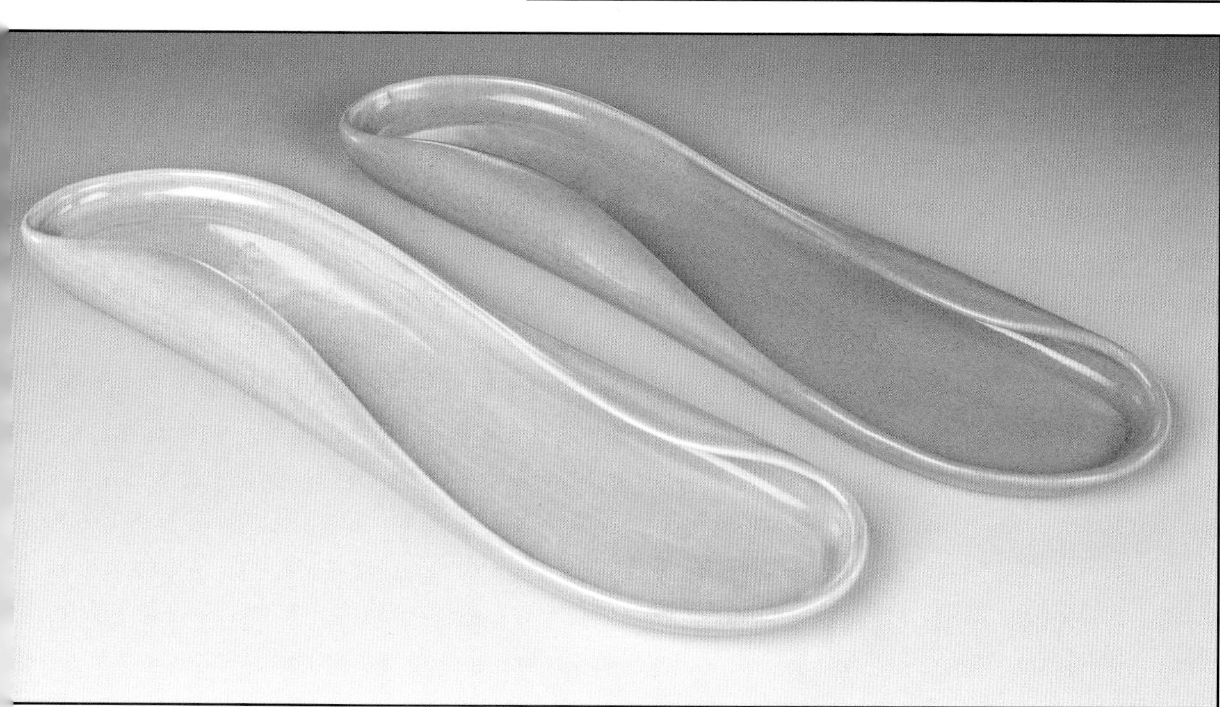

Steubenville.* ***American Modern***. *Gray & Coral.* Celery dishes, $25-35, each.

Steubenville.* ***American Modern***. *Grass Blades*. Bread & butter plate, 6", ND.

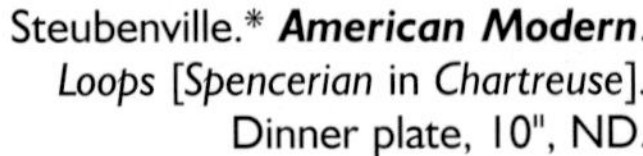

Steubenville.* ***American Modern***. *Loops* [*Spencerian* in *Chartreuse*]. Dinner plate, 10", ND.

Steubenville.* ***American Modern***. *Loops* [*Spencerian* in *Coral*]. Salad plate, 8", ND.

Steubenville.* ***American Modern***. *Matchsticks.* Dinner plate, 10", ND. These appear to be the official names used with decorated ***American Modern's*** introduction to the trade and are documented in the September 1954 issue of *China, Glass and Tablewares*. One pattern, not shown here, was called *American Leaves*. Occasionally pattern and shape names from the potteries changed by the time of introduction to the consumer.

Steubenville.* ***Raymor Contempora***. Ben Seibel. *Faun.* 1953. Large teapot, $75-100. *Mist Grey.* Water pitcher, $90-110.

Steubenville.* ***Raymor Contempora***. *Mist Grey.* Large teapot, another view.

Steubenville.* ***Raymor Contempora***. *Faun.* Cup & saucer, $14-16; dinner plate, 11", $15-20.

Steubenville.* ***Raymor Contempora***. *Faun.* Fruit [bowl], 6" x 1 7/8", $8-12. *Charcoal.* Bread & butter plate, 7", $5-8; salad plate, 8 5/8", $12-14. *Mist Grey.* Oval platter, 14 1/2", $30-45.

Steubenville.* ***Raymor Contempora***. *Faun.* Divided vegetable bowl, $35-45. *Sand White.* Nesting coffee pot, $55-75. These individual pots were designed to stack with others.

Steubenville.* ***Raymor Contempora***. *Sand White*. Party plate with well & cup, 10 1/2", $45-55. *Faun*. Salt & pepper set with stand, $40-60. *Faun*. Ash tray, $12-16.

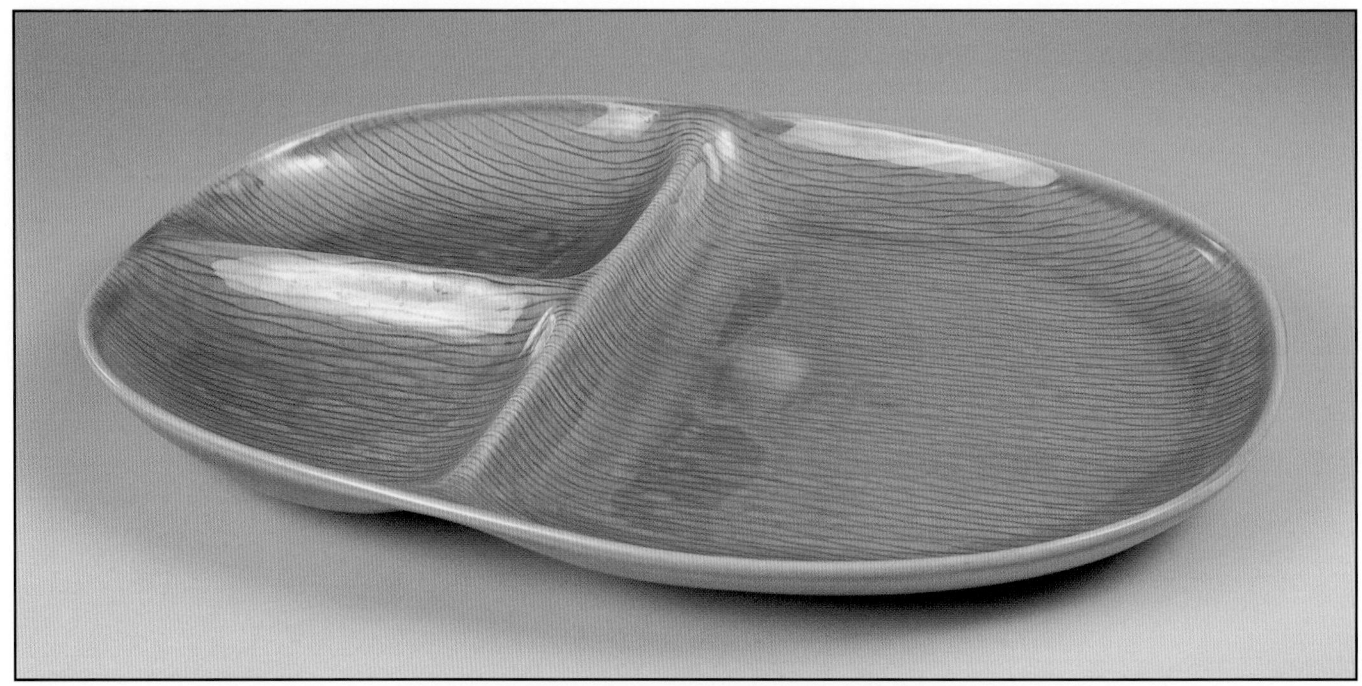

Steubenville.* ***Raymor Contempora***. *Mist Grey*. Divided food server, $50-65.

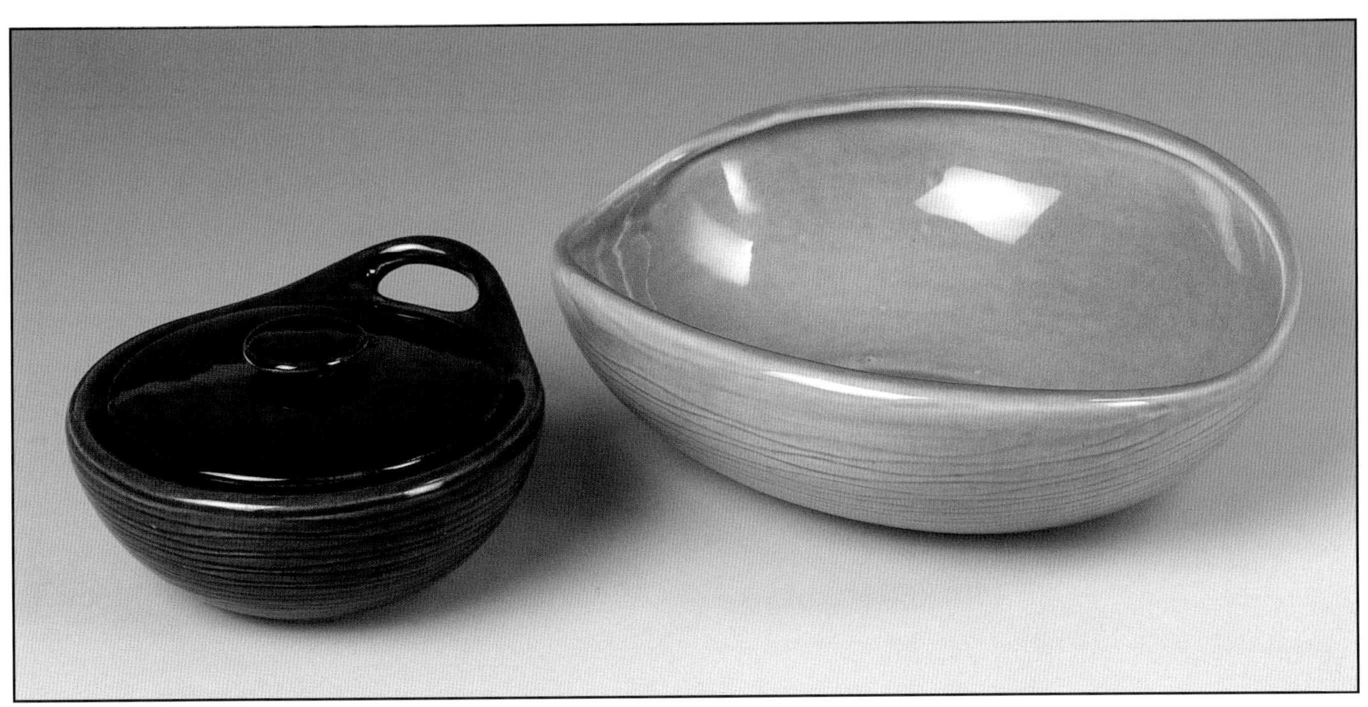

Steubenville.* ***Raymor Contempora***. *Charcoal.* Sugar, $30-40. *Mist Grey.* Vegetable bowl, 8 3/4", $20-30.

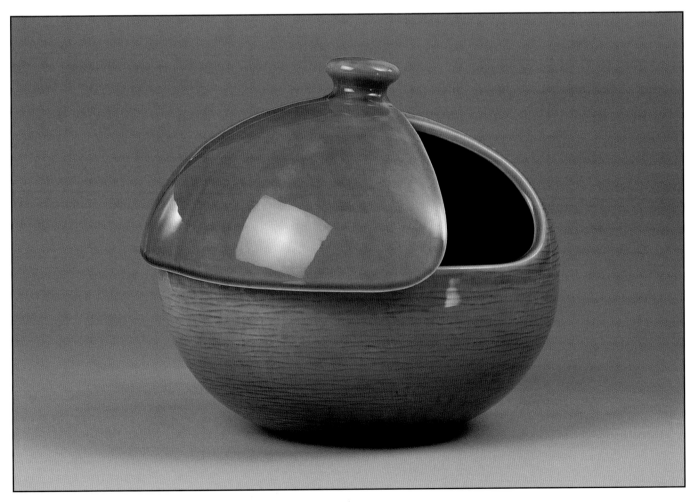

Steubenville.* ***Raymor Contempora***. *Faun.* Bun & muffin server, $175-325+.

Steubenville.* ***Raymor Contempora***. *Faun*. Covered casserole, $45-75.

Steubenville.* ***Raymor Contempora***. *Faun*. Gravy boat, $25-30.

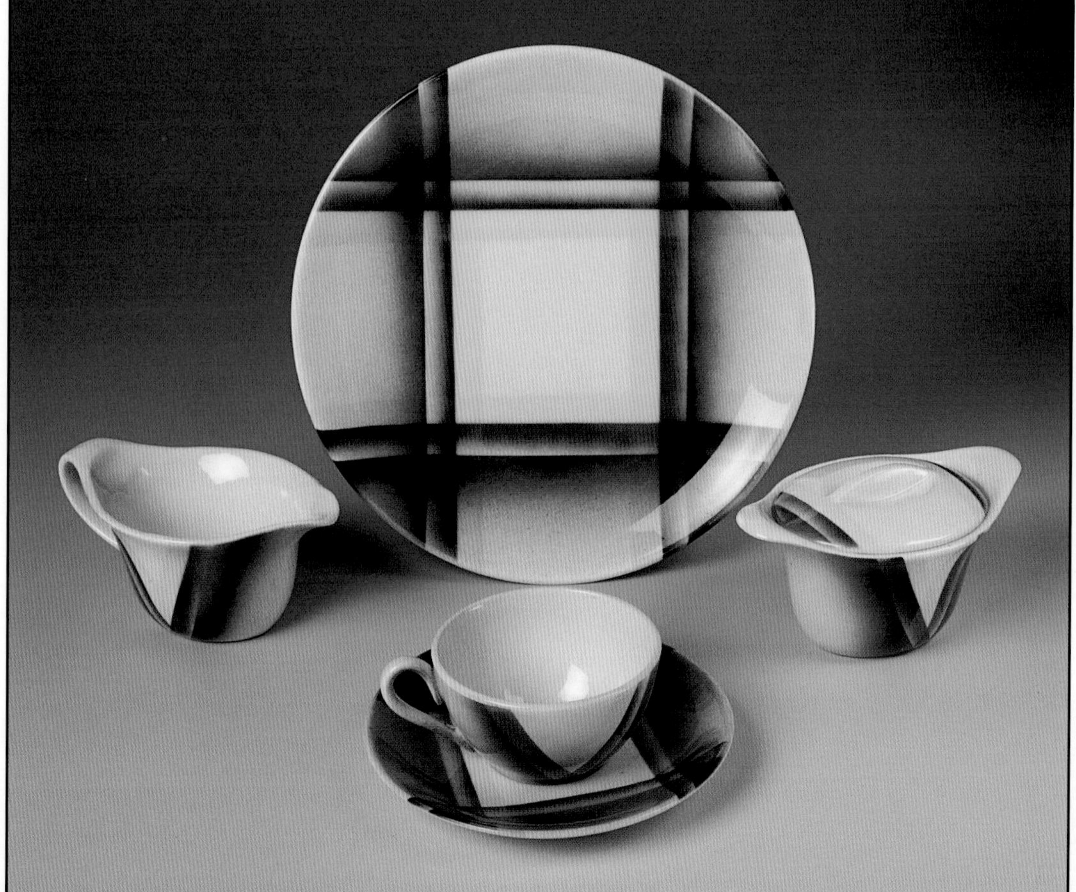

Steubenville.* **Horizon**. *Multi-colored Plaid*. <1953. Creamer, $12-15; teacup & saucer, $8-12; plate, 10", $6-15; sugar, $12-18.

Steubenville.* **Horizon**. *Sunday Afternoon.* 1954. Coffee pot, $20-25.

Steubenville.* *Sunday Afternoon.* Platter, $15-20.

Steubenville.* [**Horizon**, redesigned]. [*Cattail*], *Sunday Afternoon.* Creamers, $10-12; sugars, $12-15.

Steubenville.* **Citation**. *Satellite*. c.1956. [Cup & saucer], $8-14. **Horizon**. *Starlite*. 1954. Butter dish, $18-25. This decal appears to have been used on the **Citation** shape as well as the **Horizon** shape. Trade journals document a different pattern name with shape change. The author suspects that Vincent Broomhall may have designed both the **Horizon** and **Citation** shapes.

Steubenville. **Citation**. *Rhythm*. 1955. Plate, 10 1/4", $10-15; sugar, $18-25; creamer, $12-15. Canonsburg's famous *Temporama* pattern is featured on this shape. Soon after the Steubenville Pottery closed in December 1959, the molds and design materials were sold to Canonsburg Pottery Company (Canonsburg, Pennsylvania). Vincent Broomhall, well-known ceramic designer and pottery salesman, headed the Steubenville Division of Canonsburg Pottery.

Steubenville. **Citation**. *Delrey.* Cup & saucer, $5-12; plate, 10", $5-12. Although marked *Steubenville*, pottery made on the **Citation** shape was also marked *Steubenville* at the Canonsburg Pottery. The author has not found documentation indicating whether this was made prior to 1960.

Steubenville.* **Casual**. Vincent Broomhall. *Dimension.* 1956. Sugar (covered), $22-28; utility and relish dish (large, small), 10"; 6 1/4", $10-20, each. *Cotillion*. Beverage server, $30-50; creamer, $12-16. Steubenville's ***Casual*** line featured two other patterns: *Domino* (diamonds in gray with yellow) and *Sequence* (four-petal florets in brown and pink).

Steubenville Pottery, a division of Canonsburg Pottery. **Verve**. *Still-Life*. 1961. Creamer, $8-12; coffee pot, $30-35; sugar, $10-16.

Steubenville Pottery, a division of Canonsburg Pottery. *Still-Life*. Bowl, $5-10; dinner plate, $6-12; cup & saucer, $6-12.

Syracuse China Company™

Syracuse China Company (formerly, Onondaga Pottery. Syracuse, New York). **Round Edge** (**Rolled Edge**). Mark Haley (s). *Ancient Mimbreno.* M.E.J. Colter (p). 1937. Plate, $50-75+. This price is for original production only.

Syracuse. ***Shadowtone***. **Round Edge** (**Rolled Edge**). Mark Haley (s). *Deep Sea Fish.* Attributed to Harry Aitken (p). 1938. Bowls, $25-35, each.

Syracuse. ***Shadowtone***. **Morwel**. *Tartan*. Attributed to Harry Aitken (p). 1938>. Plate, $10-20.

Syracuse.* **Copa**. *Fanfare*. Michael J. Szymanski (p). 1956. Plate #10, [10 1/4"], $15-20. *Fanfare* was patented in 1957.

Syracuse.* **Copa**. *Flight.* Michael J. Szymanski (p). 1957. Plate #7, 9", $15-20. *Flight* was patented in 1957.

Syracuse.* **Copa**. *Driftwood.* Edward M. Otis (p). 1956. **California**. Fruit #3 1/2, [4 3/4" x 1 1/4"], $5-8. **Copa**. Plate #8, 9 3/4", $5-10. **McAlpin** teacup, 7 oz. and **Franklin** tea saucer, 5 3/4", $5-10. As can be seen, restaurantware frequently adopted items from other shape lines. American institutional lines typically took their shape name from the plate shape. The *Driftwood* pattern was patented in 1957 (Des. 180,198).

Syracuse.* **Copa**. *Driftwood.* Plate #6, 8 1/8", $6-10. **California**. Fruit #3 1/2, [4 3/4" x 1 1/4"], $5-8. **Morwel**. Dish "G", 9 5/8", $10-15. **Copa**. Plate #4, 6 3/8", $5-10. **Empire**. Jug or pitcher, 5 3/4 oz., $8-14. **St. Francis**. Unhandled bouillon cup, 7 1/2 oz. [3 7/8" x 2 1/4"], $8-12.

Syracuse.* **Trend**. *Jubilee.* 1962. Plate "H", 8 3/8", $8-10. The **Trend** shape was introduced in the mid-1950s and was designed to save space on institutional trays used in cafeterias and other facilities.

Syracuse.* **Trend**. *Jubilee.* Teacup, 6 3/4 oz. and small tea saucer (4 5/8"), $9-15.

Syracuse.* **California**. Richard Garvin (s). *Evening Star.* Ellen Manderfield (p). 1955. No. 10 plate (dinner), 10 5/8", $8-12. This fine china pattern was an award-winner at the Artists in Industry exhibition (19th Ceramic National Competition, 1956). It was still an in-stock pattern, one decade after its introduction.

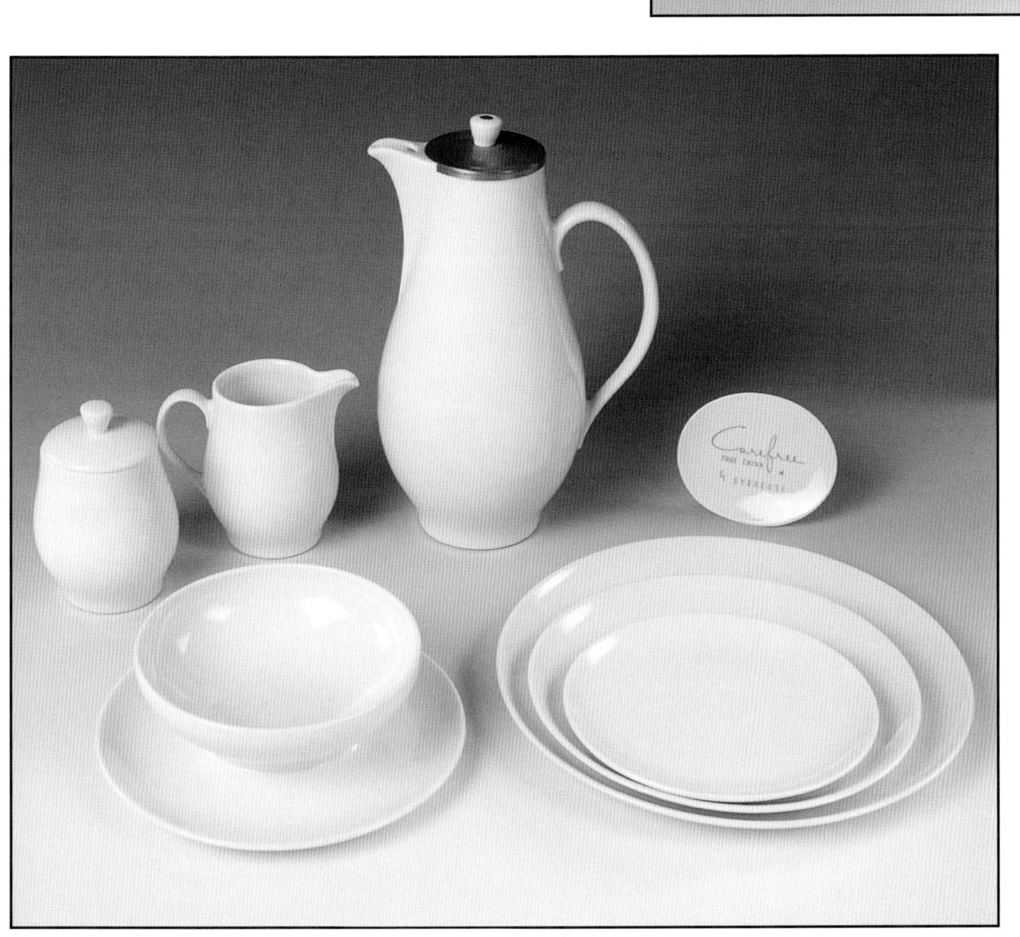

Syracuse.* ***Carefree True China***. **Carefree**. Richard Garvin. *Serene.* 1956. Covered sugar, 10 3/4 oz., $10-20; creamer, 11 3/8 oz., $8-15; beverage pot (with copper cover), 54 1/2 oz., $30-45; [dealer's sign], $25-35; gravy boat (attached stand), 16 oz., $15-35. No. 4 plate (bread and butter), 6 3/8", $4-7. No. 6 plate (salad-breakfast), 8", $4-10. No. 10 plate (dinner), 10", $5-12.

Tamac, Inc.™

Tamac, Inc. (Perry, Oklahoma).* ***Free-Form Dinnerware***. *Frosty Pine*. Barbecue plate, 15 1/2", $15-25; barbecue cup, $10-15. 1946 was the year the company was established. Actual dates for the introduction of decorations are not known. However, the order of introduction has been reported to be (earliest to latest): *Butterscotch*, *Avocado*, *Frosty Pine*, *Frosty Fudge*, *Raspberry*, and *Honey* (*Frankoma and Other Oklahoma Potteries*, 1996).

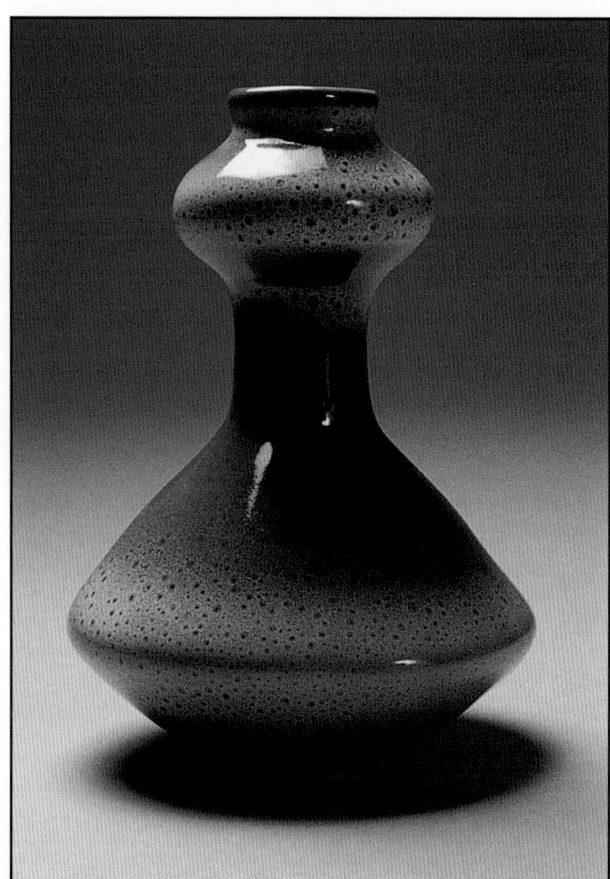

Tamac.* *Frosty Pine*. Bud vase, 6", $28-35.

Tamac.* *Frosty Fudge*. Juice pitcher, 24 oz., $45-55. *Frosty Pine*. Pitcher, 4-qt., $55-75.

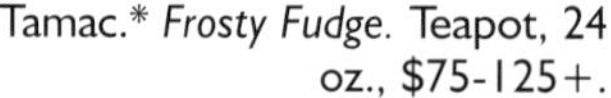

Tamac.* *Frosty Fudge.* Teapot, 24 oz., $75-125+.

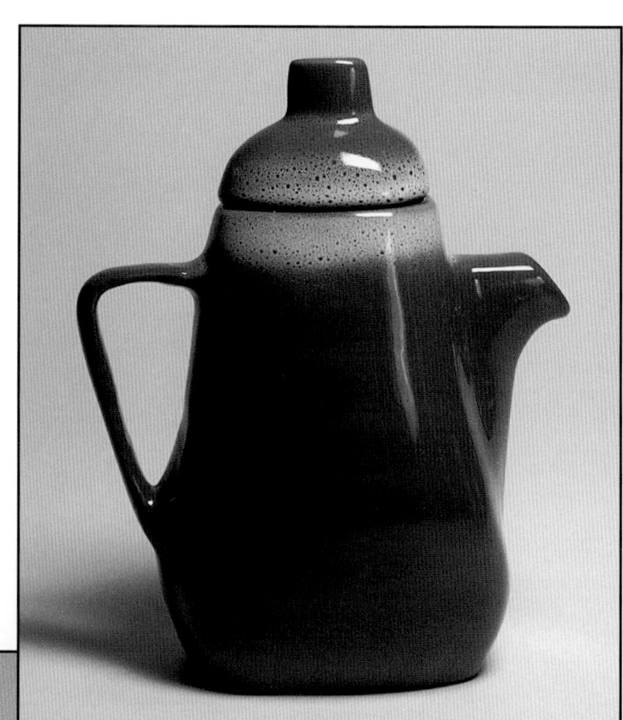

Tamac.* *Frosty Fudge.* Barbecue cup, 10 oz. and barbecue saucer, 7", $20-30.

Tamac.* *Avocado.* Cup (#19), 8 oz., & saucer, $15-20.

Tamac.* *Avocado*. Tumbler, 20 oz., $15-22. *Frosty Pine*. Dish garden, 12", $30-45. *Avocado*. Pepper shaker [3 holes], $10-12. *Frosty Green*. Salt shaker [4 holes], $10-12. *Avocado*. Soup bowl, 16 oz., $14-18.

Tamac.* *Avocado*. Sugar bowl w/ lid, $22-30. *Frosty Fudge*. Dinner plate, 10", $10-16. *Frosty Pine*. Serving bowl, 1 qt., $20-30.

Tamac.* *Avocado*. Individual cream and sugar set, $15-20, each piece.

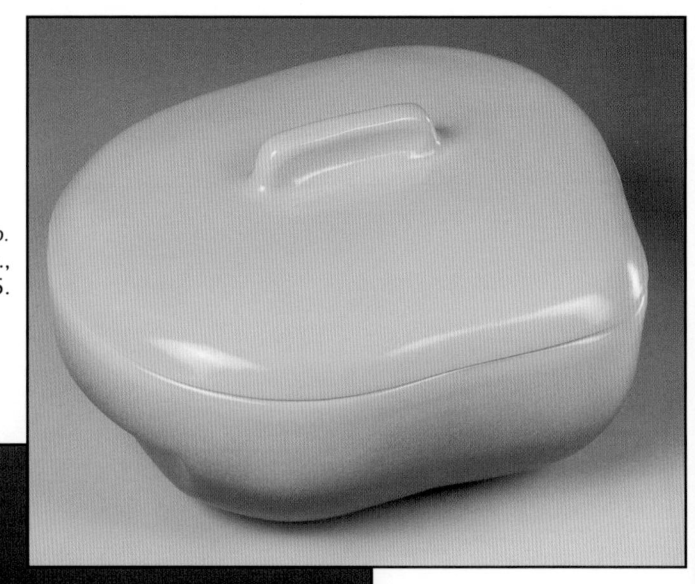

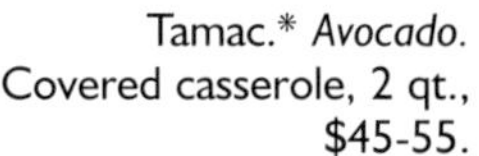

Tamac.* *Avocado*.
Covered casserole, 2 qt.,
$45-55.

Tamac.* Stack of Tamac.

Tamac.* Aerial view of Tamac stack. Notice that these organic shapes are congruent.

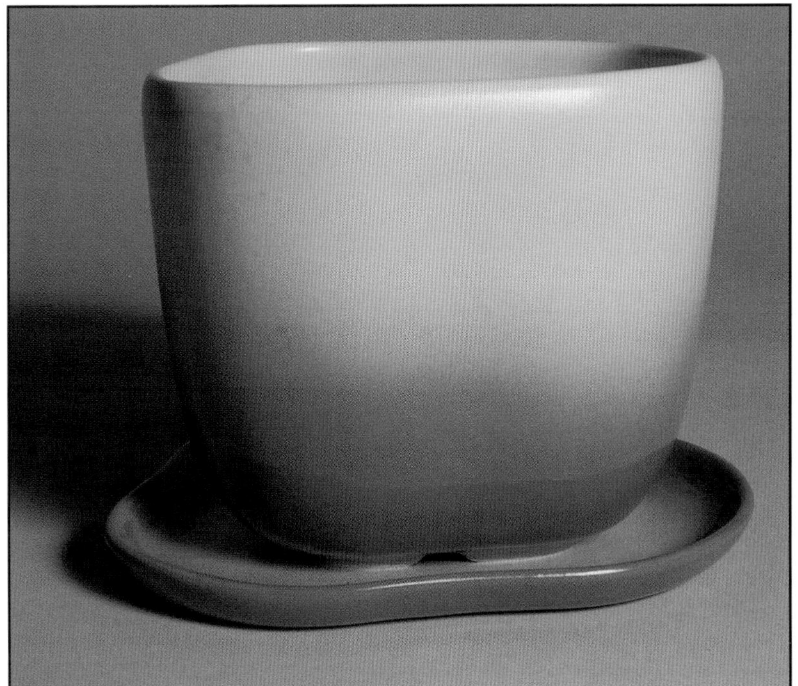

Tamac.* Planter, 5" high, $30-45.

Tamac.* *Honey.* Tumbler, 20 oz., $25-30. Mug, open handle, 12 oz., $25-35. *Honey* is a relatively hard-to-find color, but not as difficult to find as *Butterscotch* and *Raspberry*. *Frosty Pine* and *Frosty Fudge* are the most common decorative glazes.

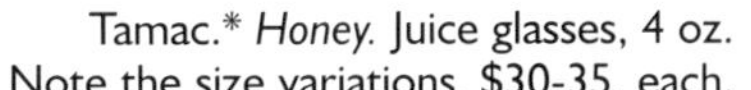

Tamac.* *Honey.* Juice glasses, 4 oz. Note the size variations. $30-35, each.

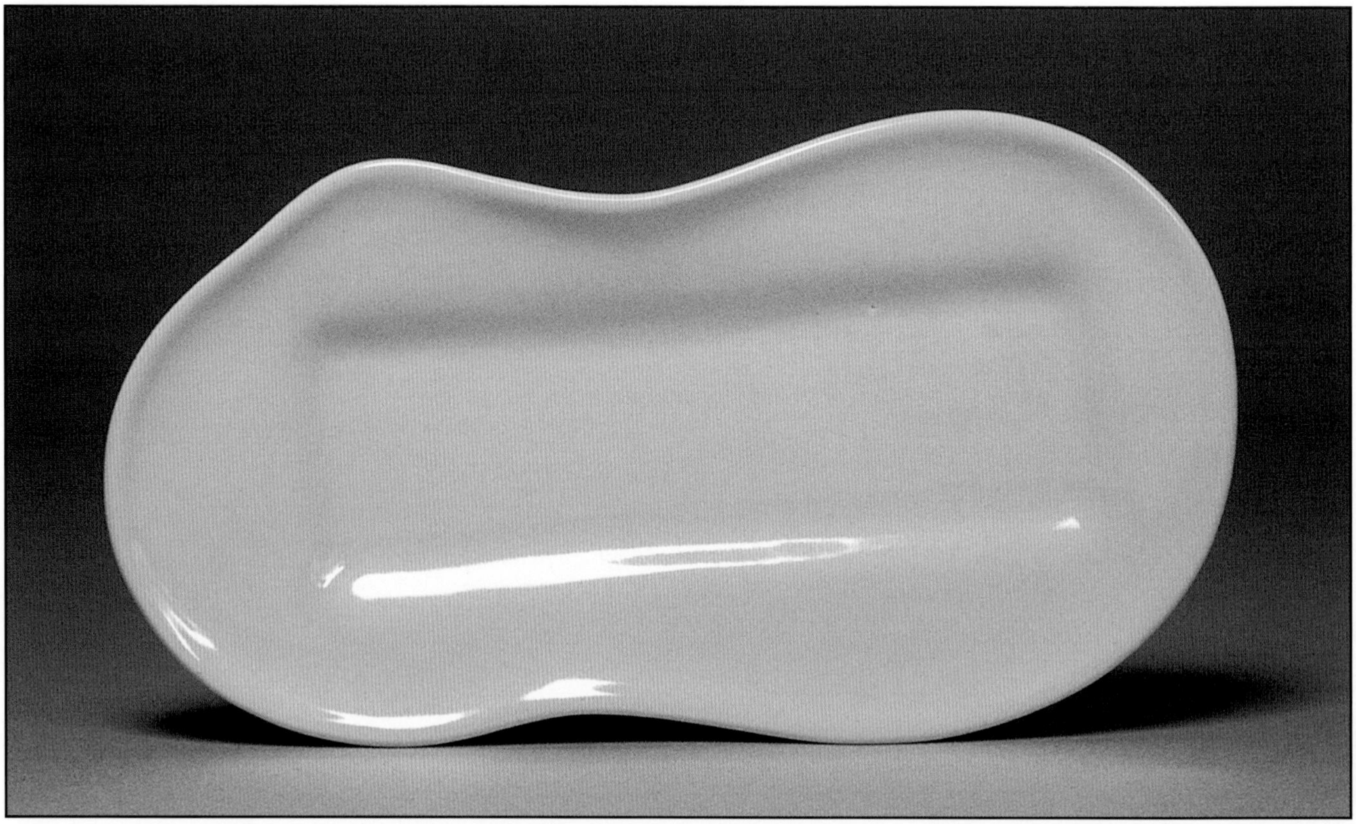

Tamac.* *Honey.* Butter dish, $60-100. Common colors, $35-45. The Tamac butter dish was lidless.

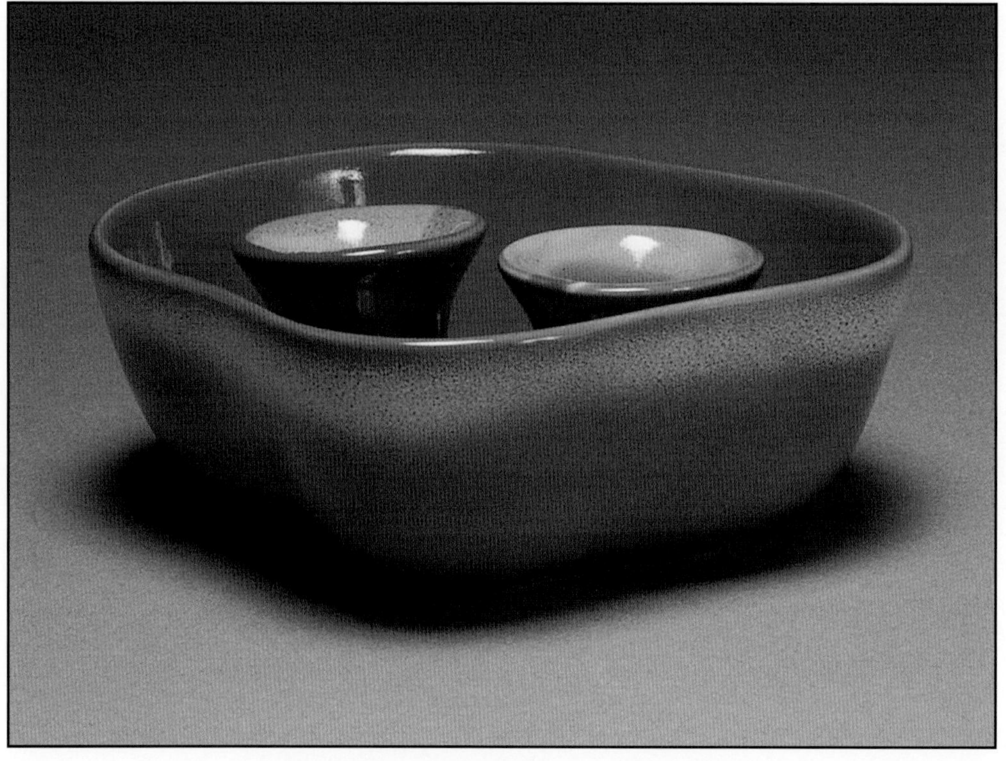

Tamac.* *Raspberry.* Double candle holder, $65-75.

Tamac.* *Raspberry.* Teacup, 6 oz. (round), ND.

The Taylor, Smith & Taylor Co.™

Taylor, Smith & Taylor.* ***Conversation***. Walter Dorwin Teague. *Meadow Tree*. Teague/ Doris Coutant (p). 1950. Coffee server, $50-60.

The Taylor, Smith & Taylor Co. (East Liverpool, Ohio).* ***Conversation***. Walter Dorwin Teague. *Meadow Tree.* Teague/Doris Coutant (p). 1950. Cup & saucer, $12-16; dish, 8" x 1 1/4", $10-14; cream, $12-18; plate, 6 1/4", $5-10; sauceboat & tray, $28-38.

Taylor, Smith & Taylor.* ***Conversation***. Walter Dorwin Teague. [*Tu-Tone Cocoa Brown*]. Teague/Doris Coutant (p). 1950. Water pitcher, $40-45.

Taylor, Smith & Taylor.* ***Pebbleford***. **Versatile**. John J. Gilkes. *White* [*Marble*]. 1953. This is the date of the introduction of ***Pebbleford***. Not all colors were introduced at the same time. Coffee pot, $25-35; water pitcher, $20-25.

Taylor, Smith & Taylor.* ***Pebbleford***. John Gilkes. *Sand, Sunburst.* Coffee pots [small lid], $25-35, each. *Turquoise, Pink, Sunburst.* Coffee pots [large lid], $25-35, each. *Teal.* Teapot, $30-40.

Taylor, Smith & Taylor.* ***Pebbleford***. John Gilkes. *Sunburst.* Divided vegetable, $15-20; relish, 9 1/2", $12-15; gravy, $10-15; cream, $8-14; sugar, $15-22.

Taylor, Smith & Taylor.* ***Pebbleford***. John Gilkes. *Mint Green, White (Marble), Teal, Turquoise.* Covered casseroles, $20-30; *Mint Green,* $25-35.

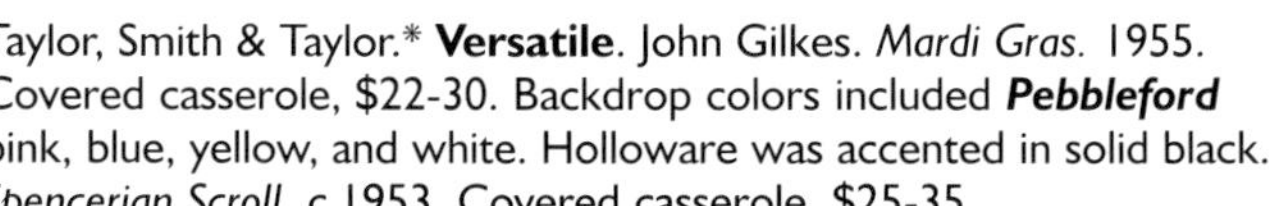

Taylor, Smith & Taylor.* **Versatile**. John Gilkes. *Mardi Gras.* 1955. Covered casserole, $22-30. Backdrop colors included ***Pebbleford*** pink, blue, yellow, and white. Holloware was accented in solid black. *Spencerian Scroll.* c.1953. Covered casserole, $25-35.

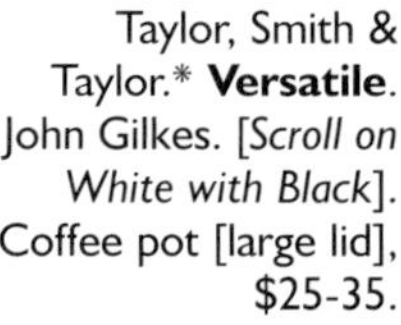

Taylor, Smith & Taylor.* **Versatile**. John Gilkes. [*Scroll on White with Black*]. Coffee pot [large lid], $25-35.

Taylor, Smith & Taylor.* ***Chateau Buffet***. *Chateau Buffet.* <1956. La Terrine Moyenne, 2 1/2 qt., $25-35. La Grande Terrine, 4 1/2 qt., $30-45. La Saladier, 3 1/2 qts., $25-35. La Fourchette a Salade, $15-20; La Cuillere a Salade, $15-20.

Taylor, Smith & Taylor.* **Versatile** [formal]. [*Pink*]. Covered casserole, $25-35. [*Blue & White*]. Coffee server, $20-25.

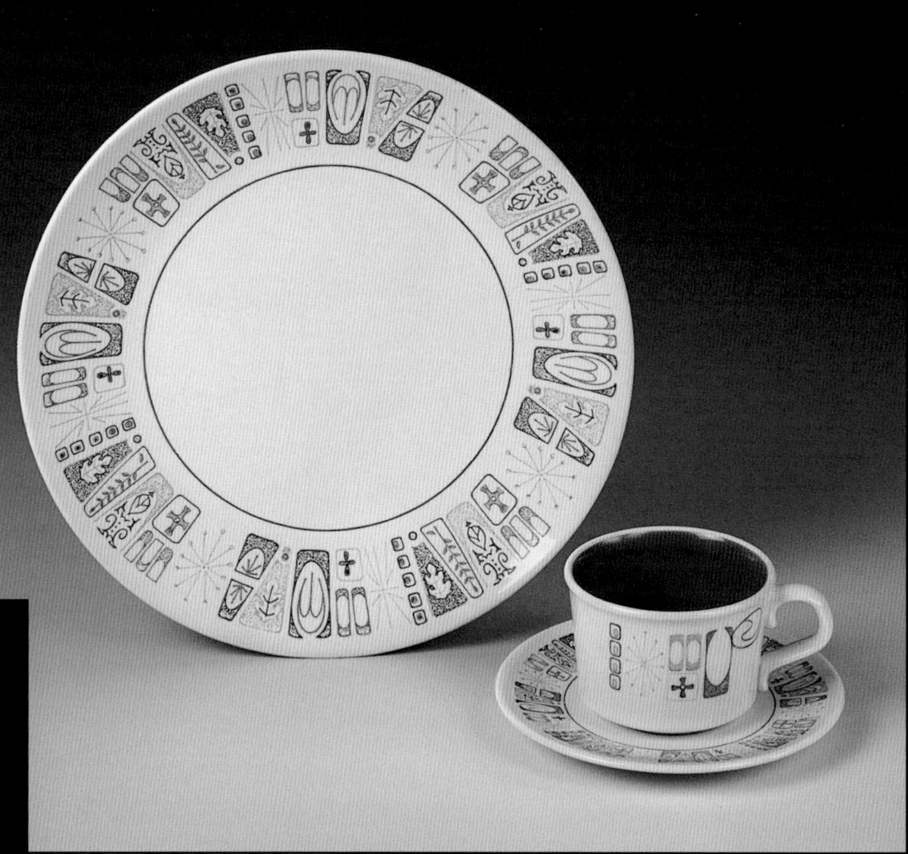

Taylor, Smith & Taylor.* ***Taylorstone***. Attributed to John Gilkes. *Moderne*. Cup & saucer, $6-10; plate, 10 1/2", $5-12.

Taylor, Smith & Taylor.* ***Taylorton China*** (***Taylorton Fine China***). John Gilkes. [*Double Gold Edge*]. Coffee server, $25-35. A pattern known as *Gold Edge* featured one line of gold trim.

Taylor, Smith & Taylor.* ***Taylorton China***. [*Double Gold Edge*]. Casserole w/ stand, $25-35.

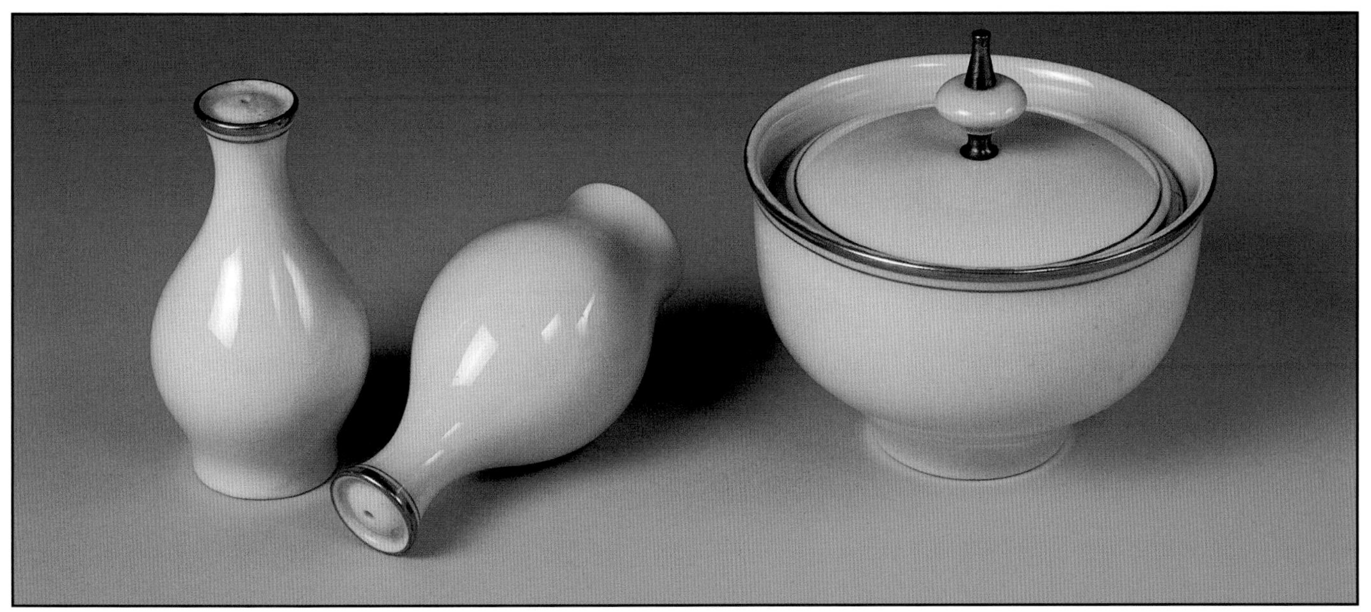

Taylor, Smith & Taylor.* ***Taylorton China***. [*Double Gold Edge*]. Salt & pepper, $10-14, pair. Sugar, $12-20.

Taylor, Smith & Taylor.* ***Taylorton China***. John Gilkes. *Happy Talk*. <1959. Covered casserole, $20-25.

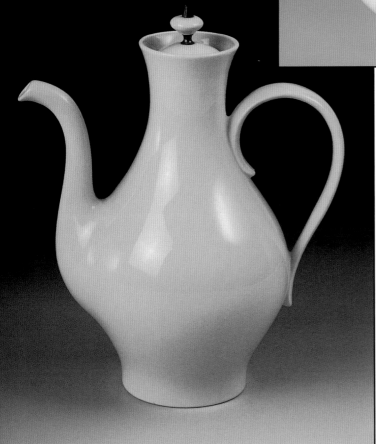

Taylor, Smith & Taylor.* ***Taylorton China***. John Gilkes. *Ivory Tower* [if all-white]. <1959. Coffee server, $30-45.

Taylor, Smith & Taylor.* ***Taylorton China***. *Ivory Tower*. <1959. Oval platter, 13", $25-35; bread tray, $30-35; large vegetable (salad), $25-35.

Taylor, Smith & Taylor.* John Gilkes. *Mint and Spice*. 1955. Cup & saucer, $5-10; plate, 10", $3-10. *Cinnamon & Honey* was another available pattern.

Taylor, Smith & Taylor.* ***Heatherton***. *"Sweet Potato"*. Plate, 10 5/8", $3-10; plate, 6 3/4", $3-6; cup & saucer, $6-10. Other patterns in the ***Heatherton*** line included: *"Radish," "Parsley,"* and *"Egg Plant."*

Taylor, Smith & Taylor.* ***Ever Yours***. John Gilkes. *Twilight Time.* <1958. Cup & saucer, $5-10.

Taylor, Smith & Taylor.* ***Ever Yours***. John Gilkes. [*White*]. <1958. Covered casserole with stand, $30-40.

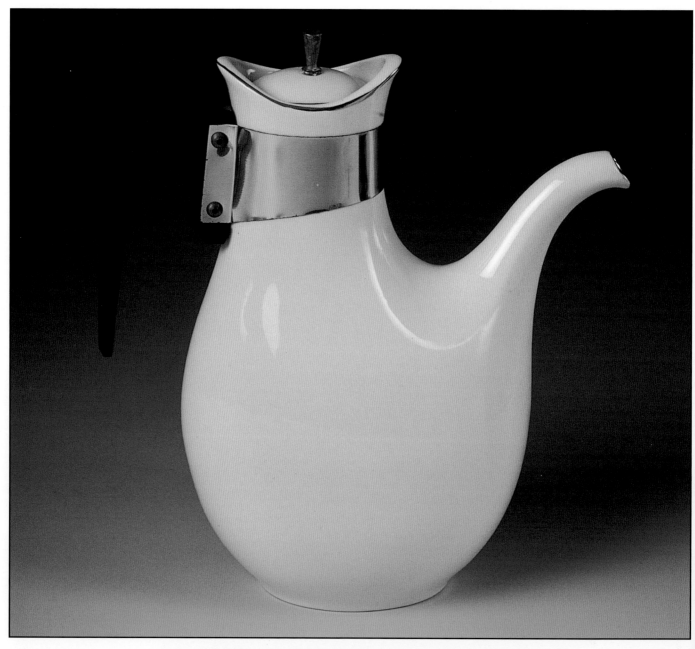

Taylor, Smith & Taylor.* ***Ever Yours***. John Gilkes. The backside of a traditionally decorated piece is shown. <1958. Coffee pot (if all-white), $40-60+.

Taylor, Smith & Taylor.* ***Colorcraft***. *Java Key.* 1962. Covered casserole, $18-30.

Taylor, Smith & Taylor for Sears (Harmony House). ***Ever Yours*** (redesigned). John Gilkes. *Del Rey* (*Adagio* is the same decoration in blue for TST). c.1960. Cup & saucer, $5-10; coffee server, $20-30; butter dish, $15-20; sugar, $12-15; salt & pepper, $8-12, pair; creamer, $8-13.

Taylor, Smith & Taylor.* ***Ever Yours*** (redesigned). *Java Key.* 1962. Cream, $8-13; sugar, $10-15.

Taylor, Smith & Taylor.* ***Colorcraft***. John Gilkes. [*Forum in Brown*]. c.1964. Coffee pot, $25-35.

Taylor, Smith & Taylor.* [*Greek Key*]. Coffee pot, $25-35.

Taylor, Smith & Taylor.* ***Taylorstone*** (redesigned). Attributed to John Gilkes. *Etruscan.* <1966. Plate, 10 1/2", $3-10; coupe [bowl], 7 5/8" x 1 5/8", $3-8; cup & saucer, $6-10.

Taylor, Smith & Taylor.* ***Taylorstone*** (redesigned). John Gilkes. *Cathay.* <1966. Cup & saucer, $6-10; nappy, 9", $3-8; plate, 10", $3-10.

Taylor, Smith & Taylor.* ***Design 70***. [*Brown Tones*]. 1966>. Sugar, $12-15; creamer, $10-13.

Universal Potteries, Inc.™

Universal Potteries, Inc. (Cambridge, Ohio). ***Stratoware***. Eva Zeisel. *San Diego Brown/Wing Brown*. 1942. Covered vegetable dishes (covered casserole), $100-125.

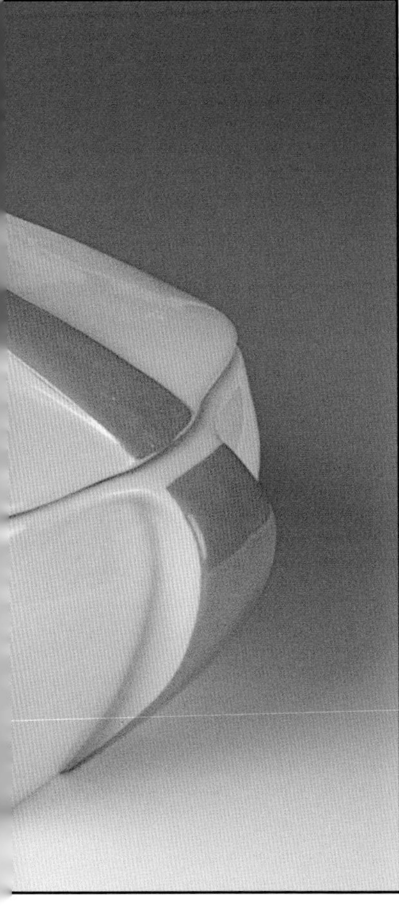

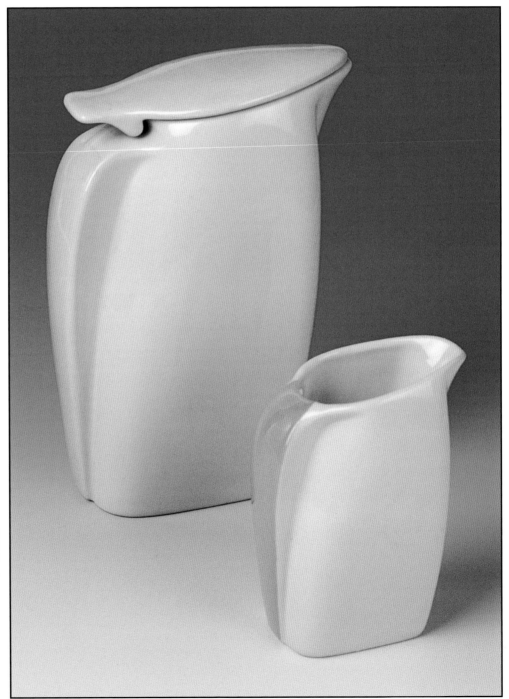

Universal for Sears. ***Stratoware***. *San Diego Brown/Horizon Blue*. Covered pitcher, $250-450+. *San Diego Brown/ Airport Green*. Creamer, $60-100+.

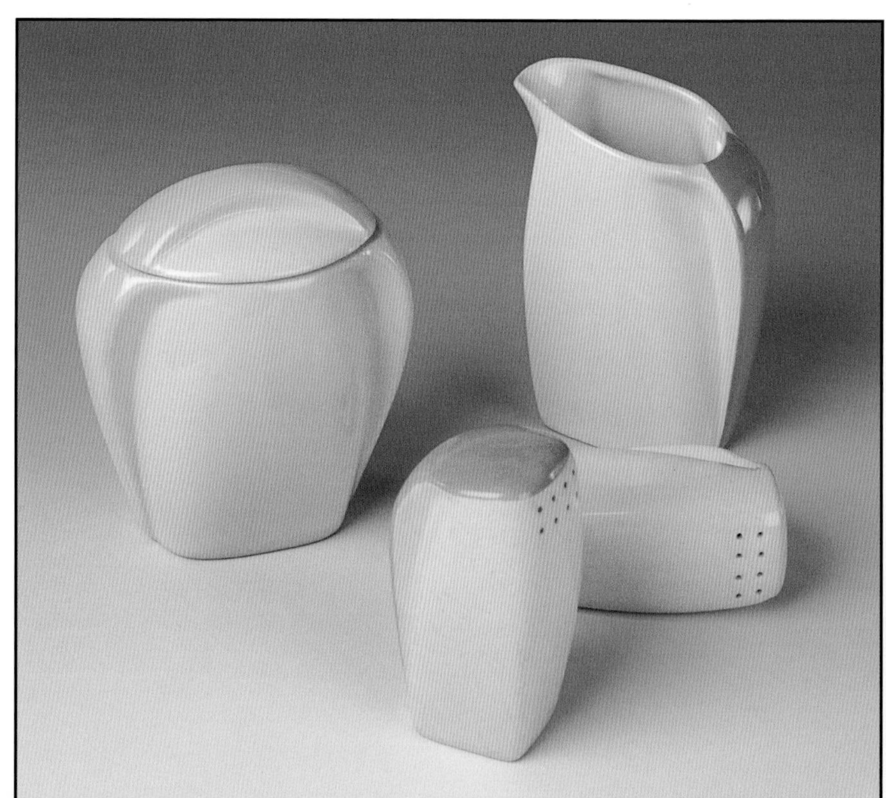

Universal for Sears. ***Stratoware***. *San Diego Brown/Flare Yellow.* Sugar [covered], $80-100. *San Diego Brown/Airport Green.* Creamer, $60-100+. *San Diego Brown/Airport Green.* Salt, $50-60+. *San Diego Brown/Flare Yellow.* Pepper, $50-60+.

Universal for Sears. ***Stratoware***. *San Diego Brown/Wing Brown.* [Bowl], 8 1/4" x 1 3/8", $60-70; [bowl], 8 7/8" x 2 3/8", $60-70.

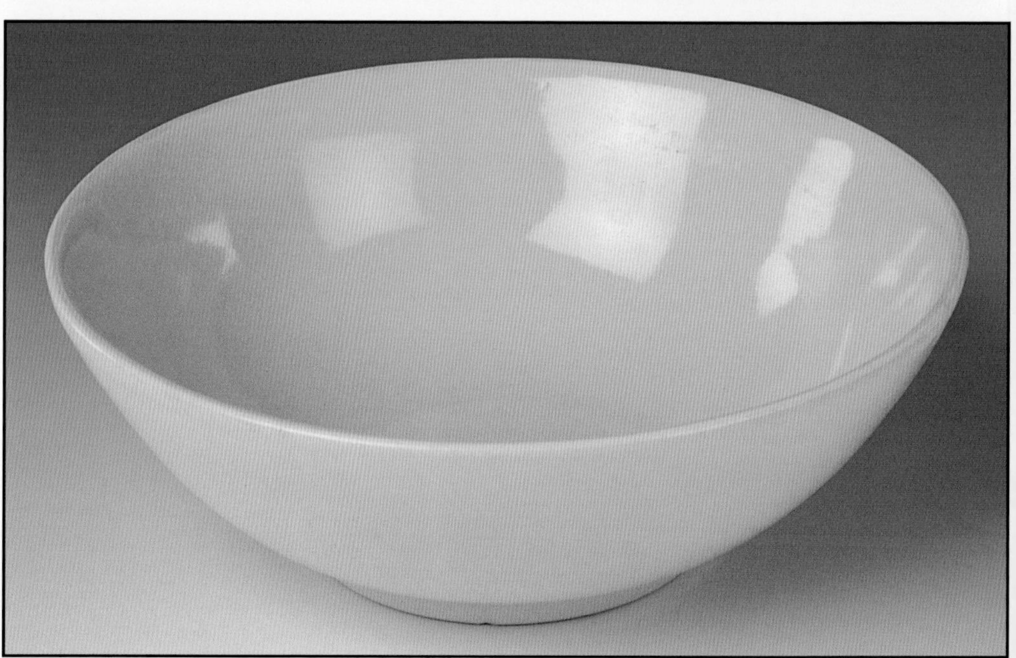

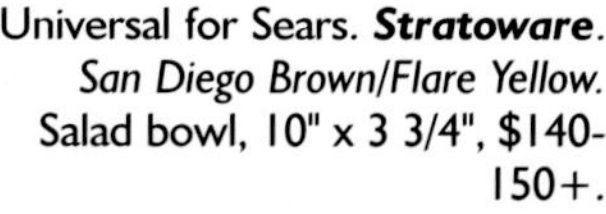

Universal for Sears. ***Stratoware***. *San Diego Brown/Flare Yellow.* Salad bowl, 10" x 3 3/4", $140-150+.

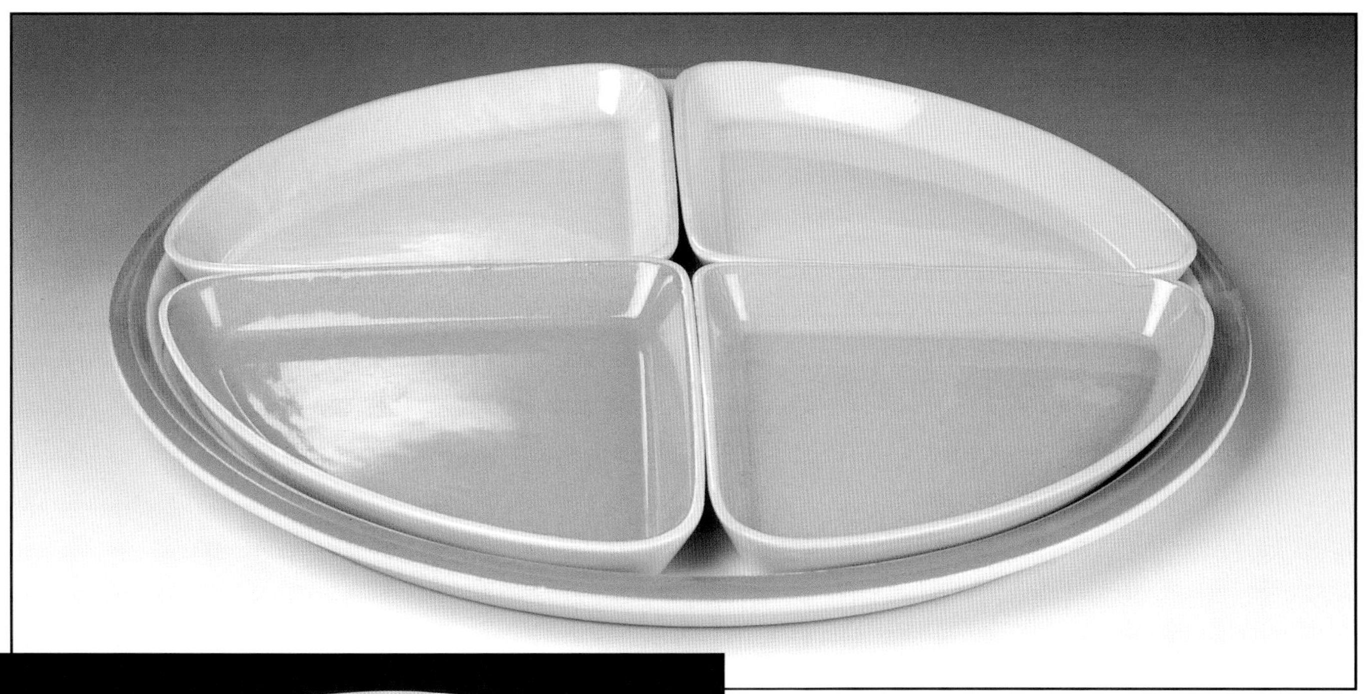

Universal for Sears. ***Stratoware***. All colors represented. Relish set, ND.

Universal for Sears. ***Stratoware***. *San Diego Brown/Flare Yellow.* Stacked cups, $30-35 each. *San Diego Brown/Wing Brown.* Saucer, $15-20.

Universal for Sears. ***Stratoware***. *San Diego Brown/Horizon Blue.* [Bowl], 5 1/2" x 1 1/4", $50-60. *San Diego Brown/Wing Brown.* [Bowl], 8 1/4" x 1 1/2", $60-70. *San Diego Brown/Flare Yellow.* Bread & butter plate, 6 3/4", $35-45. *San Diego Brown/Airport Green.* Dinner plate, 9 1/2", $55-75.

Universal for Sears. ***Stratoware***. *San Diego Brown/Flare Yellow.* [Plate], 11 3/8", $75+. *San Diego Brown/Wing Brown.* [Bowl], 8 7/8" x 2 1/2", $60-70.

Universal.* ***Vogue***. Alf Robson (s). *Mist Green/Coffee Brown.* 1952. Individual salad, 7", $6-12. *Mist Green.* Nappy (open), 9 1/8", $8-14. *Mist Green.* Regular boat [gravy], $10-15. *Coffee Brown.* Pickle, $8-12. *Mist Green/Coffee Brown.* Plates (dinner), 9 1/2", $6-12. *Coffee Brown.* Creamer, $8-12.

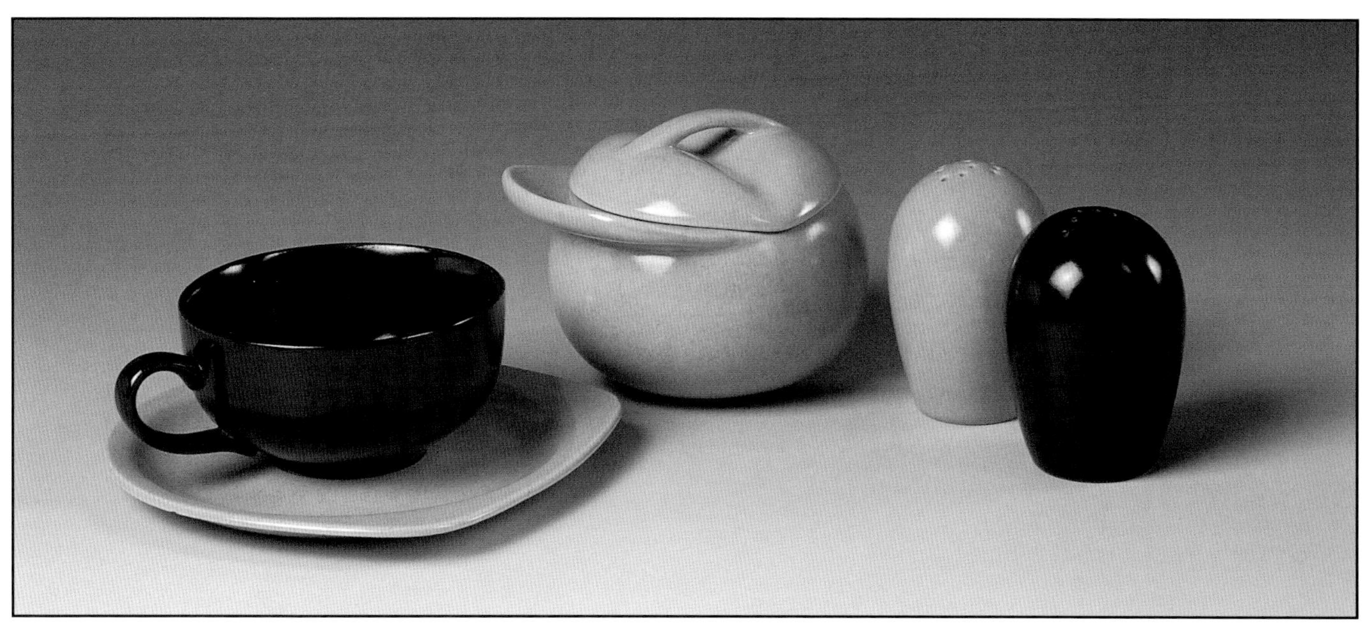

Universal.* ***Vogue***. *Mist Green/Coffee Brown.* 1952. Teacup & tea saucer, $8-12. *Mist Green.* Covered sugar, $15-20. *Mist Green/Coffee Brown.* Salt & pepper shakers, $10-15, pair.

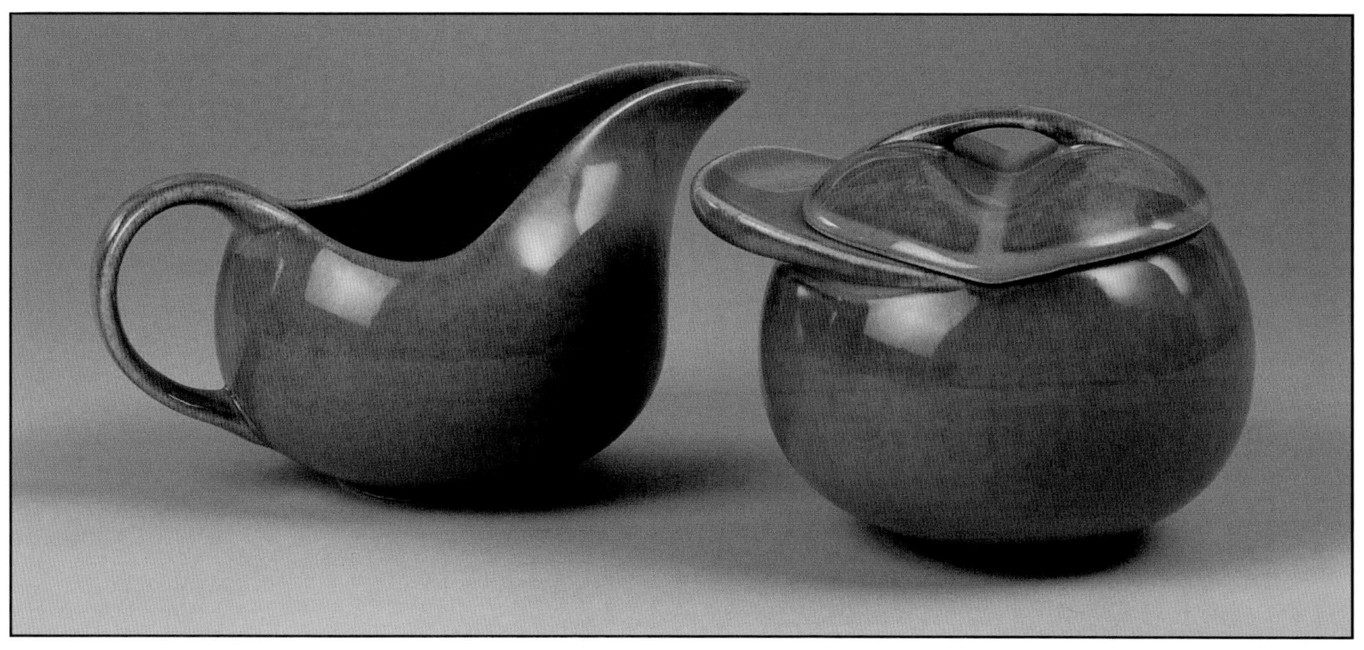

Universal.* ***Vogue***. Alf Robson (s). [*Brown w/ Overspray*]. Creamer, ND. Covered sugar, ND.

Universal.* ***Melody Series***. [**Vogue**]. Alf Robson (s). *Red Sails in the Sunset.* 1952. Lug soup, 6 1/2", $10-14; fruit, 5 1/8", $7-12; teacup & tea saucer, $14-18.

Universal.* ***Ballerina***. Alf Robson (s). *Charcoal.* 1954-1955. Creamer, $6-12. *Pink.* Covered sugar bowl, $10-18. *Pink/Charcoal.* Cup & saucer, $6-10; salt & pepper, $8-12, pair; covered butter, $12-18.

Universal.* ***Ballerina Kitchenware***. [*Pink*]. c.1954. Teapot (6 cup), $28-35. *Chartreuse.* Covered grease bowl, $20-30.

Universal for Raymor (Richards Morgenthau & Co., New York, New York).* ***Raymor Universal***. Ben Seibel. *Boutique White.* 1957. Covered coffee pot, $65-85+.

Universal for Raymor.* ***Raymor Universal***. *Boutique White.* Cream, $15-22. Water pitcher, $65-85.

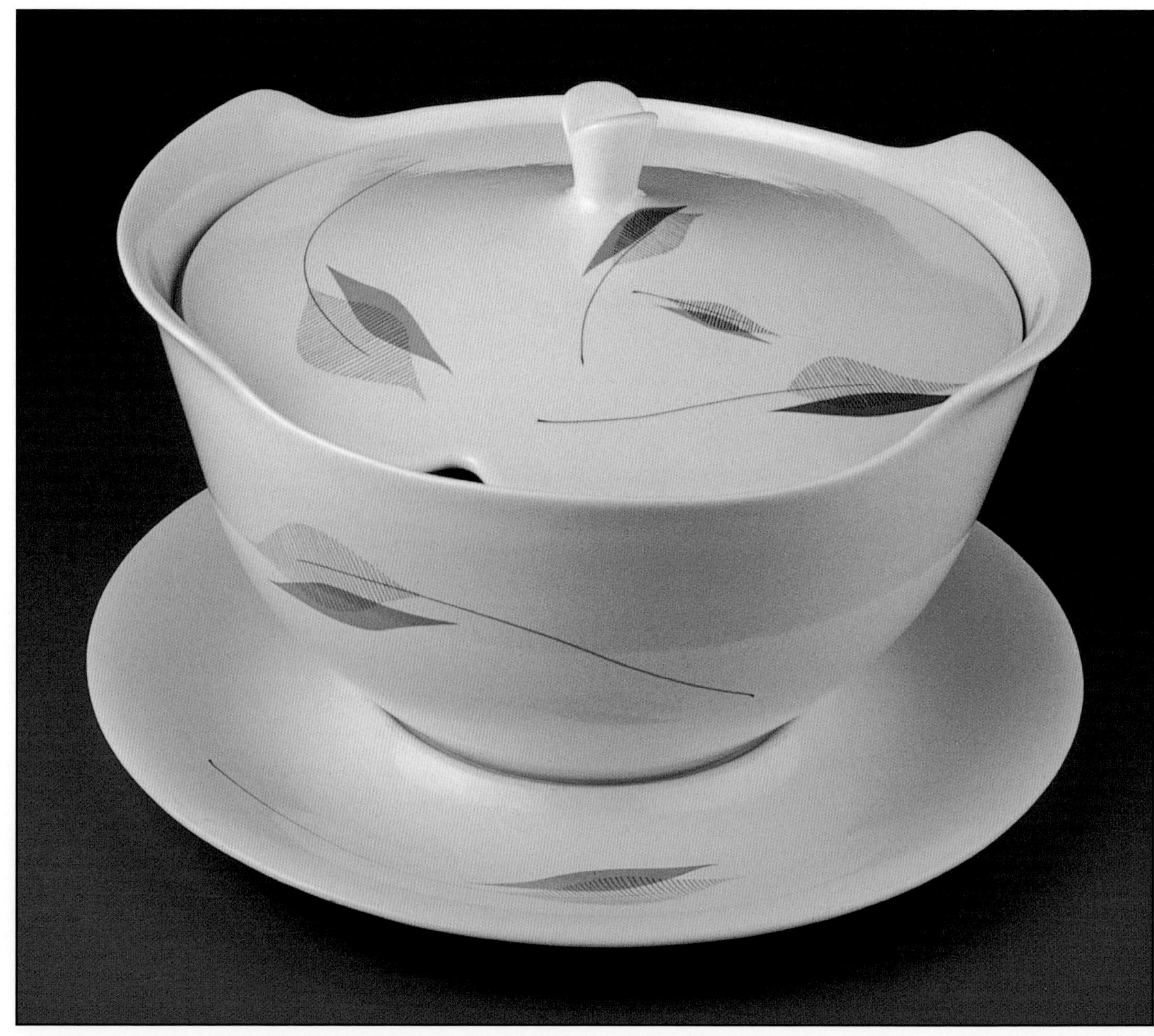

Universal for Raymor.* ***Raymor Universal***. *Festive Leaves.* Pattern attributed to having been created under the direction of Ben Seibel (p). 1957. Covered soup tureen & soup tureen tray, $100-150+.

Universal for Raymor.* ***Raymor Universal***. *Golden Burst*. Attributed to under the direction of Ben Seibel (p). 1957. Vegetable dish, 9 1/8" x 3 3/8", $20-30. Gravy boat, $15-22; cup & saucer, $10-14.

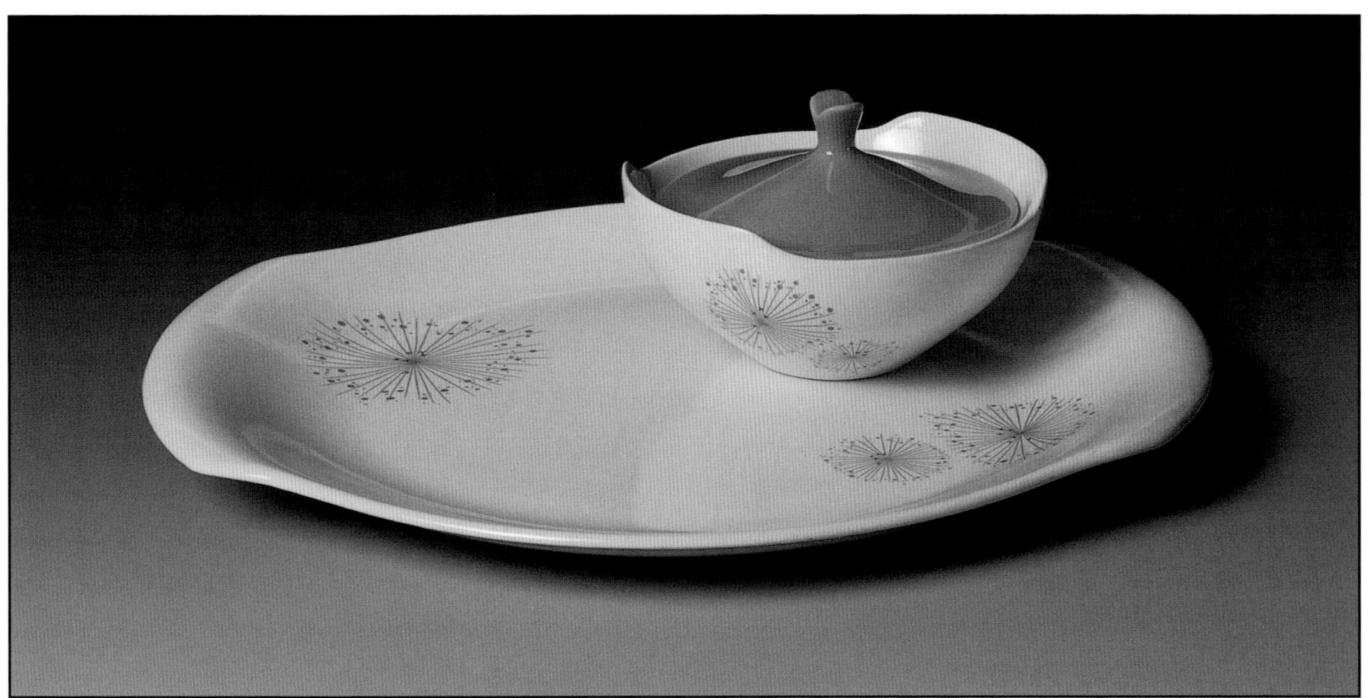

Universal for Raymor.* ***Raymor Universal***. *Golden Burst*. 1957. Platter, 13 5/8", $18-25. Sugar, $30-45.

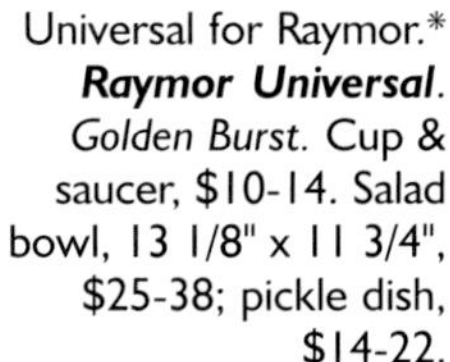

Universal for Raymor.* ***Raymor Universal***. *Golden Burst.* Cup & saucer, $10-14. Salad bowl, 13 1/8" x 11 3/4", $25-38; pickle dish, $14-22.

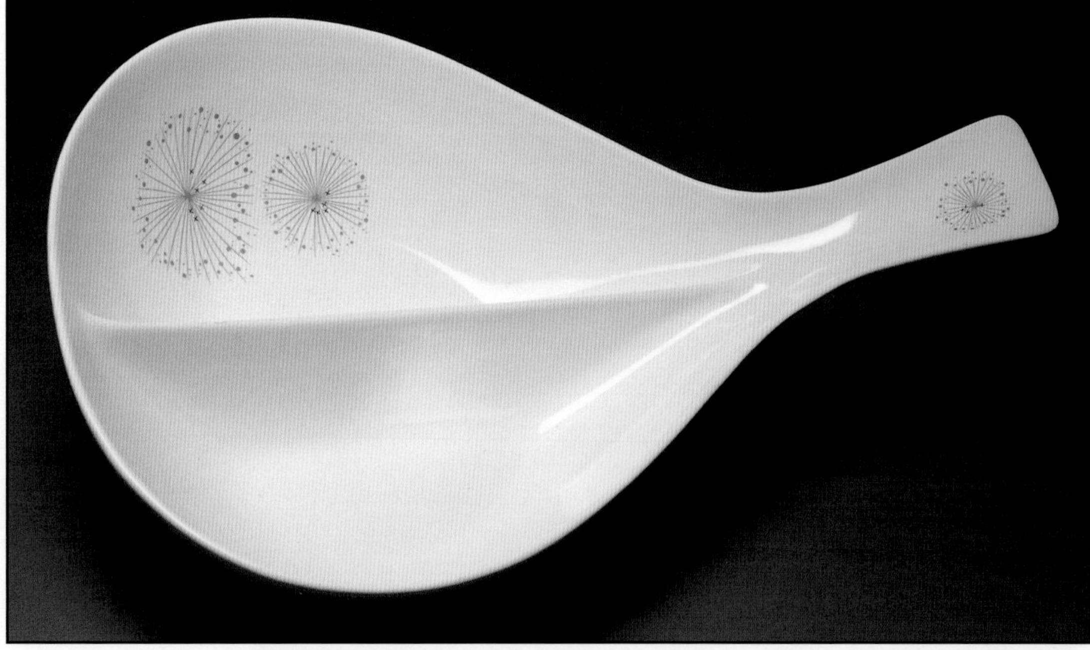

Universal for Raymor.* ***Raymor Universal***. *Golden Burst.* Handled divided vegetable dish, $25-35.

Universal for Raymor.* ***Raymor Universal***. *Sans Souci.* Attributed to under the direction of Ben Seibel (p). 1957. Salad bowl, 13 1/4", $30-40. *Golden Burst.* Gravy boat, $15-25.

Universal for Raymor.* ***Raymor Universal***. *Sans Souci*. A closer look at the *Sans Souci* pattern.

Universal.* ***Fascination***. Alf Robson (s). [*White*]. 1958. Covered coffee server, $25-35; beverage server, ice lip, $25-35.

Universal.* ***Fascination***. [*White*]. Luncheon tray, 12", $15-20.

Universal.* ***Fascination***. *Paisley.* Emma Elsner (p). 1958. Covered sugar, $8-14.

Universal.* ***Stardust***. **Fascination**. Alf Robson (s). *Dove Gray.* 1959. Desert dish, 5 1/2" x 1 5/8", $4-8; dinner plate, 10 3/8", $6-12; teacup & saucer, $6-12.

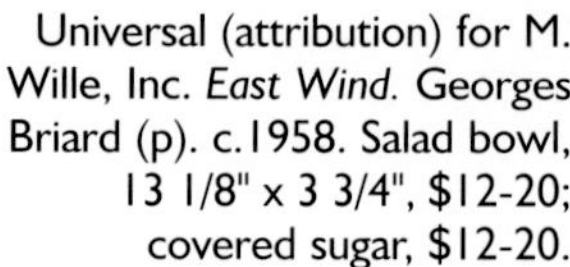

Universal (attribution) for M. Wille, Inc. *East Wind.* Georges Briard (p). c.1958. Salad bowl, 13 1/8" x 3 3/4", $12-20; covered sugar, $12-20.

Vernon Kilns™

Vernon Kilns (Vernon/Los Angeles, California).* ***Plaid group***. **Montecito**. *Organdie*. Gale Turnbull (p). 1936>. 1 Qt. pitcher [jug], $22-30; coffee server, $25-35; 1/2 pt. pitcher, $25-35.

Vernon Kilns.* **Montecito**. *Homespun*. <1950. 9 1/2" Plate, [9 3/4"], $9-12. *Tweed*. 9 1/2" Plate, [9 3/4"], $12-15. Current research seems to suggest that *Tweed*, *Homespun*, and *Calico* were introduced to consumers in 1950. A mention of these patterns in the November 1949 *China, Glass and Decorative Accessories* may represent the year of their introduction to the trade. Elucidating dates of introduction is a frequent problem in dinnerware research.

Top: Vernon Kilns.* **Montecito**. *Tweed*. <1950. Covered sugar, $15-20; creamer, $10-14.

Middle: Vernon Kilns.* **Montecito**. *Gingham*. 1950. Egg cup, $12-18. *Tam O'Shanter*. 1952. 4" Coaster, $15-22; regular salt & pepper shakers, $12-20, pair. Covered sugar, $14-18; creamer, $10-12.

Bottom: Vernon Kilns.* **Montecito**. *Tam O'Shanter*. 1952. 14 oz. tumbler, $15-23; covered teapot, $55-65. *Gingham*. 1 pt. pitcher [jug], $25-35.

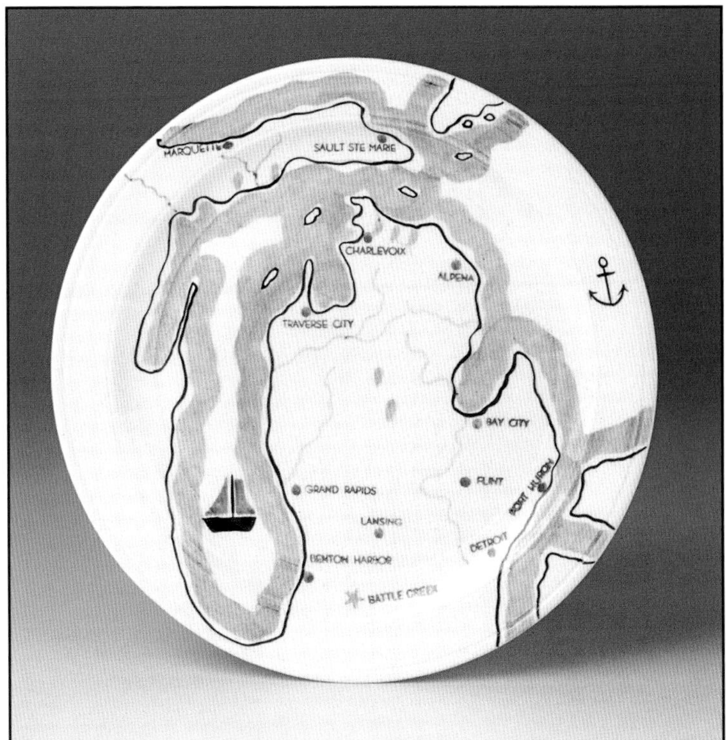

Vernon Kilns. ***Coastline Series***. **Montecito**. *Michigan Coastline.* Gale Turnbull (p). c.1937. [Plate], 9 1/2", $35-40.

Vernon Kilns. ***Native American Series***. **Montecito**. *Solitude.* Gale Turnbull (p). c.1937. [Plate], 9 1/2", $50-65.

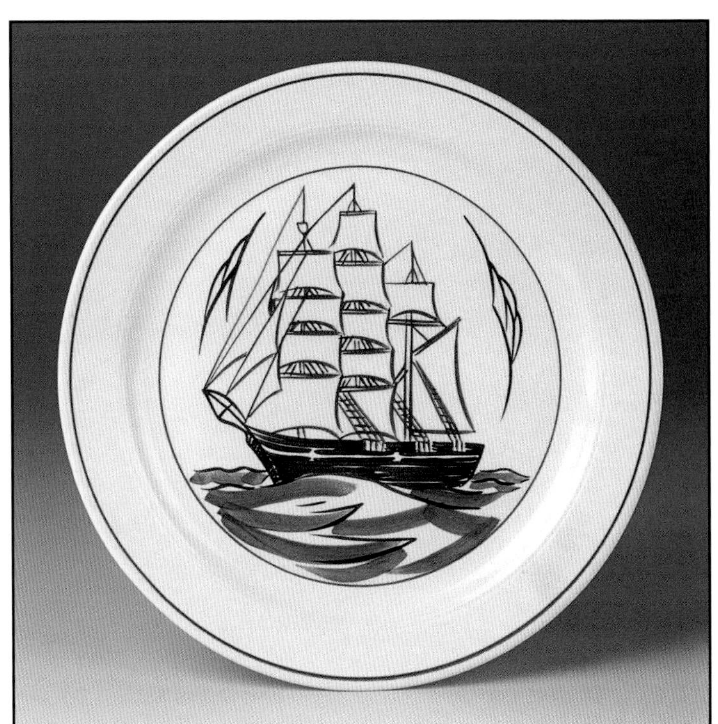

Vernon Kilns. ***Marine Series***. **Montecito**. *Whaling Service.* Gale Turnbull (p). c.1937. [Plate], 9 1/2", $40-50.

Vernon Kilns. ***Blend Series***. **Montecito**. *Blend No. 1*. Gale Turnbull (p). c.1938. 12" (Chop) platter, [12 1/4"], $30-40.

Vernon Kilns.* [**Ultra**]. Gale Turnbull/Jane Bennison (s). *Salamina*. Rockwell Kent (p). 1939. Open creamer, $75-100; 1 pint open pitcher, $200-250; sugar, $100-150.

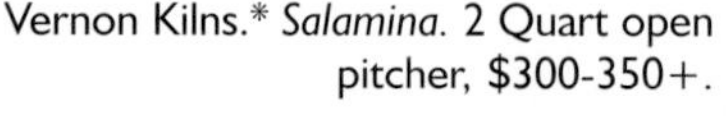

Vernon Kilns.* *Salamina*. 2 Quart open pitcher, $300-350+.

Vernon Kilns.* *Salamina.* 6 1/2" plate, $45-65; teacup, $60-70 (teacup w/ saucer, $70-100).

Vernon Kilns.* *Salamina.* 10 1/2" Plate, $115-140.

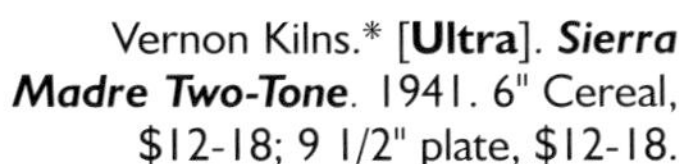

Vernon Kilns.* [**Ultra**]. ***Sierra Madre Two-Tone***. 1941. 6" Cereal, $12-18; 9 1/2" plate, $12-18.

Vernon Kilns.* ***California Heritage*** (***California Originals***). **San Marino**. *Redwood Brown*. 1950. Covered butter, $30-35; 8" Covered casserole, $40-55.

Vernon Kilns.* ***California Shadows***. **San Marino**. [*Antique Gray*]. Divided vegetable dish, 11 3/4", $20-28; *Cocoa Brown*. 1952. Creamer, $10-13; covered sugar, $13-15.

Vernon Kilns.* ***California Heritage***. **San Marino**. *Vineyard Green*. 1950. Salt & pepper shakers, $12-22. Other colors in this line included *Almond Yellow* and *Raison Purple*.

Vernon Kilns.* **San Marino**. *Gayety*. 1950. Covered sugar, $15-25.

Vernon Kilns.* **San Marino**. *Mexicana*. 1950. 13" Chop plate, $20-30.

Vernon Kilns.* **San Marino**. *Seven Seas.* 1954. 13" Chop plate, [12 7/8"], $35-$45; 1 pt. pitcher, $28-40; 2 qt. pitcher, $40-50.

Vernon Kilns.* ***California Casual***. **San Marino**. *Turquoise Blue.* 1954. 2 Qt. pitcher, $25-35. *Dawn Pink.* 1952. Salt & pepper shakers, $12-22.

Vernon Kilns.* **San Marino**. *Mojave.* 9" Round vegetable, $15-24; chowder, $12-18; divided vegetable dish, $18-28; shaker, $6-9; sauce boat, $15-20.

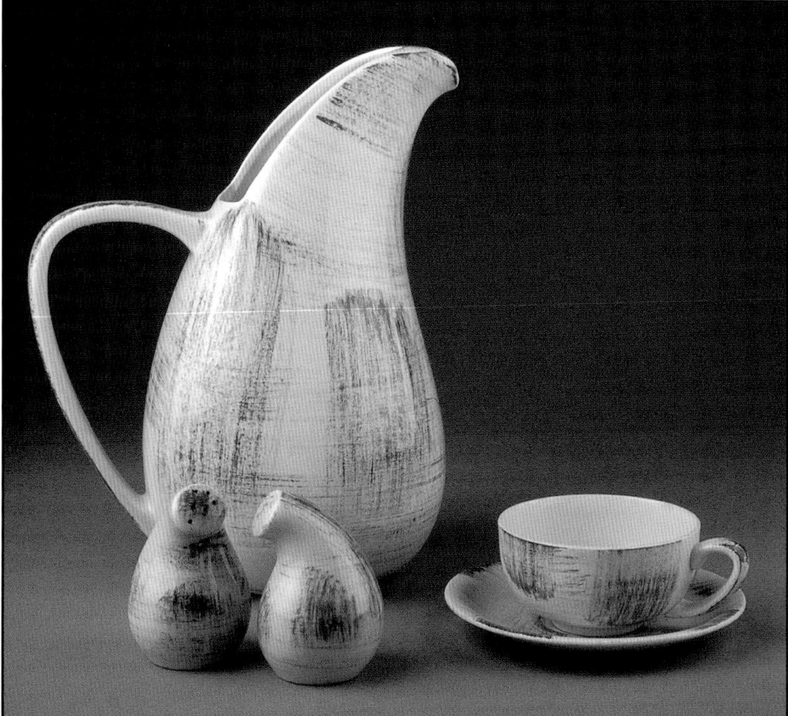

Vernon Kilns.* **San Marino**. *Raffia.* 1953. 2 Qt. pitcher, $25-35; regular salt & pepper shakers, $12-22; teacup & saucer, $8-15.

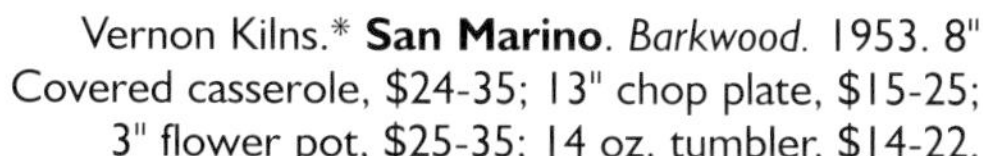

Vernon Kilns.* **San Marino**. *Barkwood.* 1953. 8" Covered casserole, $24-35; 13" chop plate, $15-25; 3" flower pot, $25-35; 14 oz. tumbler, $14-22.

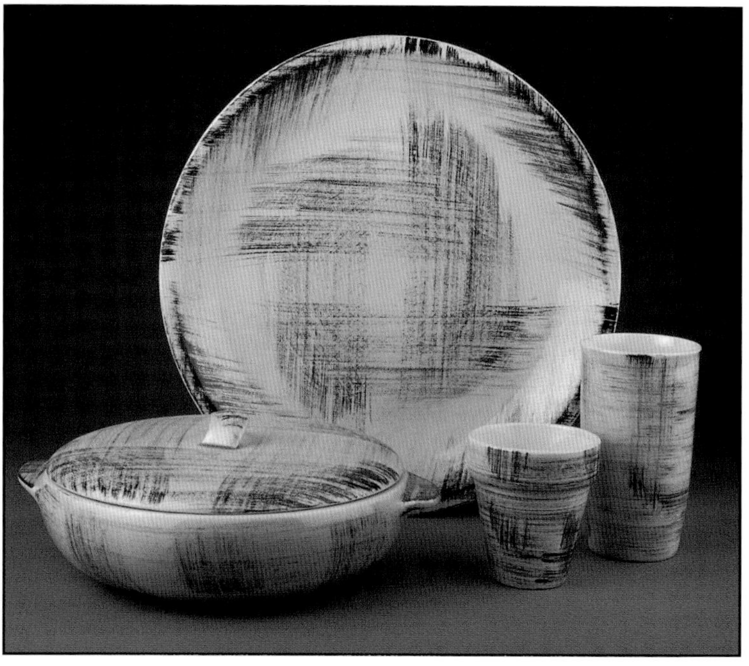

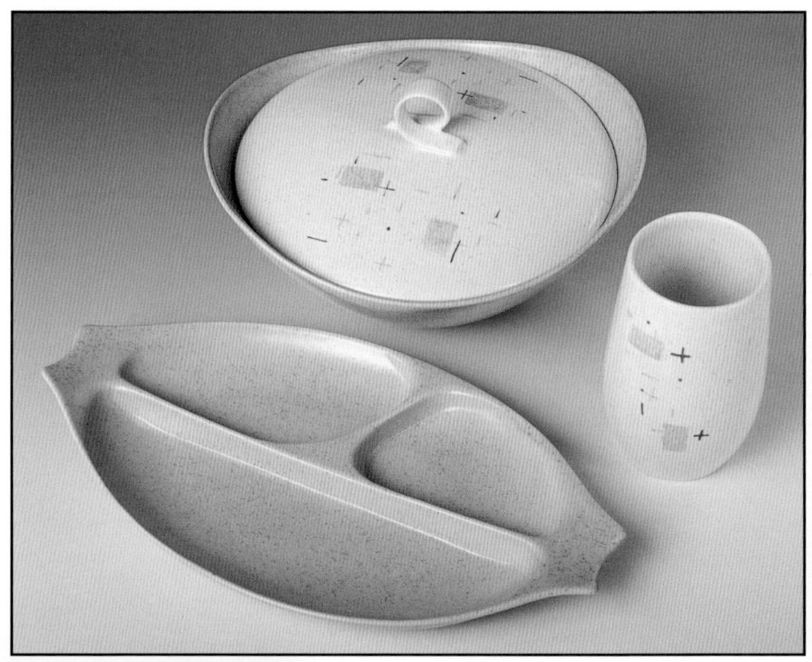

Vernon Kilns.* ***Vernonware*** (***Vernon ware***). **San Clemente** [**Anytime**]. Elliott House (s). *Tickled Pink.* 1955. An article from the *Registered California Pictorial* from October 1956, claimed that *Tickled Pink* was introduced in January 1954, however this date is unconfirmed. Relish dish (3 section), $20-30; 8" covered casserole, $45-60; 14 oz. tumbler, $25-35.

Vernon Kilns.* *Tickled Pink.* Gravy boat, $20-25; glass go-along, ND; 10" plate, $10-12; teacup & saucer, $10-15; 8-cup covered coffee pot, $45-65; 12 oz. mug, $25-35.

Vernon Kilns.* ***Vernonware***. **San Clemente** [**Anytime**]. *Heavenly Days.* 1955. 1 Qt. pitcher, $45-50; covered teapot, $45-65; 13 1/2" platter, [13 3/8"], $25-30.

Vernon Kilns.* ***Vernonware***. *Heavenly Days*. Double vegetable dish, $18-28; 7 1/2" vegetable, $8-12; 10" plate, $8-12; teacup & saucer, $10-15; 14 oz. tumbler, $25-35; gravy boat, $20-25.

Vernon Kilns.* ***Vernonware***. **San Clemente** [**Anytime**]. *Imperial*. 1955. Teacup & tea saucer, $15-20; 10" plate, $15-20; 7 1/2" plate, $9-12.

Vernon Kilns.* *Imperial*. Sugar, $35-45.

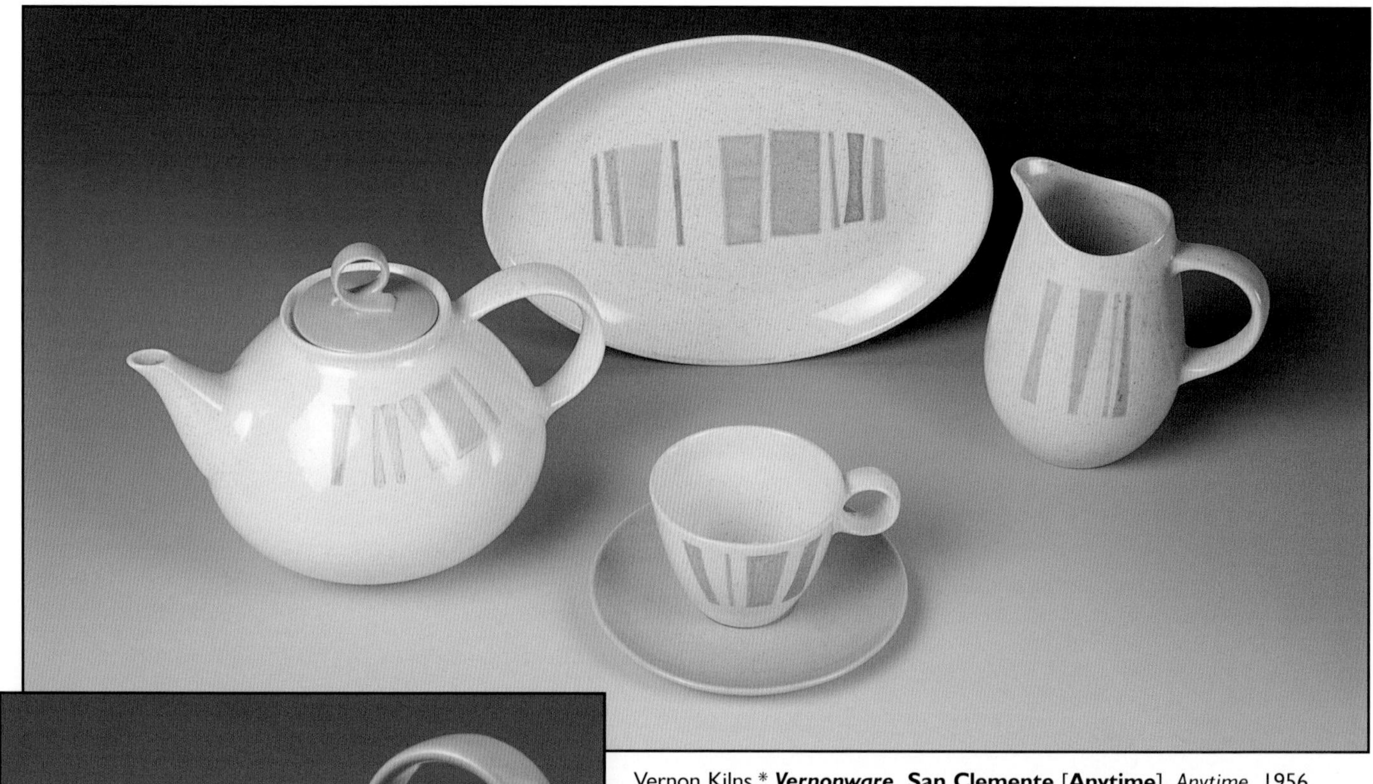

Vernon Kilns.* ***Vernonware*. San Clemente [Anytime]**. *Anytime.* 1956. Teapot, $45-65; 11" platter, [10 7/8"], $20-30; 1 pt. pitcher, $15-25; cup & saucer, $12-15.

Vernon Kilns.* ***Vernonware*. San Clemente [Anytime]**. *Aqua.* Cruet set tray, $50-100+. According to one Vernon Kilns brochure, the "Cruet Set" was available in colors of "pink, aqua, mint green and beige." The tray held the rare vinegar and oil cruets.

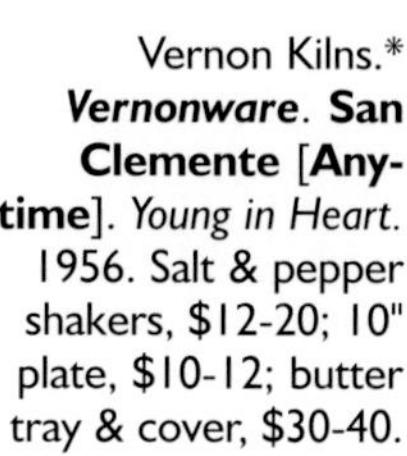

Vernon Kilns.* ***Vernonware*. San Clemente [Anytime]**. *Young in Heart.* 1956. Salt & pepper shakers, $12-20; 10" plate, $10-12; butter tray & cover, $30-40.

Vernon Kilns.* ***Vernonware***. **San Clemente** [**Anytime**]. *Dis 'n Dot.* Relish dish (3 section), $25-35.

Vernon Kilns.* *Dis 'n Dot.* 1957. 8" Covered casserole, $45-65; 2 qt. pitcher, $35-50.

Vernon Kilns.* *Dis 'n Dot.* 12 Oz. mug, $20-30; covered teapot, $55-75.

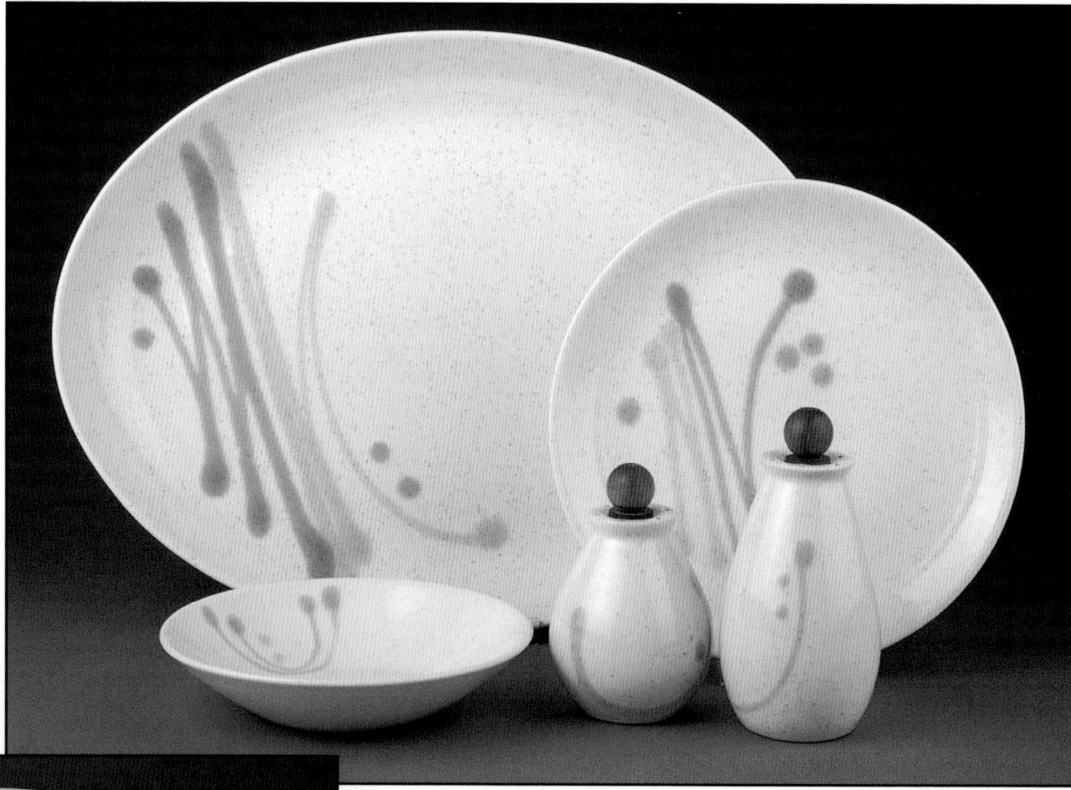

Vernon Kilns.* *Dis 'n Dot.* 13" Platter, $25-35; 7 1/2" plate, $8-12; fruit, $6-10; salt & pepper shakers, $15-25.

Vernon Kilns.* *Dis 'n Dot.* 10" Plate, $12-15.

Vernon Kilns.* *Dis 'n Dot.* Butter tray & cover, $30-45.

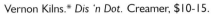

Vernon Kilns.* *Dis 'n Dot.* Creamer, $10-15.

Vernon Kilns.* ***Vernonware*. Transitional [Year 'Round]**. *Lollipop Tree.* 1957. Covered teapot, $55-75; covered beverage server, $55-75.

Vernon Kilns.* *Lollipop Tree.* Teacup & saucer, $12-15; dinner plate, 10 3/8", $12-15; covered sugar, $20-25; creamer, $15-18; salt & pepper shakers, $20-28, pair.

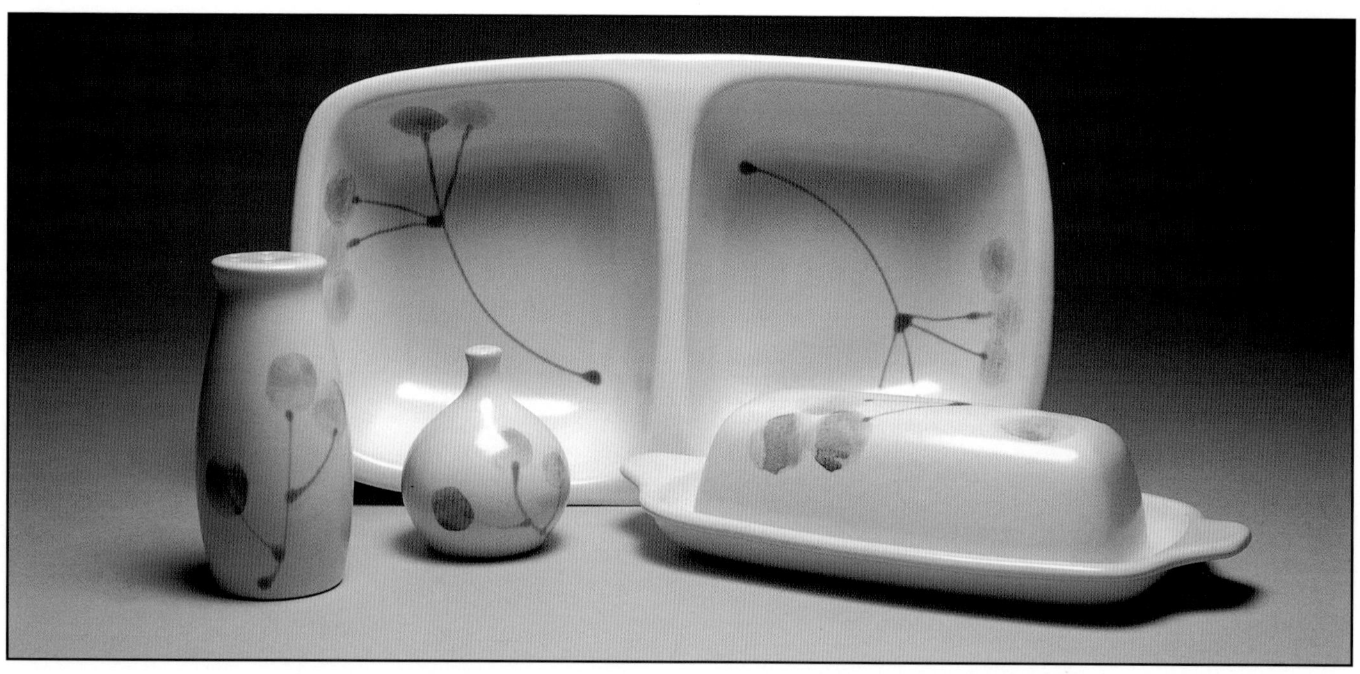

Vernon Kilns.* *Lollipop Tree.* Salt & pepper shakers, $20-28, pair. Divided vegetable dish, $25-35; butter tray & cover, $30-40.

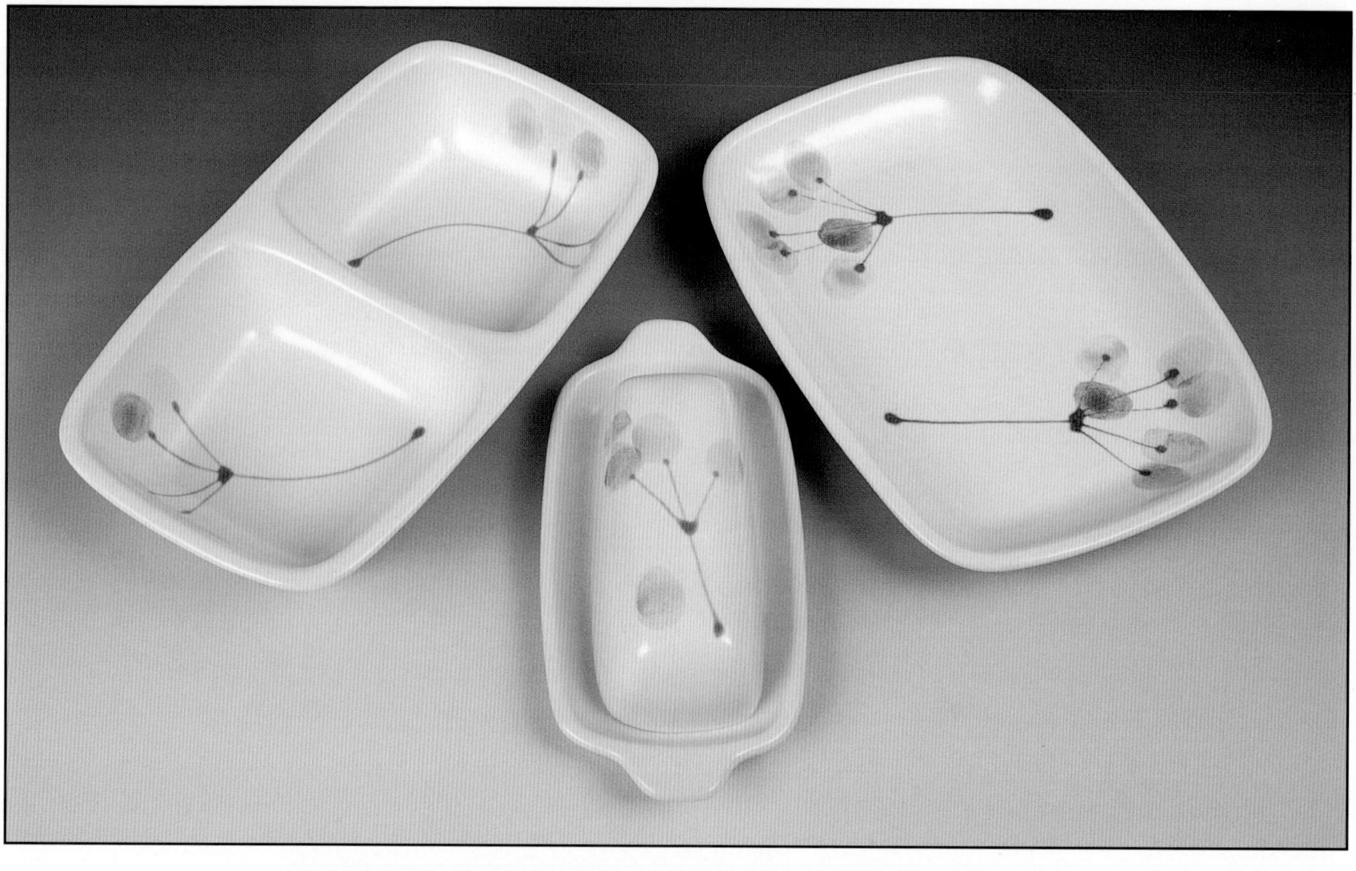

Vernon Kilns.* *Lollipop Tree.* Divided vegetable dish, 11 3/8", $25-35; butter tray & cover, $30-40; medium platter, 10 3/4", $18-25.

Vernon Kilns.* *Lollipop Tree.* Trio buffet server, $40-60.

Vernon Kilns.* *Lollipop Tree.* [2-tier tidbit], ND.

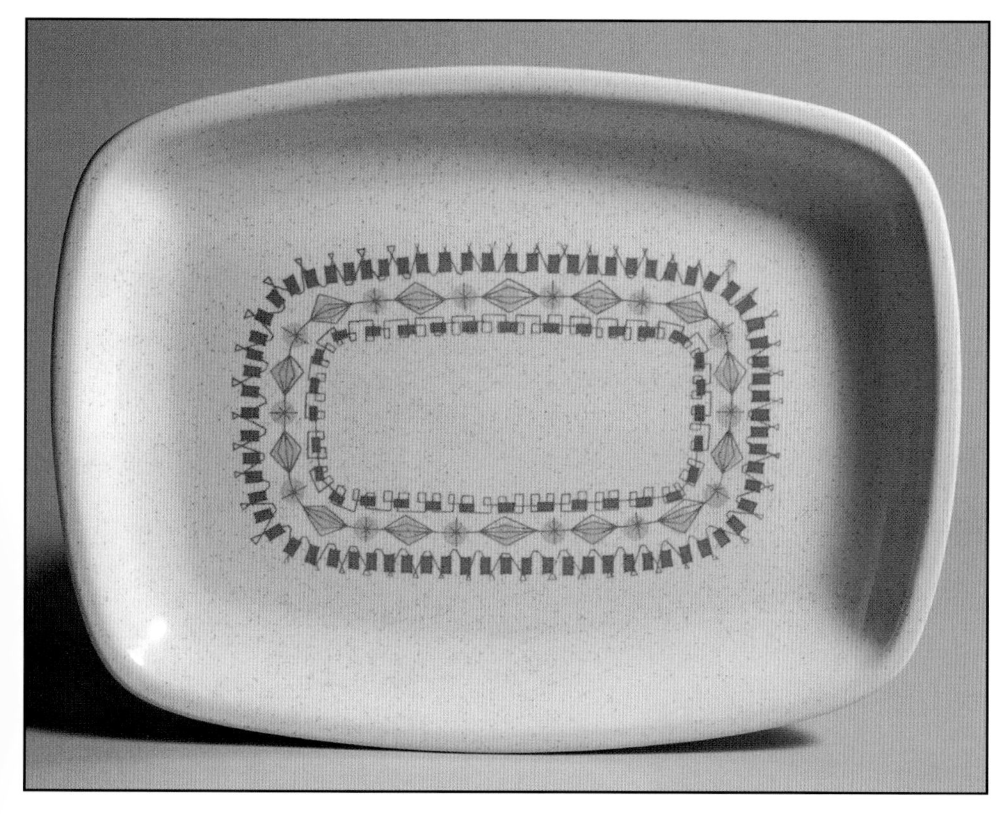

Vernon Kilns.* **Transitional** [**Year 'Round**]. *Year 'Round.* [Platter], 13 5/8" x 10", ND.

The W. S. George Pottery Co.™

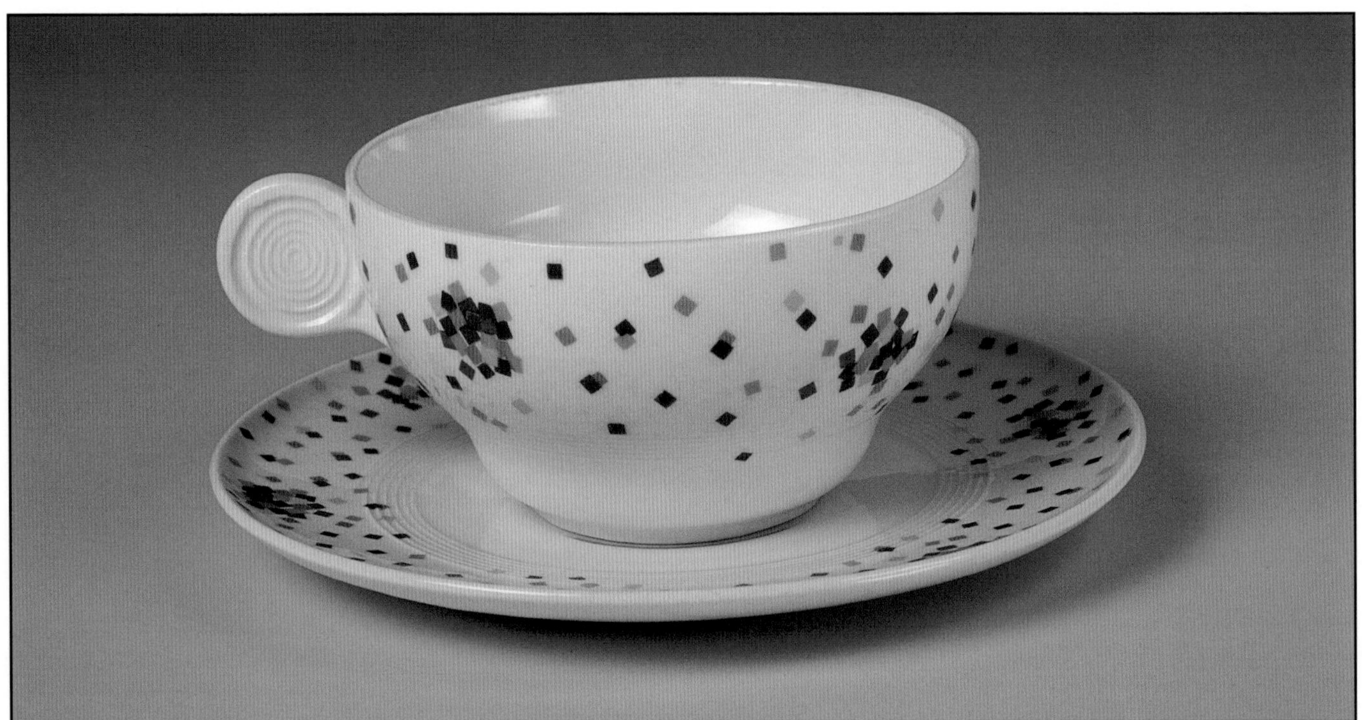

The W. S. George Pottery Co. (Cavitt-Shaw Potters [a division of W. S. George]. East Palestine, Ohio). **Vesta**. Simon H. Slobodkin (s). [*Confetti*]. 1936. Cup & saucer, ND. The plate shape in this line was patented by Slobodkin in 1935 (Des. 97,442). Simon Slobodkin, affectionately known as "doc" to the American pottery industry, was a Harvard-educated dentist who at first practiced his profession. After taking on an ailing Boston Pottery Company in 1920, he soon became not only a successful business entrepreneur and tableware salesman, but a widely respected ceramic designer. By 1934, his work was gaining recognition and was shown in the Metropolitan Museum of Art's contemporary art exhibit. Little is known about the full extent of Slobodkin's designs. The author suspects that someday, as historians learn more about his work, Slobodkin may be viewed as one of the earliest pioneers of an American style in tableware and American *mid-century modern* dinnerware design.

W. S. George (Cavitt-Shaw).* **Ranchero**. Simon Slobodkin (s). *Neptune* (Cavitt-Shaw, 1938). *Navajo* (W. S. George, 1955). Dinner plate, 10", $8-14; teacup & tea saucer, $6-13.

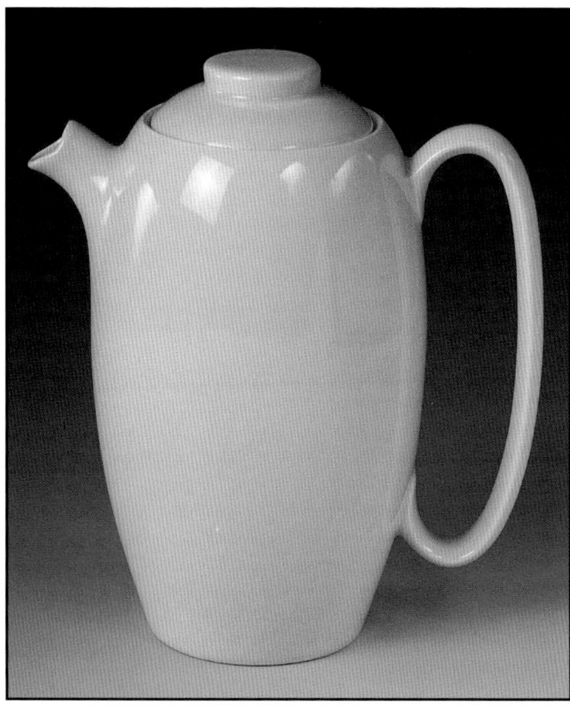

W. S. George (Cavitt-Shaw).* **Ranchero**. *Amarillo.* <1946. Coffee pot, $25-30.

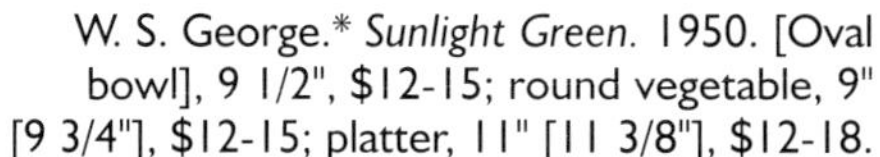

W. S. George.* *Sunlight Green.* 1950. [Oval bowl], 9 1/2", $12-15; round vegetable, 9" [9 3/4"], $12-15; platter, 11" [11 3/8"], $12-18.

W. S. George.* ***Cloudburst***. **Ranchero**. *Sunlight Green.* 1950. Teapot, $25-35; tureen and cover, $25-35; sugar and cover, $12-18.

W. S. George.* *Sunlight Green.* 1950. Ashtray, $8-12; faststand gravy boat, $14-20; regular gravy boat, $10-15. ***Cloudburst*** was also available in *Twilight Gray*.

W. S. George.* **Ranchero**. *Celeste.* c.1950. Teacup & tea saucer, $6-12; cream, $8-14; dinner plate, 10", $6-10. Luncheon plate, 9 1/4" [9 1/8"], $4-6; salad plate, 7 1/2", $3-5; sauce dish, $3-5; sugar with cover, $12-15.

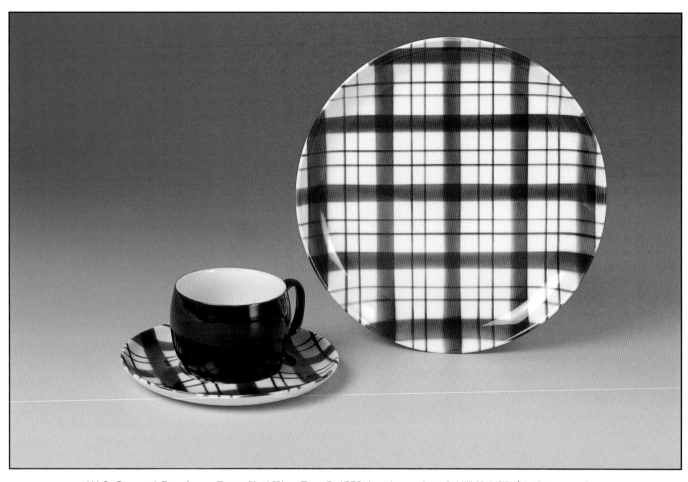

W. S. George.* **Ranchero**. *Tartan Plaid [Plum Tweed]*. 1950. Luncheon plate, 9 1/4" [9 1/8"], $6-12; teacup & tea saucer, $10-14. Similar plaids included *Angus Plaid Tweed* (Grey) and *Gael Plaid Tweed* (Green).

W. S. George.* **Ranchero**. *Holiday*. 1951>. Dinner plate, 10", $8-14.

W. S. George.* **Ranchero**. *Tango*. <1954. Dinner plate, 10" [10 1/8"], $8-14; salt & pepper shakers [round], $14-18, pair; sugar with cover, $12-18.

W. S. George.* **Ranchero**. [*Tahiti*]. <1953. Round vegetable, 9" x 2 5/8", $8-15; sauce dish, 5 1/2" x 1 1/2", $6-12; dinner plate, 10", $8-14; teacup & saucer, $5-12, platter, 11 1/2" [11 3/8"], $12-18; cream, $6-12; sugar with cover, $12-18. The color name for this line has not been confirmed, but by process of elimination this could be the *Tahiti* pattern. It has also been referred to as *Pink Fantasy.* Other striped patterns on the **Ranchero** shape included *Caravan* (chartreuse stripe) and *Carnival* (yellow-brown stripe).

W. S. George.* **Shasta**. Simon Slobodkin (s). *Shasta White.* 1951. Gravy, $10-20. The shape of this sauceboat appears similar to an earlier shape known as **Coquette**, c.1942. Slobodkin was quoted as saying that **Coquette** "is based on an ornithological formula that employs the ventral curve of the bird." (*Pottery, Glass & Brass Salesman*, January 1937). Handles and lid knobs on **Shasta** are simple, wing-like structures. A modern line named ***Domino*** featured **Shasta** in solid white mixed with black.

W. S. George. ***Community Ware***. **HandCraft**. Attributed to Simon Slobodkin (s). *Sherwood.* Platter, 13 1/4" x 11", $18-25; cream, $8-14.

Walker China Company™

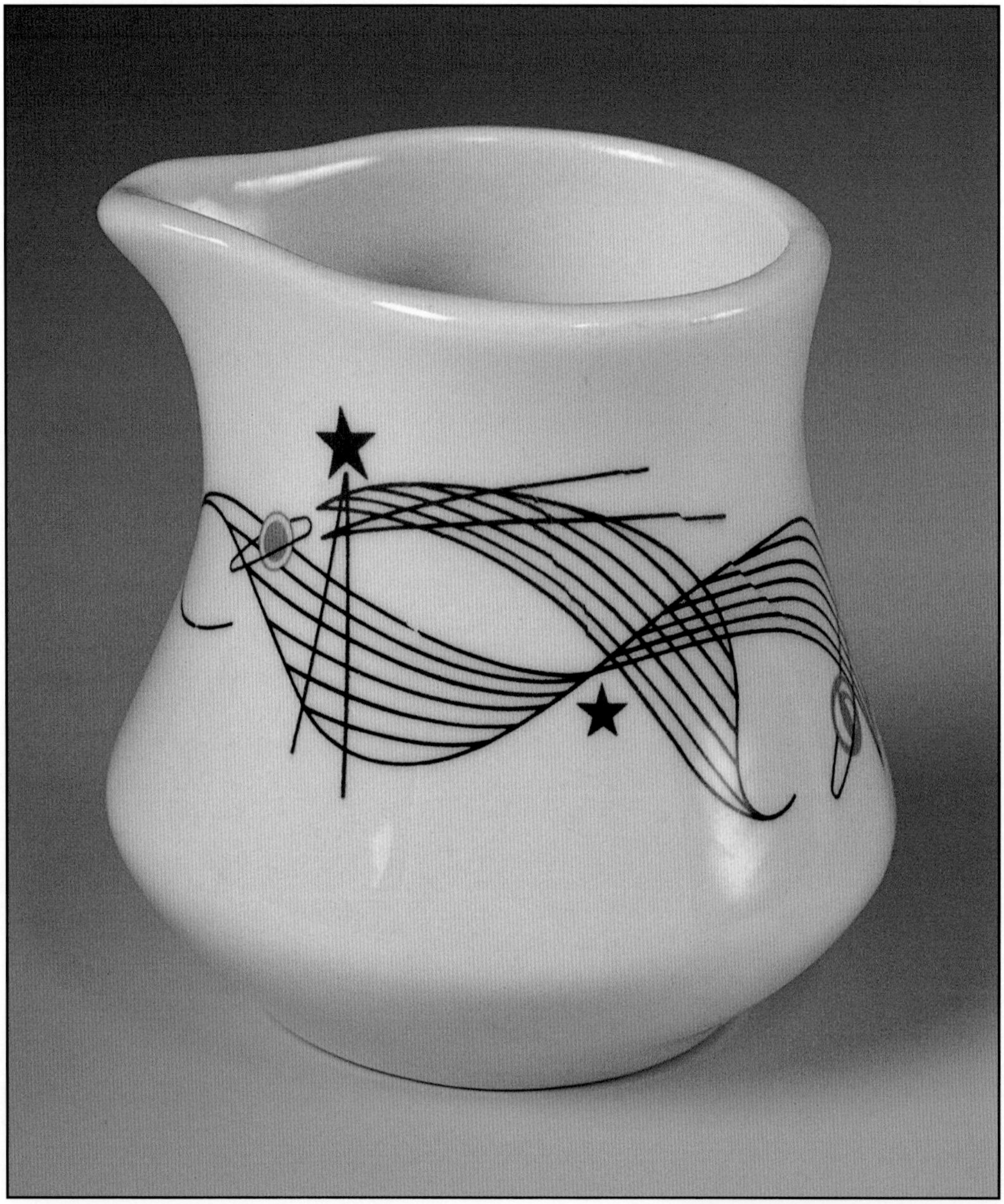

Walker China Company (Bedford, Ohio). *Satellite*. c.1949. Creamer, $8-15.

Walker China. **Narrim**. *Starlite*. <1959. Cup & saucer $5-8. The shape is apparently named after the fact that it sports a narrow rim.

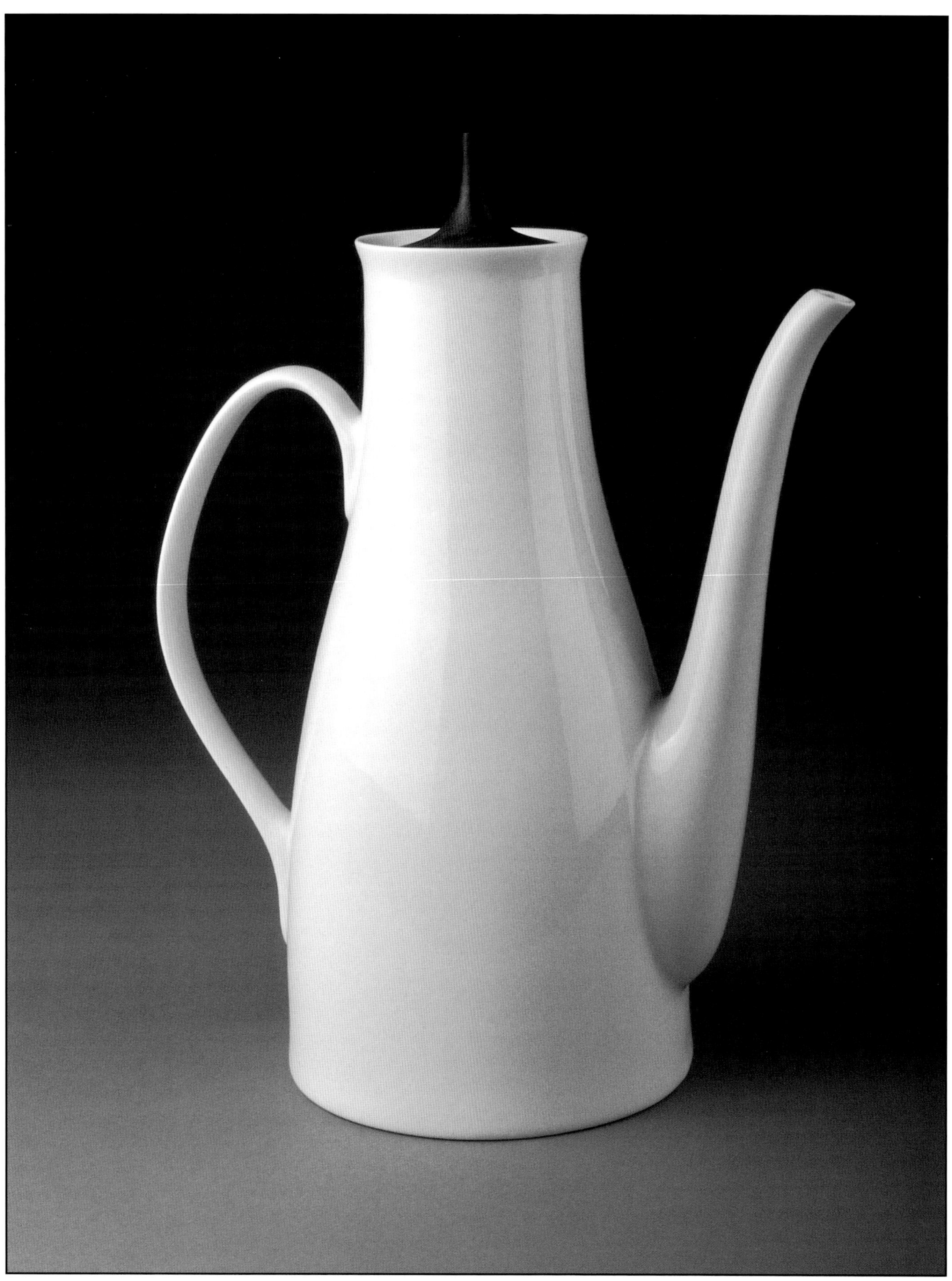

Walker China. ***Raymor Fine China***. George Nelson. [*White w/ rosewood lid*]. 1953. Coffeepot, ND. This line is very hard to find. The squatty teapot that accompanied this line was a particularly interesting, modern shape.

Wallace China Co., Ltd.™

Wallace China Co., Ltd. (Los Angeles, California). ***California Casual China***. [*Stars*]. Annette Honeywell (p). Platter, 13 1/8", $25-40.

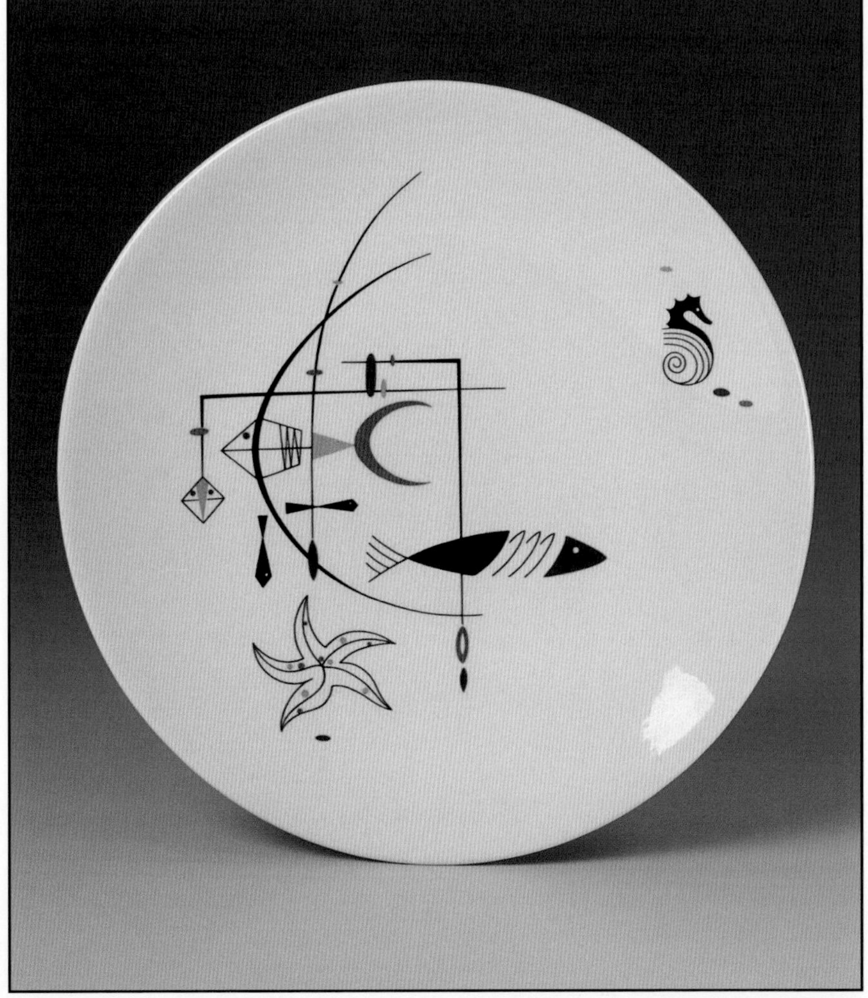

Wallace China. [*Sea Play*]. Ann F. Landau (p). c.1958. Plate, 10 1/2", $25-35+. Wallace China applied for a design patent for this pattern in 1958 and was awarded the patent the following year.

Wellsville China Co.™

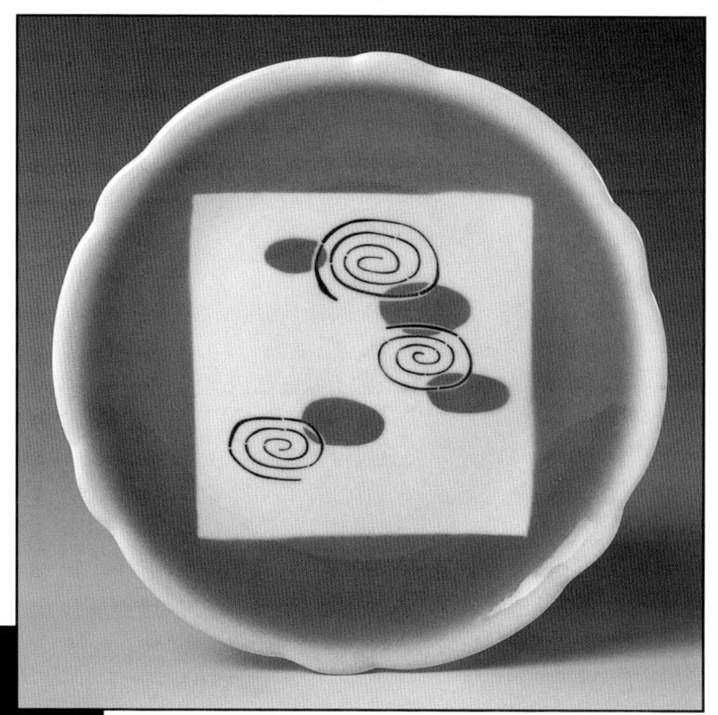

Wellsville China Co. (Wellsville, Ohio).* **Colonial Coupe**. [*Spirals & Ovals*]. Plate #5, 7 1/2", $5-13.

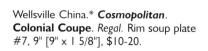

Wellsville China.* ***Cosmopolitan***. **Colonial Coupe**. *Regal.* Rim soup plate #7, 9" [9" x 1 5/8"], $10-20.

Wellsville China.* ***Cosmopolitan***. **Colonial Coupe**. [*Calypso*]. Plate #5, 7 1/2", $5-13.

Winart Pottery™

Winart Pottery (Sapulpa and Miami, Oklahoma).* **Modernair**. *Chartreuse w/ frost.* Coffee service, 4 mugs in 4 hole tray, $20-30, set. Several different mug styles existed and are easily identified based on the handle: **Husky** (rounded and thick), **Tempo** (rounded, slanted upward), **Modernair** (angular), and **Aloha** (angular with a wavy slanted segment).

Winart Pottery.* *Pink w/ brown.* Salt & pepper, $10-15, pair.

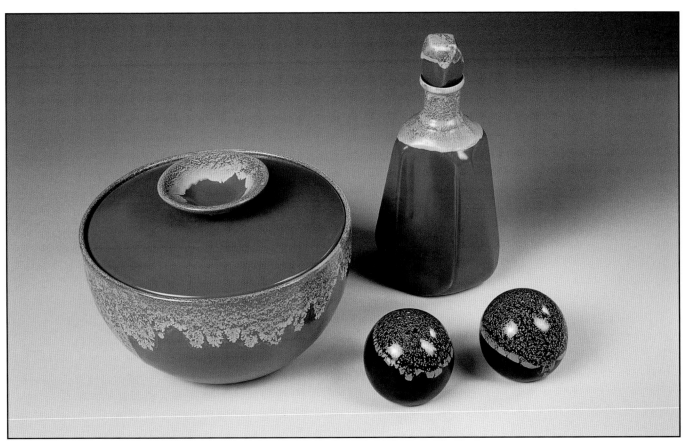

Winart Pottery.* *Avocado w/ frost.* 2 qt. casserole, $15-25. [*Black w/ frost*]. Salt & pepper, $10-15. *Avocado w/ frost.* [Stoppered decanter], $25-50.

Winart Pottery.* [*Chartreuse w/ brown*]. 8 oz. sugar bowl, $3-8. *Pink w/ brown.* 2 qt. pitcher, 11", $15-25. *Gold w/ frost.* **Tempo**. Coffee mug, 7 oz., $2-5.

Winfield China™ (Division of American Ceramic Products, Inc.™)

Winfield China (Division of American Ceramic Products, Inc. Santa Monica, and Los Angeles, California. Winfield Pottery. Pasadena, California). [*Yellow Circle*]. Plate, 10", $12-18. [*Aqua Edge*]. Plate, 10", $12-18.

Winfield (Pasadena). [*Blue Circle, Maroon Edge*]. Plates, 5 1/2", 7 1/2", 9 7/8", $6-18, each. Cup, $5-8.

Winfield (Pasadena). [*Blue Circle, Maroon Edge*]. Aerial view.

Winfield. [*Pink & Blue*]. Cup & saucer, $8-12; plate, 9", $8-12; creamer, $8-12.

Winfield.* *Gourmet.* 1953. Gravy boat, $12-16; medium round casserole, 1 1/2 qt., $20-35.

Update from *Mid-Century Modern Dinnerware: Ak-Sar-Ben to Pope Gosser*

Bennington Potters (Bennington, Vermont). Tumbler, $10-15; small jug, $12-15.

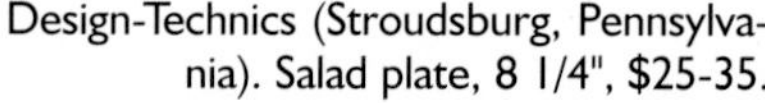

Design-Technics (Stroudsburg, Pennsylvania). Salad plate, 8 1/4", $25-35.

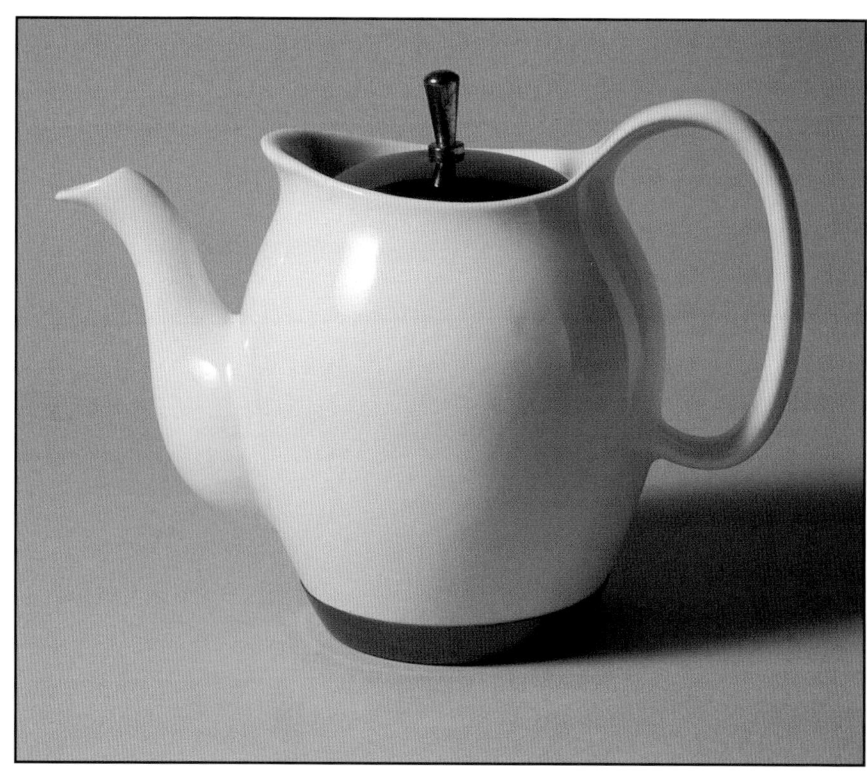

Everlast (possibly Paden City Pottery for Everlast). *Primavera.* Coffee pot, $20-35.

Iroquois China Company (Syracuse, New York). ***Primaries***. Michael Lax. *White.* Sugar bowl, $30-45.

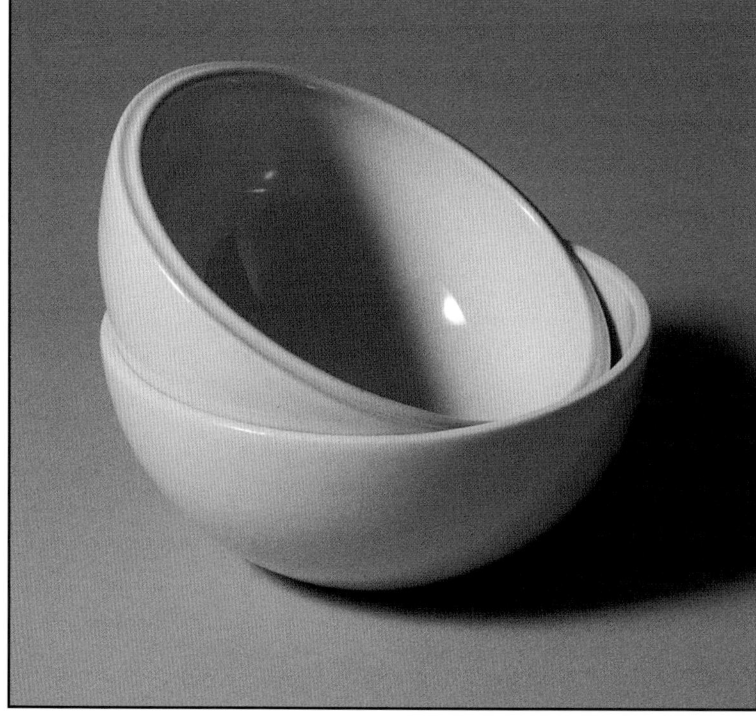

Iroquois. ***Primaries***. Michael Lax. *White.* Another view of the sugar bowl.

Iroquois. ***Primaries***. *White*. Cheese tray, $45-55.

Edwin M. Knowles China Company (Newell, West Virginia). *Equation*. Plate, 10 3/8", $12-18; cup & saucer, $12-18.

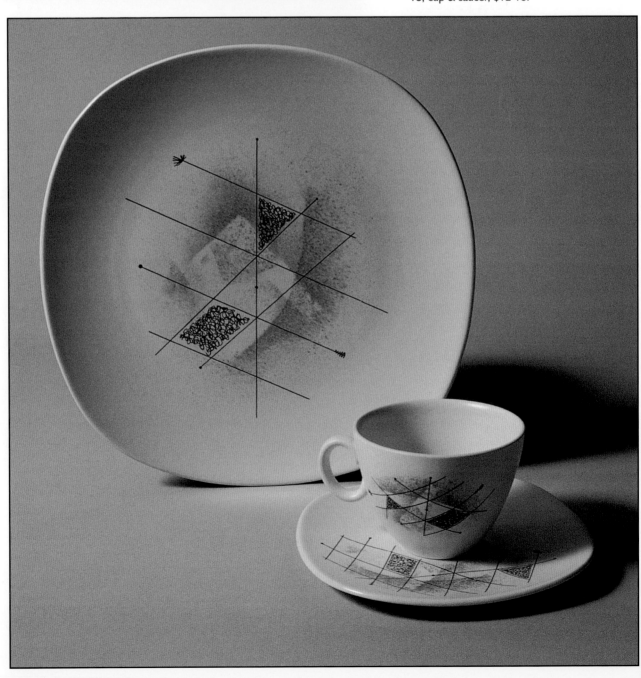

Appendix

Grading Mid-Century Modern Dinnerware

It's a simple fact that collectors want dinnerware that displays well, preferring earthenware and china in *good* to *excellent* condition. Unfortunately, *excellent* condition for the casual seller is not always *excellent* grade for the discriminate buyer. Booming e-commerce sales of vintage dinnerware through eBay and other internet auction sites, virtual antique shops, and online collector groups, have created a pressing need for a common language that accurately and succinctly communicates the condition of dinnerware. Condition significantly impacts value, making some collectors wary of purchasing items sight unseen through the internet.

During the mid-1990s, I posted my own guidelines on the internet. The guidelines were submitted with a call to collectors, dealers, authors, and onlookers for suggestions on how they might be improved. While the response was limited, I received some excellent suggestions. The grading guidelines presented here have undergone many revisions and reflect some of the input I received over the years. While it is not expected that every mid-century modern dinnerware collector will utilize this system, it is hoped that the introduction of grading guidelines will heighten the public's awareness to the importance of accurately describing dinnerware condition prior to sale.

Grading must never be a substitute for accurately describing all imperfections prior to a sale. Close inspection of dinnerware and an accurate description of all defects are essential prior to grading, and an acceptable alternative to grading. A detailed accounting of defects fulfills the primary objective: correct communication of condition. The dimensions and locations of all defects must be well explained. Simply mentioning that an item has no chips and cracks, while failing to mention the item is crazed or has some other defect, is an unacceptable practice that occurs more than infrequently. If possible, an up-close, high resolution photograph of any flaw(s) should be included in online postings. Any repairs (including refiring) should be noted in an item's provenance.

On more than one occasion, I have purchased dishes, through an online auction, that arrived covered with a layer of dirt. I have never understood how a seller can declare an item to be in *excellent* condition without ensuring the ware is free of filth. Dirt can obscure defects such as chips, cracks, crazing, decal mishaps, flecks, inclusions, stains, and pops. (For definitions of these imperfections, see the ***Grading Guidelines*** tables.) Dinnerware must be clean before describing defects and grading.

Grading is both objective and intuitive. Objectively, all ware should be examined for defects up-close (with 20/20 vision) and at a display distance (arm's length, about 3 feet). Magnification should be used to inspect any suspect areas. It is helpful to feel all surfaces with the fingertips—especially rims. A black light is sometimes useful in detecting repairs. Always inspect both inner and outer surfaces for hairline cracks and chips.

After assessing what defects the object may have, the collector should then determine how they impact the beauty or statement of the object at a display distance. Objects with flaws that do not affect aesthetics are graded more favorably than flaws having an impact on aesthetics.

Grading Guidelines

Details of the grading system can be found in the accompanying table, *Grading Guidelines for Mid-century Modern Dinnerware*. As there are no widely recognized, established standards for grading mid-century modern dinnerware, the system presented here represents the author's own guidelines. The system is presented to help the novice collector or seller develop an intuitive feeling for the various conditions that exist. The advanced collector may find that classing dinnerware is a helpful addition to an inventory database. While some collectors will find this grading system conservative, others might label it too liberal. Many, if not most, collectors *will* agree that modern dinnerware in *excellent*, *very good*, and *good* condition should have no major flaws such as chips, cracks, or crazing.

There are basically three classes of dinnerware: *A*, *B*, and *C*. (Learning these guidelines will be that simple with just a little bit of practice.) These classes refer to dinnerware that is grade A (flawless); better quality (barely blemished); and flawed (chips, cracks, crazing, conspicuous imperfections, culls). In this system, classes are subdivided into *A1*, *Excellent*; *A2*, *Excellent* (not shown in the table); *B1*, *Very Good*; *B2*, *Good*; *C1*, *Satisfactory*; *C2*, *Fair*; *C3*, *Poor*; and *C4*, *Cull*.

A1, A2—excellent condition

Class *A* represents dinnerware in *excellent* condition, with no imperfections on casual observation and only the slightest usage wear on close inspection. Dinnerware that is in *A1* condition is in perfect condition, without any signs of usage wear—even under magnification. *A2* dinnerware shows only the very slightest wear when it is closely scrutinized. *A1* refers to perfect condition and *A2* to near-perfect condition. Dinnerware in *excellent* condition is prized by advanced collectors.

B1—very good; B2—good condition

Class *B* dinnerware is typically better quality ware with only minor blemishes. These flaws are not easily seen at a display distance and do not impact the object's aesthetics. Ware in *very good* or *good* condition does not have major imperfections such as chips, cracks, or crazing. The exception to this rule is ware with a tiny, glazed factory chip, which may be graded in *good* condition (or *very good* condition if hidden or not easily seen). Class *B1* dinnerware shows only light usage wear, such as dulling or a few superficial knife marks. *B2* may have tiny defects such as unobtrusive factory inclusions or glaze pops. For guidance on grading objects with various defects, review the *Grading Guidelines* and read the *Caveats & Comments* section. Also, be sure to read the *Examples* section.

If a plate yields no flaws at a display distance, and only a few light knife marks on closer inspection, this item is in *very good* condition. (While multiple defects' sizes are added to help assess grade, don't add lengths of light markings that are invisible at a display distance.) If the plate has very small, minor imperfections that do not affect an object's overall aesthetics at a display distance, the ware is likely in *good* condition.

C1—satisfactory; C2—fair; C3—poor; C4—cull

Class *C* dinnerware consists of inconspicuous, major imperfections (chips, cracks, crazing); all conspicuous minor and major imperfections; and culls. Some flaws, like tiny chips, may not be easily seen at a display distance and may not impact aesthetics. Other flaws may be easily seen at a display distance, greatly affecting the object's overall aesthetics.

Class C ware typically has at least one problem that may be as unobtrusive as inconspicuous crazing or a tiny glaze fleck on close inspection. Ware with almost invisible imperfections is often of *satisfactory* grade.

Imperfections that are seen at a display distance and slightly impact aesthetics are found on ware in *fair* condition. Dinnerware in *poor* condition often has blemishes that significantly impact the look of the ware at arm's length. Generally, dinnerware in *poor* condition may be repairable, as with items that are totally crazed. If the defect is major, conspicuous, significantly affects aesthetics at a display distance, and is unrepairable, the object is a *cull*.

It is important to note that items in *poor* condition, or even *culls*, may retain significant collector value—especially rare items. A *Steubenville Blue American Modern* coffee cup & saucer that is totally and conspicuously crazed in *poor* condition may fetch in excess of $350. A very badly chipped saucer *cull* in this same pattern may sell for $100. Even more common items may retain significant value, especially when flaws are small or inconspicuous.

Because there is an increasing awareness that crazed dinnerware is potentially repairable with refiring (some items will break), many totally crazed items—even items that aren't rare—are retaining some value in *poor* condition. It is also important to note, that crazing on some items cannot be seen unless you are inspecting the object in sunlight or very closely. In this case, aesthetics rule: an object with total surface crazing, that is invisible under normal lighting at a display distance, may be graded in *satisfactory* condition, barring other defects.

Remember, if you mention a *grade* prior to a sale, never forget to mention all flaws. Grading dinnerware, for now, remains somewhat subjective—utilizing both objective and intuitive criteria. An accurate description of flaws (and photographs, if possible) is more objective. It is hoped that grading will, at the least, help sellers better understand the meaning of *excellent* grade: ware without flaws on very close inspection. Classing dinnerware—A1, B2, C4, etc.—is useful to collectors who want to easily track their expanding inventory.

This chapter is taken from the author's book entitled: *Mid-Century Modern Dinnerware: An Encyclopedia of American Design & Production (Ak-Sar-Ben, Denwar Ceramics, Iroquois China Company, Laurel Potteries of California, Royal China Company, Stetson China Company)*. Atglen, PA: Schiffer Publishing Ltd.

Grading Guidelines for Mid-century Modern Dinnerware

Class	Grade	chip	crack	crazing	decoration mishap	fleck	scratches, light	scratches, heavy	stain	factory chip	factory inclusions	factory pop	factory skip
		A1 condition. Pristine. Flawless. Perfect. No imperfections.											
A1	*Excellent*	no	no	no	no	no	no	no	no	no	no	no	no
A2	*Excellent*	no	no	no	no	no	x small	no	no	no	no	no	no
		Better quality. Bon plat. Barely blemished. Aesthetics not impacted at display distance.											
B1	*Very Good*	no	no	no	no	no	x small	no	no	no	no	no	no
B2	*Good*	no	no	no	x small	no	small	no	no	x small	x small	x small	x small
		Chips, cracks, crazing, and culls. Conspicuous flaws. Aesthetics often, but not necessarily, impacted at a display distance.											
C1	*Satisfactory*	x small	no	small	small	small	medium	small	small	small	small	small	small
C2	*Fair*	small	small	medium	medium	medium	large	medium	medium	medium	medium	medium	medium
C3	*Poor*	medium	medium	large	large	large	x large	large	large	large	large	large	large
C4	*Cull*	large	large	x large	x large	x large	x large	x large	x large	x large	x large	x large	x large

Subjective Defect Size Guidance

X Small or Pinpoint	Typically inconspicuous. Miniscule. Not prominent. Not easily seen at a display distance. Does not affect overall aesthetics. Very small in size or number.
Small	Typically inconspicuous. Not prominent. Not easily seen at a display distance. Does not affect overall aesthetics. Small in size or number.
Medium	Typically noticeable but not prominent. May slightly impact overall aesthetics. Moderate in size or number.
Large	Typically prominent. Easily seen at a display distance. Impacts aesthetics. Large in size or number.
X Large	Typically prominent. Easily seen at a display distance. Impacts aesthetics. Extra large in size or number.

Definitions

Chip: avulsion of the ceramic body.
Crack: fracture of the ceramic body.
Crazing: fracture of the glaze over the ceramic body.
Decoration mishap: cuts, fading, placement flaws, smudging, or other imperfection.
Display distance: arm's length, about 3 feet.
Factory chip: chip under a factory finish; possibly factory second.
Factory inclusions: stray grit found under the glaze.
Factory pop: pinhole openings in the glaze.
Factory skip: area devoid of glaze, missed in the original glazing process.
Fleck: glaze chip, not affecting the ceramic body.
Inclusion: stray grain of particulate matter under the glaze surface.
Scratches, light: very superficial utensil marks. *Heavy*: gouges.

Caveats & Comments

1. Always thoroughly examine an object up-close (with 20/20 vision) and at a display distance (arm's length, about 3 feet). Magnify any suspect areas. Feel all surfaces. Inspect all inner and outer surfaces.
2. An object is graded based on the defect type, size, and how it impacts the object's aesthetics. Common sense should prevail. An object with multiple flaws is not in *very good* or *excellent* condition.
3. A repaired object is not graded. The repair is either flawless or flawed. All repairs (including firing) must be included in an object's provenance.
4. Most important is defect prominence and how the flaw affects an object's aesthetics and display.
5. Objects with defects that are hidden and/or seen only on very close inspection, may warrant upgrading. Upgrading may occur only within the same class.
6. Minor factory flaws are viewed somewhat more forgivingly by today's collector.
7. Always list *all* imperfections of an item when buying and selling. **Dinnerware grade is not as important as accurate communication of condition and flaws.**
8. Always give defect dimensions when buying and selling. Close-up photographs of any defect(s) are helpful.
9. A blemish of the unglazed underside of a body or lid is not usually considered in grading unless the imperfection affects the integrity of the body or extends into the glaze.
10. Normal pin marks are not considered flaws.

Bibliography

Contemporaneous sources have been vigorous pursued for the majority of information contained in this book. In addition to these materials and individuals, a number of reference works have been utilized. The following books, magazines, ephemera, archives, libraries, and online sites have been sourced in the compilation of factual information for this book. Some listings, especially in the *Select Bibliography*, are presented primarily as additional sources of reference for the reader.

Reference Books

Bassett, Mark. *Introducing Roseville Pottery*. Atglen, PA: Schiffer Publishing Co., 1999.

Bassett, Mark. *Understanding Roseville Pottery*. Atglen, PA: Schiffer Publishing Co., 2002.

Bougie, Stanley J. and David A. Newkirk, *Red Wing Dinnerware*. St. Cloud, Minnesota: Volkmuth Printers, Inc., 1980.

Carney, Margaret L., *The Binns Medalists*. Alfred, New York: The Schein-Joseph International Museum of Ceramic Art, New York State College of Ceramics at Alfred University, 2000.

Chipman, Jack. *Collector's Encyclopedia of California Pottery*. Second Edition. Paducah, KY: Collector Books, A Division of Shroeder Publishing Co., Inc., 1999.

Conroy, Barbara J. *Restaurant China*. Volume 2. Paducah, KY: Collector Books, A Division of Shroeder Publishing Co., Inc., 1999.

Conti, Steve, A. DeWayne Bethany, and Bill Seay. *Collector's Encyclopedia of Sascha Brastoff*. Paducah, KY: Collector Books, A Division of Shroeder Publishing Co., Inc., 1995.

Cunningham, Jo. *The Best of Collectible Dinnerware*. Atglen, PA: Schiffer Publishing Co., 1995.

Cunningham, Jo. *The Collector's Encyclopedia of American Dinnerware*. Paducah, KY: Collector Books, A Division of Schroeder Publishing Company, 1995.

Duke, Harvey. *Official Price Guide to Pottery and Porcelain*, Eighth Edition. New York: House of Collectibles, 1995.

Duke, Harvey. *Stangl Pottery*. Radnor, PA: Wallace Homestead, 1993.

Huxford, Sharon and Bob. *The Collectors Encyclopedia of Roseville Pottery*. Paducah, KY: Collector Books, A Division of Schroeder Publishing Company, 1995.

Keller, Joe and David Ross. *Russel Wright: Dinnerware, Pottery & More: An Identification and Price Guide*. Atglen, PA: Schiffer Publishing Co., 2000.

Kerr, Ann. *Collector's Encyclopedia of Russel Wright*. Paducah, KY: Collector Books, A Division of Shroeder Publishing Co., Inc., 1998. Also Third Edition, 2002.

Lehner, Lois. *Lehner's Encyclopedia of U.S. Marks on Pottery, Porcelain & Clay*. Paducah, KY: Collector Books, A Division of Shroeder Publishing Co., Inc., 1988.

Meehan, Bill & Kathy. *Collector's Guide to Lu-Ray Pastels*. Paducah, KY: Collector Books, A Division of Shroeder Publishing Co., Inc., 1995.

Nelson, Maxine. *Collectible Vernon Kilns*. Paducah, KY: Collector Books, A Division of Shroeder Publishing Co., Inc., 1994.

Newbound, Betty & Bill. *Best of Blue Ridge Dinnerware*. Paducah, KY: Collector Books, A Division of Shroeder Publishing Co., Inc., 2003.

Newbound, Betty & Bill. *Collector's Encyclopedia of Blue Ridge Dinnerware. Volume II*. Paducah, KY: Collector Books, A Division of Shroeder Publishing Co., Inc., 1998.

Newbound, Betty & Bill. *Southern Potteries Incorporated: Blue Ridge Dinnerware*. Revised 3rd Edition. Paducah, KY: Collector Books, A Division of Shroeder Publishing Co., Inc., 1996.

Piña, Leslie. *Pottery: Modern Wares 1920-1960*. Atglen, PA: Schiffer Publishing Co., 1994.

Pratt, Michael. *Mid-Century Modern Dinnerware: An Encyclopedia of Design & Production. Ak-Sar-Ben Pottery, Denwar Ceramics, Iroquois China Company, Laurel Potteries of California, Royal China Company, Stetson China Company*. Atglen, PA: Schiffer Publishing Co., 2002.

Pratt, Michael. *Mid-Century Modern Dinnerware: A Pictorial Guide, Ak-Sar-Ben to Pope Gosser*. Atglen, PA: Schiffer Publishing Co., 2003.

Racheter, Richard G. *Tableware Design of Ben Seibel: 1940s-1980s*. Atglen, PA: Schiffer Publishing, 2003.

Reiss, Ray. *Red Wing Art Pottery*. Chicago, IL: Property Publishing, 1996.

Reiss, Ray. *Red Wing Dinnerware Price and Identification Guide*. Chicago, IL: Property Publishing, 1997.

Ruffin, Frances and John. *Blue Ridge China Today*. Atglen, PA: Schiffer Publishing Co., 1997.

Runge, Jr., Robert C. *Collector's Encyclopedia of Stangl Dinnerware*, Paducah, KY: Collector Books, A Division of Shroeder Publishing Co., Inc., 2000.

Smith, Timothy J. *Universal Dinnerware and its Predecessors: Cambridge Art Pottery, The Guernsey Earthenware Co., The Oxford Pottery Co., The Atlas-Globe China Co.* Atglen, PA: Schiffer Publishing Co., 2000.

Trade Journal/Magazine Bibliography

(Issues primarily from 1935-1965.)

Ceramic Age. Cleveland: New Jersey Specialty Clay Workers Association.

Ceramic Industry. Boston: Cahners Pub. Co.

Ceramic Trade Directory. Newark, NJ: The Ceramic Publishing Co., Inc.

China and Glass Redbook. Pittsburgh, PA: China and glass.

China, Glass & Tablewares. Clifton, NJ: Doctorow Publications.

China, Glass and Decorative Accessories: see *China, Glass & Tablewares*.

Craft Horizons. New York: American Craftsmen's Cooperative Council, et. al.

Crockery and Glass Journal. New York: Haire Publishing Co., Inc.

Everyday Art Quarterly. Minneapolis: Walker Art Center.

Gift & Tableware Reporter. New York: Billboard Publications.

Giftwares and Home Fashions. East Stroudsburg, PA: Haire Pub. Co.

Home Furnishings Daily. New York: Fairchild Publications.

House Beautiful. New York: Hearst Corporation.

Industrial Design. New York: Design Publications.

Interiors. New York: Billboard Publications.

Lippincott's Monthly Magazine. Philadelphia: J.B. Lippincott.

Pacific Coast Ceramic News. Beverly Hills, California.

Pottery, Glass & Brass Salesman. New York: O'Gorman Publishing Co.

Registered California Pictorial. Los Angeles: Registered California, Inc.

Restaurant Management. New York: Ahrens Publishing Co.

Retailing Daily. New York: Fairchild Publications.

The Gift and Art Buyer. New York: Geyer.

Manufacturers' Brochures and Catalogs

A research collection of brochures, catalogs, archival materials, and facsimiles.
Red Wing Potteries Specialty, Inc.
Royal China.
Rubel & Company Decorative Accessories, Inc.
The Salem China Company.
Sascha Brastoff Products, Inc.
Shenango China, Inc.
Stangl Pottery.
Sterling China Company.
Stetson China Company.
Steubenville Pottery Company.
Syracuse China Company.
Tamac, Inc.
Taylor, Smith & Taylor Company.
Universal Potteries, Inc.
Vernon Kilns.
The W. S. George Pottery Company.
Wellsville China Company.
Winart Pottery.
Winfield (American Ceramic Products, Inc.).

Archival/Reference Materials

The American Ceramic Society Library. Columbus, Ohio.
Cooper-Hewitt National Design Museum Library. New York.
Lawrence County Historical Society. New Castle, Pennsylvania.
Morris County Public Library. Morristown, New Jersey.
Museum of Modern Art Library. New York.
Newark Public Library. Newark, New Jersey.
New York Public Library. New York.
Ohio Historical Society. Columbus, Ohio.
Ohio Historical Society's Museum of Ceramics archives. East Liverpool, Ohio.
Onondaga Historical Association. Syracuse, New York.
Scholes Library and Archives at Alfred University. Alfred, New York.
Sterling China Company archives. Wellsville, Ohio.
Stetson China Company archives. Philip Stetson.
Smithsonian Institution. Washington, D.C.
Department of Special Collections, Syracuse University, Syracuse, New York.
Syracuse China Company (Mayer China). Syracuse, New York.
Thomas J. Watson Library. New York.

Online Informational Resources

Beedenbender, Paul. *abenseibeldesign* (www.abenseibel design.com).
Colling, Tim. *The Vernon Kilns Website* (www.colling.com).
Gonzalez, Mark. *Ohio River Pottery* (www.ohioriver pottery.com).
Hintz, Todd and Ivy Loughborough. *Red Wing Dinnerware.* (www.redwingdinnerware.com).
The Lawrence County Historical Society. *The Shenango China Collection* (www.ilovehistory.com/Collections/collections.html).
Lenling, David. *Red Wing Tips* (www.redwingnet.com/index.htm). Byron Bush, founder.
Moore, Pat. *Zeisel, Mostly* (www.zeiselmostly.com).
Pratt, Michael. *Modish.net* (www.modish.net).
Runge Jr., Robert C. *Stangl Pottery* (www.stanglpottery.org).
Sacksteder, Dorrie L. *The W. S. George Pottery Company*. (wsgeorge.jdfiles.org).
The Schein-Joseph International Museum of Ceramic Art (nyscc.alfred.edu/mus).
Souza, Kevin. *Vernon Kiln's Plaid Dinnerware* (www. geocities.com/WestHollywood/6027).
Sterling China Company. *Sterling China* (current products: www.sterlingchina.com).
Libbey® Inc. *Syracuse China* (current products: www. syracusechina.com/libbey/html.nsf/Pages/SyracuseChinaSite).
Way, Doug. *Town & Country by Eva Zeisel* (www.mind spring.com/~dway/town.html).

Select Bibliography

Adams, Henry. *Viktor Schreckengost and 20th-Century Design*. Seattle, Washington: The Cleveland Museum of Art and the University of Washington Press, 2001.

Albrecht, Donald, Robert Schonfeld, and Lindsay Stamm Shapiro. *Russel Wright: Creating American Lifestyle*. New York: Harry N. Abrams, Inc., 2001.

Barber, Edwin AtLee. *The Pottery and Porcelain of the United States*. New York: G. P. Putnam's Sons, 1909.

Eidelberg, Martin, et al. *Design 1935-1965 What Modern Was*. New York: Harry N. Abrams, 1991.

Eidelberg, Martin. *Eva Zeisel: Designer for Industry*. Montreal: Le Château Dufresne, Inc., Musée des Arts Décoratifs de Montréal, 1984.

Friedman, William. *20th Century Design: U.S.A.* Buffalo, New York: Buffalo Fine Arts Academy, 1959-1960.

Greenberg, Cara. *Mid-century Modern*. New York: Harmony Books, 1995.

Hiesinger; Kathryn B. and George H. Marcus, eds. *Design Since 1945*. Philadelphia: Philadelphia Museum of Art, 1983.

Hennessey, William J. *Russel Wright: American Designer*. Cambridge: The MIT Press, 1983.

Kaufmann, Jr., Edgar. *What is Modern Design?* New York: The Museum of Modern Art, 1950.

Manitoga/The Russel Wright Design Center. *Russel Wright: Good Design Is For Everyone: In His Own Words*. New York: Universe, A Division of Rizzoli International Publications, 2001.

Prime, William C. *Pottery and Porcelain*. New York: Harper & Brothers Publishers, 1878.

Stern, Bill. *California Pottery: From Missions to Modernism*. San Francisco: Chronicle Books, 2001.

Venable, Charles and Ellen Denker, Katherine Grier, Stephen Harrison. *China and Glass in America 1880-1980: From Tabletop to TV Tray.* New York: Harry N. Abrams, Inc., 2000.

Wingler, Hans M. *The Bauhaus*. Cambridge: The MIT Press, 1978.

Index